Finding Your Harmony

Finding Your Harmony

Dream Big, Have Faith, and Achieve More Than You Can Imagine

Ally Brooke

DEY ST.

An Imprint of WILLIAM MORROW

FINDING YOUR HARMONY. Copyright © 2020 by Rising Sun Productions, LLC. All rights reserved. Printed in the United States of America. No part of this book may be used or reproduced in any manner whatsoever without written permission except in the case of brief quotations embodied in critical articles and reviews. For information, address HarperCollins Publishers, 195 Broadway, New York, NY 10007.

HarperCollins books may be purchased for educational, business, or sales promotional use. For information, please email the Special Markets Department at SPsales@harpercollins.com.

FIRST EDITION

Library of Congress Cataloging-in-Publication Data has been applied for.

ISBN 978-0-06-289577-6

20 21 22 23 24 LSC 10 9 8 7 6 5 4 3 2 1

Mom and Dad

Mom, you are the light of my life. You are my hero. My compass. My road-map. My queen. My heart. My everything. You taught me the true meaning of love and belief. You always put your family first. Your strength and bravery constantly leave me awe-inspired. I would not be where I am without you. I thank God every day for you and your tender heart. I will always be your "Sunshine Bird." Thank you, from the bottom of my heart, for everything you have done for me my entire life. You helped me to spread my wings and fly. I love you with all of my heart.

Dad, you are the sun of our family. I am so grateful to be your daughter. Thank you for always being there for Mom, Brandon and me. For always being the first to help, to make us laugh till our stomachs hurt, and to give us hope and joy. Thank you for showing God's love to everyone you encounter, in every minute of the day. Since you first held me in the palm of your hand, you've shown me love. Thank you for all of the sacrifices you've made to make my dreams come true, and for always believing in me. I love you more than words, and I am forever proud to call you my Dad.

Contents

Introduction

Thank you so much for picking up my book. It represents the culmination of a process that's been ongoing (sometimes painfully) for nearly a decade now—where I'm finally coming into my own, as a performer and a woman, and finding myself at a place in my growth where I can fully accept who I am.

It is my honor and privilege to share my story with you. I remember looking up through the window of my room or my parents' car, and I was always dreaming.

I've always been a dreamer. I've always been a girl of faith.

My family raised my brother and me with the foundation of Jesus and faith. I grew up going to church, and I carried my beliefs on with me as an adult. As you will see, God has carried me through my entire life. He has shown up in ways that left me awe-inspired and forever changed; in ways that I never even thought were possible. That is what I'm most excited to share with you. I hope this story can inspire your faith. It is time for me to let my true voice and heart shine out, so that's what I'm going to do, every day of my life and on every page of this book. This book is for all of those little girls (and boys) who look up at the night sky, searching for the dazzle of a falling star, daring to hope that their wish will come true.

All I've ever wanted to be, since I was a little girl, is to be a light—a light in this dark world and in this dark industry. One of my favorite Bible verses of all time is Matthew 5:16, which says, "Let your light shine so before men, that they may see your good works and glorify your Father in Heaven." I hope that this book can be a light to you. And I hope it leaves you changed, the same way that my own story has left me changed.

ONE

The Worst Best Day of My Life

I t looks like everybody's here!" I called out.

I was in my usual spot in the backseat of my parents' car, staring out the window at everything we passed, thinking and daydreaming, as I always did. When we parked, I swiveled around, noticing the familiar cars that belonged to all of my family members, parked in front of my aunt's house on a street of oak trees and single-story homes, in the South Side of San Antonio, Texas. Abuzz with nervous energy, I couldn't sit still. Bubbles of excitement rose within me; I felt as if they might float me away.

I've always been a deep feeler. When I'm happy, I explode, and when I'm sad, my heart is completely broken—my soul aches. When I witness unfairness in the world, I just can't bear it. And when I'm looking forward to something, I burst with anticipation. This September evening in 2012 was a combination of every kind of high and low—all at the same time. Yes, on this night, my excitement and emotions were off the charts.

Most everything was as normal as could be, except that this was the biggest night of my life. Although it was officially fall on the calendar, the air when I stepped out of the car was a hot, damp blanket of humidity—once again, the seasons would take their sweet time changing. In my beloved hometown of San Antonio, we only have two seasons—really hot, or warm to cool in the winter, if we're lucky. We were gathering as a family at my aunt's house—with its fun "everyone's welcome" vibe—as we'd done my entire life, for countless holidays, birthday parties, weekend barbecues, and any other excuse to get everyone together. My aunt's house was cozy and warm, the perfect place for everyone to gather. I think it has a lot to do with our Mexican culture—I've always been raised that all we needed was family, food, love, and faith. With those four essentials in our lives, we don't need anything else, really.

But what was different on this particular evening was that tonight, after ten years of focus and more than a few sacrifices—from my parents and me—while pursuing my dream of making it as a singer, I was going to see the broadcast of my audition for the reality television music competition *The X Factor*. Along with the more than eight million Americans who would be tuning in to watch—no pressure, right? I'd had trouble thinking of anything else all day, and now that it was almost go time, I practically skipped out of the car. My family and I all knew the outcome of the audition, which I'd done in Austin back in the end of May, but we'd been sworn to secrecy until the results aired in September. So we'd been waiting for this moment for four months—a decade, really, if you counted all of the years since I'd seriously started chasing my singing dreams when I was nine years old.

Standing on the sidewalk, I could see the glow of TVs in a few neighbors' houses. How crazy and amazing it was to think that in a few minutes, my face would be staring from some of those screens as I sang my heart out for them. The thought made me wonder how I would look and sound in front of the cameras—and would people like me? All I'd ever wanted was to connect with an audience through what I loved most, singing out into the world with my voice, and here finally was my chance. Only, would people want to connect with me, too? I couldn't wait to find out!

As eager as I was to race inside and get this party started, I automatically paused to give my mom time to get out of the car. My family and I have always been sensitive to my mom's severe scoliosis and the limitations it has put on her because of her chronic back pain. She took an extra beat to slide from under the seat belt and unfold herself to stand by the open door. Without my mom, none of this would have been possible. She'd encouraged me to audition for *The X Factor* in the first place. And in the years before that, she and Dad had dedicated a tremendous amount of time, money, and effort—even selling the property where they'd planned to build their dream home and living part-time in LA—to support my singing. I helped my mom pull the special cake she'd gotten for tonight out of the car, and we made our way across the street. As we rang the doorbell, the three of us exchanged excited smiles. This was it. As soon as the door swung open, a cheer exploded from the room, catching us up in their spirited joy.

"There she is!" someone called out.

I screamed, giddy with all of the anticipation inside of me. There was the familiar delicious spread of refried beans, homemade rice, beef tacos, and chalupas, all piled onto a long table, along with giant bottles of soda, especially Big Red, because we're from Texas, and it's pretty much the state soda. Grinning ear to ear, I was swept up into the welcoming arms of my family—my grandma, my aunt Rose and my other aunts and uncles, my cousin BJ and a dozen other cousins, my brother and his girlfriend, who's now his wife. We're extremely close, and we've always celebrated our victories as a unit and comforted one another in hard times. They are home to me, so there was nowhere else I would have wanted to be for this biggest night of my life, so far.

"Hi, Mama!" shouted one of my aunts. (My mom, aunts, and even my dad often call me Mama, a term of endearment in our Mexican culture.) Her eyes wide with excitement, she smothered me in the biggest hug. My aunts are always fun and full of emotion, and they were not shy about expressing how happy they were for me.

"Oh, my goodness, mija, we are so excited for you!"

"Go, Ally!"

A chorus of voices called out to me, wrapping me up in the warmth of their love and enthusiasm, like a hug. Always loud, my family was extra exuberant tonight. I looked around the room at the beautiful faces of my loved ones. They'd all shown up to so many of my singing events, as far back as I could remember. And now they were here for me as I made my debut appearance on national TV, which seemed like the pinnacle of all of my performances. Or might it actually be the real beginning of my career—the first of many such steps onto bigger stages around the world?

My brother, Brandon, nudged my arm to get my attention.

"Are you sure it's really showing tonight?" he asked, grinning.

I held up my phone.

"One of the producers texted me, saying that we should watch tonight," I said.

We'd tuned in to every episode, since the second season had begun airing twice a week in mid-September, hoping to see the footage of my audition. And now the moment had finally arrived. Just thinking back to how it had felt to stand in front of that season's judges—only some of the biggest names in music: Simon Cowell, Britney Spears, Demi Lovato, and L.A. Reid—gave me goose bumps of anticipation.

"It's starting!" BJ shouted, and we gathered around the TV, straining to catch a glimpse of my hometown and any of our faces. All of us who were crowded together at my aunt's house already knew the result of my audition and all of the amazing moments I'd experienced on that stage in Austin, but we were anxious to see how it would all come together on TV.

In the four months since I'd tried out, my imagination had run wild, wondering what of all the footage they'd shot would actually make it onto the air. When the camera had started rolling, I'd dared to share so much of my true self—what I cared about most, and all of my dreams, not just to succeed as a singer, but to help others—and the very real struggles that we'd overcome as a family from my earliest days on this earth.

As the familiar theme music blasted through the living room, quieting those around me, I wondered what parts of my story would be aired. Surely, they'd include some mention of the many sacrifices my parents and brother had made to support my dreams, including how my mom had traveled with me extensively for years, despite the constant horrible pain she suffered from her severe scoliosis. I couldn't wait for my mom to finally be acknowledged, for the whole world to hear just how remarkable and inspiring she was. And they had to keep in my love of my beautiful hometown, which I knew would bring joy to my fellow San Antonians, including my old teachers, pastors, voice coaches, family members, and everyone from my community who'd believed in me and cheered me on since I first began singing out around town as a kid.

I'd also shared my story of being born a premature baby—how by a miracle I defied the odds and survived my birth with no major health complications. I gave a shout-out to other kids born prematurely. Maybe seeing me on the show would encourage them to go after the impossible. I imagined other preemie kids watching tonight, starting to believe that their dreams could come true as well. The idea of inspiring others filled my eyes with tears.

"Oh, look, there we are!" someone said.

At last, after so many weeks of waiting, the moment was finally here. We recognized the red T-shirts with "Shining Star Ally Brooke" across the front that my family had worn that day. It was the sweetest thing ever. My dad had asked a lady in San Antonio to make these shirts for us. That's how much my parents supported me—they always went the extra mile. They'd been nearly as excited as I was. My mom, who often helped style me, had put together my outfit for my audition.

As we saw ourselves on the screen, everyone in the room broke out in screams and shouts of excitement. Then everyone hushed immediately to hear what was being said. I covered my mouth in disbelief. The moment I'd been waiting for was finally here.

Then my opening introduction came on.

"Hi, I'm Ally Brooke from San Antonio, Texas. Knowing that L.A. Reid and Simon Cowell are going to give me feedback is ah! [I let out a little scream], it's amazing! I want to do it all. I want to do film and to act. Have, you know, my own perfume line, my own clothing line, singing. Do things that nobody's seen before."

That was my opener? I got worried. This wasn't the best start, but maybe I was being too critical of myself? Everyone kept smiling and looking toward my aunt's large TV, and then to my face, and back to the image. There I was again, filling the screen.

"My ultimate dream is I wanna be as big as Beyoncé."

My heart froze in my chest. "I didn't say it like that," I muttered.

Little did I know how much I would pay for that, especially the line about Beyoncé. I remembered the producers asking me questions like "Do you want to own your own clothing and perfume line?" I'd responded yes. But they'd been the ones who'd gotten me to say it. My focus had been on expressing deeper and more personal dreams and goals. Where were the important things I'd shared with the interviewer? Where were the topics like my mom's strength? Being a preemie? The love of my family and of Texas? I swallowed hard, waiting for them to air the good parts. But there was nothing. They didn't show any of it.

"They didn't make me sound very good," I said.

My family rallied around me, trying to reassure me. My heart was racing now as I tried to get over my deep disappointment and the underlying sense that the show was trying to make a fool out of me. Their edits made me sound shallow and ditzy. That wasn't me. But I knew the power of my actual audition, at least. I hoped that would save me.

Then it was time. I watched myself on TV, walk out onstage. I felt my heart beating as it had when I'd stopped in front of those four judges, all giants in the music industry and some of my biggest inspirations. It was a little encouraging that at least, dressed up cute in my high-waisted black shorts, pink crop top, black fedora, and open-toed heels with neon socks, I didn't appear as nervous as I'd felt that day. As I watched, my heart pounded. I knew the outcome, and all that came after the audition that I couldn't share with anyone yet, but the thought that millions of people were watching my performance right now felt like a tidal wave sweeping over me.

I saw myself answer the judges' questions and then start singing. *Here it goes.* When the camera switched to my mom crying as I sang, tears came to my eyes. But then something happened. On the TV version, as I sang on, after the music stopped, the camera cut to the judges, and Simon looked annoyed. Other judges made cringing faces at me. The producers cut to people in the audience laughing. The camera cut back to me as I sang, but the magic was shattered. Simon appeared even more irritated. This version of events was nothing, and I mean nothing, like what I'd experienced in real life. It didn't seem powerful for me to keep singing. It almost seemed arrogant. But this wasn't how it had happened at all. Instead of being beautiful, as the moment had been, it was embarrassing.

"No, he didn't do that. That's not what happened," my mom said, referring to Simon's reaction—or at least the one that showed on TV.

My family had been there; they knew the truth. Now everyone was talking around me, though some quieted and leaned forward to hear the judges respond when I finished singing. My cousin was insisting that Simon didn't roll his eyes like the show made it seem. I could hear my family's upset conversation, but they all seemed very far away. I just felt cold.

I felt like I was watching from a great distance. My excitement was gone. It was as if I had tunnel vision. Faces turned my way, then back to the screen, as the judges gave some great compliments and their unanimous yeses. I could hardly hear what they were saying, though. I felt too sick to my stomach. Their words didn't reach me.

"That wasn't good," Mom said, disappointment in her voice. I wanted to burst into tears.

She had given up so much for this. The show hadn't used any of the parts about how amazing my parents had been while trying to make my dreams come true. Right before my eyes, they had taken one of the most powerful days of my life and tweaked it into something else—something no longer glorious, no longer elevated, but instead, empty and trivial.

Dad and a few others tried to cheer me up, putting their arms around me. "It wasn't that bad. The judges all said great things. Simon said he was looking at a future star."

Someone else came up to encourage me, saying that these shows always did things like that to stir up some drama, and that it didn't matter because I had made it.

"But that's not me," I said, my voice small. I knew everyone was looking at me. The disappointment cut through me. I felt hollow.

"A future star," Dad said again.

"Yeah," I muttered, fighting back the tears.

Maybe I'd built it up too much in my mind over the past months. Everyone had been wonderful to me on the show, so why had they done this? Tonight's edit, which had aired to all of those millions of people across the country and around the world, made me look like a joke.

God, why is this happening? I asked silently. It's a question most of us ask God, often in moments when our thoughts are too loud to catch his answer. I was probably too upset to hear from Him or find solace in this moment. Unfortunately, it was about to get worse.

I managed to hold it together until we got out to our car. I hadn't come across how I'd hoped. I couldn't hold it in anymore, and I broke down. My mom started to cry, too. My dad did his best to comfort us as he drove us back to our house.

When I got home that night, I pulled out my computer and went to my audition on YouTube, hoping we'd been wrong to expect a strong negative reaction. Maybe I'd learn that I'd seen it all wrong, and I'd actually find some comfort from what I found there. This proved to be the worst decision possible. I began scrolling through the comments, and my heart felt like someone had grabbed hold of it and crushed it to pieces. The cruel comments were devastating. I was called annoying, cocky, irritating, terrible, stupid, a b****, ugly, fame hungry—basically, everything terrible.

I saw a few good comments, but mostly negative ones. And I couldn't stop reading them, through tear after tear. I wanted to tell each of those people that this wasn't who I am. What they'd seen on TV didn't represent me. With some creative editing, the show had turned the best day of my life into a nightmare. And now for the rest of the show, that's who everyone would think I was. That had been my one chance to make a first impression, and I'd been made to look like this. My faith was seriously tested in that moment. When I prayed that night, I had many questions and doubts in my mind. *Why, God? We've been patient for so long. We've been following you for so long—your plan and your path. We've waited for this moment basically my entire life. Why did this have to happen like that?*

Have you ever experienced something like this—a moment that makes you feel like you're in a spotlight of shame and humiliation? It's one of the worst feelings in the world, especially when you didn't do something to cause it yourself.

Deep inside, I tried reminding myself of the truth of who I was. I'd gotten those four yeses from the judges, and there was so much ahead. But on that night, I felt too broken to take in the gratitude.

I'd gone from being completely infused with joy to wanting to hide and cry. Maybe the episode wasn't as bad as it seemed, but I kept running the scene through my head, making it worse and worse. The annoyed look on Simon's face, the awkward glances, the shallow personality they'd made me appear to have, and the cruel, uncaring responses it had led to online. It hurt so much that I wanted to quit and walk away from it all.

But I knew the rest of the show that hadn't aired yet. There was much more to come, and soon it would be time for me to compete on the upcoming live shows. Yet how was I going to even try when it felt as if the world saw me as an annoyingly self-centered and silly girl? This was not the big start I had dreamed of or worked so hard for. In that moment, I couldn't be excited about what else happened even if the future of the show was about to completely change my life.

All I felt was humiliation and heartache. I crawled into bed, and when my faithful cat Bobbi padded up and hopped on, I wrapped my arms around her and cried myself to sleep. Bobbi had entered my life when I was fourteen. She was a little stray Manx cat in our neighborhood. The first time I saw her, she walked right up and curled up with me. I knew immediately that she was my baby. No other animal had ever interacted with me with such an abundance of affection and love, which she would give me so much of in the years to come. She always knew when I was sad, and she would sleep with me then, close by my side. Because I'd been homeschooled while pursuing my singing, I didn't really have a best friend that I saw often at the time, other than my parents. So Bobbi became that for me. She was always there for me. She never broke my heart or used me or hurt me. She didn't ever judge me or shame me, and in this moment of my public humiliation, her unconditional love was more valuable to me than ever.

Even though it felt like the end of the world, it wasn't, of course. Sometimes the first step toward surviving a truly horrible experience is to find a way to pick yourself back up after a big fall. What I didn't know at the time was that there would be many more occasions to pull myself out of a low place, just as there'd been throughout my childhood. I did that then, and I'm sure I'll do it again. I'm here to say that you can do it as well. No matter where you started from or where you are right now, you can get back up. You can reach your dreams. You can face hardships, and with the strength you find within yourself, you can actually achieve even greater heights.

So how did I get through that awful night when *The X Factor* aired? That story is coming, and many more. But first let me tell you about how my life began—or rather, how it almost didn't.

TWO

Singing from the Start

S he came into the world singing." That's what my parents like to say. God has been showing me miracles all of my life—literally, since my birth. My entrance to this world was definitely full of them. But no matter how scary my arrival was for my parents, they have always focused on the marvels it entailed, which tells you everything about the optimism and faith with which they raised me.

It was early July 1993, and my mom, Pat, who was twenty-eight at the time, was still three months shy of her due date in mid-October. She'd already had my brother, Brandon, four years earlier, so she was familiar with the normal stages of pregnancy. She could tell that something wasn't right when she started feeling unwell and having cramps. She called her doctor, who told her to wait at home, monitoring the situation.

The next morning, when her condition had not improved, she and my dad called her doctor back, and he told them to go straight to the hospital. It was much too early for their baby to be born, so my parents were concerned and wanted to hear that everything would be okay. Instead of reassuring them, after assessing Mom's condition, her doctor grew more serious. She had lost her amniotic fluid, which was far from ideal for her baby.

"Let's admit you into the hospital so we can watch you and the baby and see if the amniotic fluid will replenish itself," her doctor said. "I think it will, but you may be on bed rest for a while."

Mom had felt like something was wrong. But she had assumed it was something minor, and she'd expected to go to her appointment and then return to her normal life. The doctor's decision to keep her in the hospital surprised and worried both of my parents.

As my dad, Jerry, who was thirty at the time, gently pushed the wheelchair with my mom in it into the hospital elevator, a nurse walked in beside them. Suddenly the nurse paused and looked from my mom to my dad.

"You know, I'm really feeling led that we should pray together," he said. "Is that okay with you?"

"Oh yes, thank you so much," my parents said.

What the nurse didn't know was that they'd already been praying for a healthy second baby for several years. They'd been so happy when Mom found out she was pregnant with me, and everything had gone well until now. But it was hard not to worry along the way, and now my mom's being admitted to the hospital was definitely upsetting enough to redouble their prayers.

As the nurse bowed his head and began to pray, my mom felt an indescribable peace descend over her. After the prayer, my parents were no longer scared. They had complete faith that the tiny baby in my mom's womb was in God's hands and was going to be okay.

My parents would need that reassurance because after a day in the hospital, the prognosis quickly became much more ominous.

"The amniotic fluid isn't replenishing itself," Mom's doctor said. "We need to get you into surgery. We are going to have to get her ASAP."

"Her?" This was the first time my parents were told I was a girl. They were overjoyed by the news, especially since they already had a little boy at home.

"I have my boy and my girl!" my mom said.

But I was only twenty-six weeks along, and the survival rate for a baby born this early was unfortunately very low. My parents were terrified that they might lose me before I arrived.

The doctor gave my parents more difficult news. He said that if I survived, I'd most likely have learning disabilities, developmental problems, possible vision and hearing issues, and other challenges. The list of all that might be wrong with me was long and frightening. But my parents' faith was and is incredibly strong. In addition to their own prayers and those of their close family members, they'd asked the members of their church for prayers, and that request had spread to include people praying for our family all around the world.

My mom has told me many times that while she listened to her doctor's terrible list of all the many problems I could have, she still felt calm. It was unexplainable, a peace that can come only from God, and which is described in Philippians 4:7 as one that surpasses all understanding. In her heart and soul, my mom somehow knew that I was going to be okay.

Mom was rushed into surgery, and thanks to an emergency C-section, I was born on July 7, 1993. For as long as I can remember, seven has been my favorite number. When I got a little older, I realized that my birthday was actually 7/7, which felt like such a special day to me. Also, seven is considered by many to be a blessed number, and there were seven days in which God created the earth. I weighed only one pound and fourteen ounces—so small that I fit in the palm of my dad's hand. As soon as my mom regained consciousness, her first thought was of me.

"Is she okay?" she asked.

One of the greatest dangers for premature babies is that their lungs are not yet developed. The lungs are one of the last parts of the body to form in the womb, since they aren't needed until birth. Because of this, many premature babies don't survive. But as soon as I took in my first gasps of air, I miraculously started screaming—or singing, as my parents say—loud enough that my mom could hear me, through the door, inside the operating room. She began to cry, so relieved and overjoyed that I was alive and already fighting. My parents are still amazed by this story, to this day, and they love to point to how I've always been blessed to beat the odds.

One of my dad's favorite stories is about the doctor coming out from surgery and updating him about my well-being. "Well, she's one pound and fourteen ounces," he said. "To be honest, we are in awe that she came out screaming like that because her lungs should not be that developed."

My dad was speechless. He, too, cried tears of joy.

"Right now she's breathing on her own, but don't be afraid when you see her," the doctor said. "She'll have tubes down her nose and throat because she shouldn't be breathing on her own, and we expect her lungs to get tired soon. She's going to need artificial breathing."

Later, the doctor came back from the neonatal intensive care unit with another update.

"I have some news for you," he said. "Your daughter has two things going for her. One, she's a girl. For some reason, girls have a higher survival rate than boys. And two, she came out screaming and is still breathing on her own."

The doctor again warned my parents that my lungs would eventually get tired, and I would need to be intubated to help me with my breathing. But then another day would pass, and the miracle continued.

"We just can't believe it," the nurses and doctors said. "All babies born this small have to be intubated. But by tomorrow morning, most likely, she'll get tired and will need help breathing."

Day after day it happened the same way, until finally my parents got some good news.

"It looks like her lungs are strong enough on their own," the doctor said. "And she will not need to be intubated."

Over the course of the weeks and months that followed, my parents and other family members were at the hospital every day. Another visitor who made a daily trip to the NICU was my precious brother,

Brandon. He was four years old at the time, and my parents would lift him up and point at me in the incubator.

"That's your baby sister," they said. "There she is. You have to help take care of her. You have to always love her and protect her—don't ever forget that, mijo."

These were words that Brandon would take to heart. From that first sight of his tiny sister to this day, my brother has been very close to me, and we have shared a special bond. Throughout our childhood, our parents taught both of us to love and take care of each other, and my big brother is one of the people I am closest to.

At the time I was born, Brandon's favorite movie was *The Karate Kid,* with the actor Ralph Macchio. Brandon especially liked the female lead character, named Ali. So although he still wasn't even old enough to attend kindergarten, my brother decided I should be called Ally. My parents were very touched by this. So there I was—Ally, or Allyson Brooke Hernandez, my full name. I ended up giving my brother a name as well, because I couldn't say Brandon right. Since as far back as I can remember, I've called him Bobo.

Love has always been front and center in our family. Both of my parents grew up in large Mexican American homes. Even though they didn't meet until they were young adults, when they did, they quickly realized that they had a lot in common. They were both Catholic, both raised in San Antonio, and were both one of nine siblings, after having lost a sibling early on. How crazy is that? They also both grew up pretty poor. My mom slept in a bed with four of her sisters. Dad's mother was a single mom, and they lived off government assistance. Growing up, he slept on the floor or the couch, and he did not have his own bed until he got married. My dad tells stories of how when he got home from school, he'd wonder what utility was going to be shut off that day, because they hadn't been able to pay the bill.

Both my parents were raised with strict rules and were taught to respect their elders and themselves. My grandma would say to my dad, "We don't have much, but we're always gonna love each other, and family is all you need." My grandma from my mom's side used to say to her and her siblings, "Always work hard and be good to people and love with all your might." Even though my dad's father didn't live in the home, my grandfather taught my dad a lot about life, also stressing the importance of working hard and having a good attitude and heart.

I love hearing my parents talk about how they met, especially because they each have a different version of the story. Dad will say, "If you want to know the real story, listen to me." He describes how my mom and her sister came shopping for shoes at the store where he worked, Bakers Shoes, at the McCreless Mall on the southeast side of San Antonio. It was right at closing time, on a night when Dad happened to have a date with another girl. My mom and her sister were checking out all the different styles, not realizing that the store had already closed. My dad couldn't help but notice how beautiful my mom was, but he was getting anxious about being late for his meet-up with the other girl. Finally Dad spoke up.

"I'm really sorry, but we're closed, and I have a date tonight," he said. "How about if you come back Wednesday, and I'll buy you those shoes you're looking at?"

Clearly my dad had game. Nice job, Dad!

This seemed like a good deal, so they agreed and left. Sure enough, they did return on Wednesday, and when my dad saw them, he realized he had to buy them their shoes! He noticed again just how beautiful my mom was, but she hardly talked, compared to her sister. After my dad made good on his word and bought them their shoes, they thanked him and left. That could have been the end of the story right there. But my dad noticed a makeup compact on the bench cushion where they'd sat. He hurried out the front door to find them. When he didn't see them, on a hunch, he went out the back and there they were, headed toward the parking lot.

He called out to them and then ran up and returned the compact.

My aunt played matchmaker, giving my mom's phone number to my dad. He teases my mom to this day that she left her compact there on purpose. My mom insists that she wasn't even interested in him, and that it actually took Dad a few tries before he could convince her to go out with him. But whichever version of the tale is true, they've been happily together ever since.

During the difficult days and weeks after I was born, I grew stronger, helped by the powerful connection between my parents, as well as the strength of my family, their faith in God, their prayers, and my own resilience. It was not an easy or straightforward road. I had to have surgery to fix two hernias. I actually needed three hernias repaired, but the doctors were worried that being under anesthesia for too long would be too dangerous for me, since six weeks after my birth I still weighed less than three pounds.

My dad sometimes jokes that I'm their million-dollar baby, because I remained in NICU for a total of two and a half months, and the hospital bills were astounding. Thankfully they had good health insurance that covered some of the cost. And the hospital was kind enough to recommend programs that could help them with their remaining medical debt, but it took them years to pay off the bills completely. This was challenging for their young family, but thankfully, they had the support of their larger families, their friends, and their church community. They also received assistance from the March of Dimes.

Two and a half months may sound like a long time, but this was actually a small miracle in and of itself. Most premature babies born as young as I was have to stay in the hospital much longer. My doctors continued to marvel at my fighting spirit.

When I was finally strong enough to go home, my parents were elated. But I was not completely out of the woods yet. I had to be sent home with a heart monitor, as I had sleep apnea. The machine would sound an alarm if I stopped breathing, notifying my parents to give me a small touch to remind me to inhale. Of course, this was terrifying for them. And they didn't sleep properly for a long time. They were too afraid that if they were asleep, my breathing would stop, the monitor wouldn't go off, and I would die. They sometimes moved me gently, just to make sure I was okay.

As the months passed, it became clear that by the grace of God, I didn't have any disabilities or residual issues. The doctor warned my parents that I might have either hearing loss or acute hearing, but they wouldn't know for sure until I was older. It turns out I do have acute hearing, which means I have sensitive hearing. I'll go into all of that in more detail later. It's mostly a blessing, but not always.

Many of us have challenges in our lives. We have no control over what family we are born into, our initial gifts and talents, or the circumstances of our early lives. Some people undoubtedly have it easier, while others come into this world via difficult situations. But regardless of how your life started out—whether the cards were in your favor or the deck was stacked against you—know that you can achieve so much that's amazing.

Sometimes the very thing you see as a weakness or a challenge will actually lead you to excel. The first step is to believe that no matter what obstacles you may have to overcome, you can pursue excellence and be successful. In fact your early struggles may actually have gifted you with special tools and strengths that will enable you to reach your goal. So much of your future is about having the right mind-set and finding the courage to have faith in yourself, even if you were not as fortunate as I was to have such a wonderful support system in place at birth. I can honestly tell you, with all of my heart, you have value and beauty. God created you on purpose with love. As it says in Psalm 139:14: "I praise you because I am fearfully and wonderfully made; your works are wonderful, I know that full well."

I am so thankful for the blessings in my life. I credit God and my family for getting me to where I am now. That's a huge part of why I have chosen a life path where I can pay it forward by being there for as many people as I can—with my music, of course, but also with my story, and our online and in-person connections, which mean so much to me. It's hard to get by when you feel alone. I've been there, as you're about to read. We all need each other. We can't do this walk through life by ourselves. I certainly required a lot of support to face everything that was to come. But first I had to discover my true passion.

THREE

Where We Come From

Where I grew up is the foundation of who I am today. Whenever someone asks me where I'm from, there's always pride in my voice when I say, "I'm from San Antonio, Texas!" It's not just a location; San Antonio will always be a huge part of my soul, along with my family, my faith, and the power of music. In order for you to fully understand me, I need to tell you more about the forces that shaped the woman I am today.

Everyone has probably heard of the Alamo and the famous battle that took place there in 1836, a pivotal event in the Texas Revolution. It's definitely an important local landmark, and one that I visited in school when I was a little girl. We also have a deep admiration for our hometown heroes, the San Antonio Spurs. Our city really comes together to support our legends. Some of my happiest childhood memories are of going to games with my family—in my Spurs jersey, nachos in hand, of course. And I still go today when I can.

Along with the rest of downtown, one of my favorite places in the city is the River Walk, or Paseo del Rio, a network of walkways along the San Antonio River. The River Walk is lined with shops, restaurants, historic missions, art stands, galleries, bars, bridges, and all sorts of culture.

There's no better time to visit the city than the spring, when we celebrate our history and heritage with an enormous ten-day event called Fiesta San Antonio. I remember learning that it started back in the 1880s, and that today three million people attend more than a hundred events across the city each year. What I can tell you from firsthand experience is that it is a joyous celebration that the whole city comes together for, and it is so fun to be a part of. There are day and night parades in the streets of downtown, river parades, live music, food trucks, fairs, carnivals, and brightly colored costumes and decorations. If you live in San Antonio, you go.

I grew up attending with my entire family. We looked forward to it all year long. Nothing compares to Fiesta—it's so exhilarating and such a massive celebration. There were always so many fun events, and we loved going downtown to the market square for one of the most important parts of all—the food, of course! Under a rainbow of tents, they served up all the most delicious Mexican and Tex-Mex dishes, from elote (Mexican street corn) and tamales to nachos and, my favorite, gorditas—puffy tacos, stuffed with refried beans and cheese, or beef and cheese, and lettuce and tomato. I can almost just taste it now!

The most famous and oldest attraction of Fiesta is the Battle of Flowers Parade, which celebrates our diversity and honors the heroic spirit of our city. There's also the Fiesta Flambeau Parade, which begins at sunset and features floats, bands, horses, women wearing gorgeous princess-like dresses, and dancers illuminated by colored lights. My family would always be ready way in advance for both of these parades. We'd set up twenty or thirty lawn chairs along the route. And then everyone would crowd in together—my grandma, my aunts and uncles, my parents, my brother, all of my little cousins—with, of course, plenty to eat. My aunts would make their own tacos, and we would devour them along with whatever food we bought at the parade.

Throughout Fiesta, there's also a blend of live rock and Tejano music so people can dance together. And there are live flamenco shows and other fun events along the River Walk to enjoy. Nothing compares to Fiesta—it's amazing. I've always felt a thrill when I looked up to all of the beautifully dressed local heroes who passed by on the beautiful parade floats, waving at everyone lined up to cheer them on. I dreamed of one day being up there myself. It was the honor of a lifetime when I was asked to be the honorary grand marshal of this year's Fiesta Flambeau Parade. Now I'll be the one waving out into the crowd at all of the little wide-eyed girls and boys with big dreams, just like I used to be.

Actually, if there's one thing that can top Fiesta, at least for me, it's the holidays. Not only is Christmastime my favorite time of year, but it's the most magical moment for the River Walk, when it's all lit up with lights twinkling for as far as you can see. No matter the season, there is so much to do here. What I love most about San Antonio is that it's so rich in culture, and that we always come together around our local pride for this majestic city.

You can't come to San Antonio or to any gathering my family throws without planning to *eat*. The food I was raised on is part of my DNA. Tex-Mex is a fusion of American and Mexican cuisine, known for handmade flour tortillas, spices, a hot sauce we call chilé, rice, beans, the best tacos ever, chorizo, enchiladas, tamales, and lots more. In my family, we had many get-togethers at the holidays, but also at any time there was an excuse—like a birthday celebration or a football game. My aunts would make chalupas, beans, rice, beef tacos and fideo, which is Mexican spaghetti. The food is glorious, and even though we can all eat like champions, there was never any shortage of leftovers.

My dad is an excellent cook, too. He makes flour tortillas from scratch—the best tortillas on the planet. He also bakes amazing pies, and no family celebration during the holidays would be complete without them. And just about every weekend when I was growing up, he'd make delicious breakfast tacos—chorizo and egg, potato and egg, or sausage and egg. They were definitely a hit with my friends and anyone who came over. I would sometimes help my dad to get out the cheese or crack the eggs. I do now know how to make homemade tortillas myself. I'm very proud that I learned how to do so recently. But I still can't seem to mimic Dad's magic. And one day I will learn to make them as well as he does.

On Christmas Day, tamales are a tradition, not just at our house, but for lots of Mexican families. Sometimes my family makes them from scratch. My parents also found the sweetest Mexican lady who makes them for locals, and hers are the best in the world. My dad also makes mouthwatering chilé con queso dip, which is a Tex-Mex dip served with tortilla chips. For breakfast, my mom does a quiche— sometimes with French toast or biscuits on the side, and always delicious. I'm in charge of making hot chocolate for my brother and me. We make Mexican wedding cookies and thumbprints, which are some of my all-time favorite desserts.

Not surprisingly, given how much they love Christmastime, my parents always went all out on decorations. My dad actually earned the nickname of Clark Griswold—the character Chevy Chase played in the National Lampoon movies—because at Christmastime, he acted just like him, covering the outside of our house with so many lights and decorations that people would come from all over to see his annual displays. Inside, the Christmas tree was the main focus, and every year my mom chose a different theme—it might be snowmen, elves, angels, or a particular color. Of course we always put out our nativity scene, too. And the whole house became a wonderland.

On Christmas, we'd spend all morning in our pajamas, taking turns opening gifts, and watching our favorite holiday movies. Then we'd meet up with our whole family—my grandma and Grandpa Paul, aunts, uncles, all of our cousins, and enjoy ourselves. Those qualities at the heart of who we are as a family—food, love, family, and faith—

are especially important during the holidays. Christmas is my absolute favorite time of the year. I love the reminder of Jesus's birth, the child-like wonder felt by people of all ages, the love in my heart, the nostalgia, the music, and the traditions. I wish every day was like Christmas.

When my family gathers for any reason, almost every weekend, it's sure to be a good time. I grew up with dozens of aunts, uncles, and cousins, and our get-togethers are filled with laughter and storytelling. Oh, and amazing music—usually oldies, or Spanish and Tejano, which is a blend of numerous types of music including Mexican, country, polka, waltz, pop, blues, mariachi, and cumbia that originated among the Mexican American cities of central and southern Texas.

At our family's heart is my grandma, and we also had so much love for my grandpa Paul, who was her second husband. I loved going to my grandma and Grandpa Paul's house as a little girl and watching telenovelas, Mexican dramas similar to soap operas. She would make me beans, pork chops, tortillas, and huevos (eggs) and the best chilé or hot sauce. If I had to choose my last meal, it would be my grandma's tortillas and cooking. Grandma would sit with me and talk in Spanglish, and I would try to figure out what she was saying. We would talk about so many things—from family and school, to boys, my friends, and music. Even today, whenever I visit home and can see my grandma, we do the same exact thing. I always cherish time with my grandma.

My Grandpa Paul was a special man. He was always outside, working on the yard, wearing a cowboy hat, Wrangler jeans, cowboy boots, and a big smile. He was kind to everyone and had the greatest laugh. I would sometimes help him with jobs around the house. Or I would give him a hand, cleaning out his little garage, and we would listen to Spanish and country music and talk. He loved George Strait with all of his heart. He also loved Selena as much as I did, and he kept a little poster of her in his garage, which is still there to this day.

Sometimes my grandparents and I would go out for a meal at a Mexican restaurant near their house or go to the grocery store together.

Our local grocery store is called H-E-B, which stands for "Here Everything's Better," the store slogan—and it really is the absolute best. Our whole family has always shopped there. I think my parents make a trip there pretty much every day. And when I'm home, even when we don't need anything, I always ask if we can go to H-E-B.

I'd also spend time with Grandma and Grandpa Paul at family get-togethers. But mainly we made our memories at their house, with food prepared from the heart and lots of laughter. Grandma's little house was like a second home to me, and she still lives there. My grandpa is in Heaven now, but I'll always hold him and my memories of him very close. I miss him every day. He was an angel on this earth. He was one of the most wonderful men in the world.

From childhood on, I was lucky enough to receive the kind of unconditional support from my family that would sustain me through the many lows and highs to come. A strong family bond, my faith in God, and our Mexican American culture became the foundation for everything else.

I've also had great spiritual mentors over the years. I especially think of those from Oak Hills Church, my home church in San Antonio. My parents were drawn to this congregation because Max Lucado was the pastor, and they had heard wonderful things about the church. Not to mention that Pastor Lucado is a passionate and articulate man with a great heart who has written many bestselling books on faith. I remember being read his books in elementary school, especially *You Are Special.* To me, he radiates the heart and spirit of Jesus. As soon as we joined the church, we immediately felt right at home. It happened to be in our neighborhood as well.

On Sundays, my parents, brother, and I went to service in the big church, and then when I was in high school, I started going to youth services at the youth ministry, which was overseen by the youth minister Brett Bishop. My youth leaders became a huge part of my life: Chris Butler; Deneen Goeke; Deneen's husband, Tim; Brett Bishop and his wife Jenna Lucado, who was Pastor Lucado's daughter. She was someone I really looked up to and admired, who had a great influence on me. In fact, I am still very close to all of these wonderful people to this day.

Although I was very shy when I was young, I started to come out of my shell in these years. I immediately felt right at home at the church. They were so welcoming and showed me God's love. They became a big part of my life. I even had the honor of singing at the youth service, and then eventually, the big church over the years. When I'm home, I always love to go back to Sunday service at Oak Hills with my parents whenever I can.

A love for music runs deep in my family. For as long as I can remember, my parents brought an array of sounds into our home that influenced my own passion for music. I grew up on so many of the greats, including such varied talents as Dolly Parton, Gloria Estefan, the Carpenters, Frank Sinatra, Barbra Streisand, Elvis Presley, Aretha Franklin, Chicago, Sade, Céline Dion, Santana, Amy Grant, Elton John, George Michael, Taylor Dayne, Rosemary Clooney, Whitney Houston, Judy Garland, Diana Ross, Cher, Stevie Wonder, Crystal Lewis, and Louis Armstrong. These are just some of the magnificent artists we would listen to. Our home was always a mix of priceless, eclectic, timeless music. They raised me on everything from Motown to music from the seventies, eighties, and nineties. That was one of the biggest gifts my parents could ever give me—the gift of music. Real music. The classics. I cannot emphasize just how important having this musical foundation has proven to be for me. I am deeply thankful that my parents raised me on such great artists.

One of my mom's favorite songs of all time is "What a Wonderful World" by Louis Armstrong. Hearing those strings swell at the start of the song never fails to give me goose bumps. It is now one of my favorites, too. You can hear the smile in his voice and feel the magic of the instruments coming together just perfectly, really lifting you up. That's what I love about music. It warms the soul and enwraps the listener in the beautiful spirit of the music, creating a deep connection between us on a soulful level. I also love the magic of "Somewhere Over the Rainbow" and "Moon River." Those will forever be my favorite songs.

While I was growing up in San Antonio, there were always mariachi bands and Spanish music playing at events and restaurants. This music is part of our city and our culture. It is who we are. It influenced me in ways that I am still discovering to this day. Latin/Spanish music has been around forever, but only recently has it gained popularity all over the world. The beautiful, highly emotive lyrics, infectious rhythms, and intricate melodies are now being heard internationally. It is being appreciated more than ever, and it is finally being given the spotlight that it deserves. This is because of groundbreaking artists like Selena, Gloria Estefan, Jennifer Lopez, Shakira, Enrique Iglesias, Ricky Martin, Marc Anthony, and so many others.

They have paved the way for artists like me, and I love the music made by all of them and draw on it for inspiration every day. I am able to sing in Spanish and reflect Spanish influences in some of my music, because of the trailblazing artists that made this possible. Now I hope to expand the possibilities even further by finding new ways to honor and draw on my musical heritage. My family couldn't be prouder.

Of all the extremely talented Latin artists out there, one star has always shined the brightest for me. Ever since my earliest childhood, my favorite singer and biggest inspiration of all time has been Selena Quintanilla. Selena was a Mexican American singer from Lake Jackson, Texas, not too far from my hometown of San Antonio. She had the most majestic voice in the world. Everything she sang came from the depths of her heart. As an entertainer, she lit up the stage like no other, gracing it with charisma and presence. And as a person, she had an extraordinary spirit. She was so beautiful, and what made her even more so was her radiant, one-of-a-kind soul. She was down-to-earth and funny, had a trademark laugh and a signature vibrant smile, and she loved her family and truly adored her fans. Selena was so special, and it was a tragedy for millions of people around the world when her life was cut short at the age of twenty-three. Her tremendous spirit shines brightly to this day, even more than two decades after she was so tragically taken from us. If anyone embodied how music can touch people with genuine passion and heart, she did.

Our family would play Selena's music all the time—at barbecues, around the house, in the car. I would dance and sing along for hours, until I sometimes fell asleep mid-song, having worn myself out. From a very young age, I loved Selena with all I had. She was everything to me. And I truly mean for as long as I can remember, because she passed away when I was two.

Some of my earliest memories, from when I was four or five years old, are of watching the biopic about her life, *Selena,* starring Jennifer Lopez. I've seen that movie countless times—more than I've watched any other movie, ever. My mom and dad had to buy me three different copies of the DVD of the film, because I wore out our copy more than once. No matter how often I had seen it before, whenever I got to the heartbreaking scene of her passing, I would sob and sob. Every time, I felt the same deep sorrow and emptiness that she was gone. Going to find my mom in the kitchen where she was cooking dinner, I would wrap myself around her legs and press my tear-stained face into the fabric of her pants.

"Mom, Selena died," I said.

"Oh, Mama, I'm so sorry you're sad," she said, even though we'd gone through this same grief just the night before. I'd want her to lift me up and comfort me, and she would.

It always made me feel closer to Selena, knowing that some of her most famous performances and important career highs had occurred right in my hometown, and it still fills me with pride. Our city is honored to have welcomed her so many times. Her music video for "No Me Queda Más" was filmed at the River Walk and Sunset Station. She opened one of her boutiques, Selena Etc., in San Antonio and held one of her fashion shows for her clothing line here. Over the years, she also held numerous concerts and interviews here. Also, her biopic was filmed at several different locations in San Antonio, including the Alamodome, where Selena had performed in real life.

Do you want to know something else that's amazing? There is a famous video out there of Selena holding a baby girl, and that baby is my cousin, Destiny! My aunt and uncle used to follow Selena around Texas and watch as many of her concerts as they could, because they also were big fans. They have a large framed photo of the special moment. Since I was little, I've often asked them to tell me their stories of meeting Selena in person. As a family, as a city, and as a culture, we hold Selena forever in our hearts. And the impact all of this had on me cannot be stressed enough: having witnessed a Mexican American woman like me reach her dreams at such an early age helped me to believe that it could happen for me someday as well. It was so powerful to have an early hero who was also Latin and looked like my family and me.

It's just amazing that someone you've never met could have such a big impact on your life. Selena definitely played that role for me. I admired her so much—not just for her stunning voice, but also for the way she connected with millions of people across the world. And for her beautiful smile and laugh, and how she seemed to radiate pure light and goodness at all times. Also, Selena helped me with my first obstacle to performing—my shyness. Because I watched her movie and interviews over and over, I learned through her example to be more outgoing. I would not have the personality that I have today without her positive influence on me. I wanted to be like her—to touch people and to change their lives—and I really modeled my dreams after her. Not long ago, my parents found an old home video of me in front of our Christmas tree when I was around four or five, talking to the camera about my dreams. "This is me, Ally, and I love to sing," I said. "And I love to sing! And I want to do a show, and I wanna sing in front of lots of people, lots and lots and lots of people, a beautiful song."

That vision of my future definitely came from Selena, and she has been a guiding force to get me here. Whenever I hear Selena's music, it still brings me an indescribable joy. To this day, I watch Selena's videos and listen to her music almost every day. There will never be another like her. Her legacy gives me the courage to spread my own wings and fly.

FOUR

Finding What You Love

Not only did I come out singing, but I never stopped.

My dad and mom tell stories of me as a two-year-old singing along to the radio in the backseat of our car. They recorded videos of me singing around the house. I loved wearing my mom's heels, dancing around in my diaper, or even just singing along to the music my parents had on in the background. Other friends and family began mentioning what a good voice I had for such a little girl. My parents were flattered by these compliments, and of course they thought I was great at pretty much everything I tried, but it didn't fully register with them that I might have a gift for music—at least not right away.

And then when I was about three years old, my secret superpower began to reveal itself. We'd gathered around a cake for a relative's birthday, and there was that feeling of anticipation in the air, just before the singing starts. The candles were all lit and flickering, and then everyone joined in for "Happy Birthday to You," singing along and smiling at one another. Everyone but me. As soon as the singing began, I clapped my hands over my little ears as if they were hurting me and started shaking my head.

"No, stop, stop!" I called out.

The first time this happened, everyone thought it was cute and they laughed as they tried to reassure me that there was nothing to be upset about—we were all having fun, and the singing would be over in a few moments. And then the same thing happened at several other family birthday gatherings. Finally my parents had a realization: *She doesn't like the sound!*

It wasn't just that. The singing wasn't just too loud. I was upset that people were off-key. You know how it is: in a group that's singing "Happy Birthday," it rarely sounds perfect—there are usually a few flat notes from tone-deaf people. They began to realize that even though I was young, my musical abilities were already starting to develop.

My parents also thought back to my doctor's warnings when I was a tiny preemie—that I might have either hearing difficulties or acute hearing from being born prematurely. That's exactly what this was. My ears are very sensitive. Sudden loud or banging sounds have always been extremely painful for me. Fireworks, thunderstorms, and even just balloons popping bring major pain to my ears. Every Fourth of July while I was growing up, instead of watching the fireworks outside with all the other kids and their families, I stayed inside our house, trying to protect my ears from the loud pops that hurt me enough to make me cry.

This sensitivity to sound might be annoying every once in a while, but in other ways, it actually turned into a gift, allowing me to hear notes and inflections with great clarity and to identify certain sounds with precision. I can't tell you how many times I've been able to catch when someone is even a little off-key, an instrument is not in tune, or something is not quite right in the mix in recording sessions. Especially when I was younger, people have doubted me, raising their eyebrows when I first pointed out the issue I was hearing. But eventually we'd all listen together very closely and discover that, yes, what I said I'd heard was absolutely accurate. I can't tell you how many times I've had producers, engineers, and other musicians ask me, "How did you hear that?" (This also comes in handy if my phone rings in another room—even if it's on vibrate, I can always pick it up. I really can hear that well.)

My hearing is such a great example of how God can take our biggest challenges and limitations and flip them around into something positive. Over the years, I've seen so many cases of how a weakness can actually become a strength. And when I'm faced with doubts about my abilities or a situation that seems insurmountable, I try to remind myself to have faith that there very well may be a gift contained in this situation, even if it's not visible yet.

I was always singing and putting on mini shows around the house. And then when I was around six years old, I sang at church for the first time. Before my family attended Oak Hills Church, we went to this sweet little church that held services at a local movie theater. My parents were good friends with our pastor, and he told my parents that I was welcome to sing during Sunday service, if I wanted to. They asked me how this sounded to me. "Oh yeah, I'll do it! I'll do it!" I said.

We chose "This Little Light of Mine" for me to sing, and I practiced it at home. On Sunday morning, my mom dressed me up in a pretty sundress and put bows in my hair. I was all ready to go—until we got to church. I was so shy and I immediately got stage fright.

"I don't want to sing anymore, Mom," I whispered.

"You'll be okay, Mama, don't worry," my mom said, keeping her voice low.

"You'll be great," my dad said.

When the pastor saw I was nervous, he smiled and held out his hand to me. "Come on, Ally, I'll help you," he said.

"No, I don't want to," I said, shaking my head harder.

Of course everyone thought this was adorable. But I was really frightened—the thought of having everyone staring at me was too much, even though these were our parents' friends and everyone there was so loving and supportive. It was quite scary for me. On the other hand, I *loved* to sing.

Finally I went up to the front. I gave my parents a look that said: *Help. I don't want to do this.*

The pastor, seeing how anxious I was, had a brainstorm.

"How about if you just turn around and look to the back of the room and sing into the microphone?" he said.

The pastor's wife had come up to the front, too, and they were both hugging me and encouraging me with their presence and support.

"Don't worry, you're singing about Jesus," he said. "You're going to be great."

The pastor's wife gave me one final squeeze and kiss on the cheek, and they both took their seats, leaving me alone up there.

I looked at my mom one last time. She gave me a look that said: *You can do it, Ally!*

The music started. I clutched the microphone and turned my back to the audience, staring at the white screen where movies were projected. I started singing "This Little Light of Mine." I was so nervous, I started crying and shaking into the mic. But then, when I was done, everyone clapped for me, and it made my little heart so happy. I felt so elated as I scampered back to sit between my parents, who were beaming.

"They liked me!" I said.

"Of course, they liked you, Mama," my mother said. "You sang beautifully."

I'd definitely felt triumphant after my unofficial debut at our church. But my nerves were so bad that even though I was always singing something around the house, I mostly just left it at that. And my parents were casual about my voice. Still, anyone who did hear me sing was always exclaiming to my mom, "Pat, Ally can really carry a tune!"

So my mom tried again and put me in a music recital when I was a little older. This time I was also nervous, but somehow I was able to sing and my voice was the loudest.

And then someone close to me spoke words that would change my life forever. Not that any of us realized it at the time. It was 2003, I was nine years old and attending third grade at a private school in San Antonio. My grades were great, and I had a wonderful, close group of friends, including Kayla, Aaron, and Kristen, as well as a few others, and who are still my friends today. Overall, I had a blast in school. My favorite part was music and English class, recess, lunch (of course!), and PE. These were the good ol' days of being a kid, when life was simple. I absolutely hated the idea of getting in trouble, so I was always very obedient. Most of the time, my teacher didn't need to ask me to do something more than once. I was early for everything (my parents had raised both my brother and me to be this way). I was always prepared for whatever the day's lesson was, and I tried to be as helpful in the classroom as I could be.

I had a wonderful teacher named Mrs. Merrill, and little did I know how important she would become to my life journey and career. Not only was she very gifted when it came to leading her classroom, but she also cared enough to go above and beyond the basics of her job, speaking up when she saw something special in someone. I will always be grateful to her for that. One day Mrs. Merrill sent me home with a letter, requesting a meeting with my mom. My mom often volunteered in my classroom, so she was familiar with my school and already had a close bond with my teacher, but this was something unexpected. They met after school the next day.

Mrs. Merrill was clearly excited as she sat down with my mom and prepared to tell her why she'd called her in that day. "I wanted to talk to you because Ally has been asked by her music teacher to sing at chapel," she said. "We wanted to see if that is all right with you."

My mom was pretty surprised. As much as she knew I loved to sing and had always earned compliments for my voice, she'd never thought of my singing as anything more than something sweet that she and my dad enjoyed recording for family home videos. But she was very flattered by my teacher's request. Of course my mom said yes and expressed her excitement about this opportunity for me to shine.

"Ally has a gift," Mrs. Merrill said. "She has such a beautiful voice."

"We are always hearing that," my mom said. "This will be great for her."

A few weeks later, the day came for me to sing in chapel. Around my family, and with close friends, I was outgoing and fun-loving, but with strangers or in crowds, I remained painfully shy. My parents and I both had a clear memory of how bad my stage fright had been when I'd sung for our church, and I think they were a little worried that my nerves might get the best of me once again.

When it was time, I was able to walk right up to the front of the chapel, stand there proudly, and sing. Looking out at my classmates, Mrs. Merrill, and my parents in the audience, I let my voice soar up to the sky. As I finished, it was amazing to see the audience clap and cheer.

My parents were amazed. For the first time they realized, *Oh my gosh, she has a beautiful voice.* It was at this very moment that my mom and dad realized that my path forward was not necessarily going to be the same as that of most other kids my age. Mrs. Merrill had helped my parents to realize that I had a gift for music. Thanks to the inspired words of my beloved teacher, Mrs. Merrill, and what my parents witnessed firsthand during that chapel service, my life was forever changed.

My mom and dad felt they had to do something with my voice. They had to nurture it. They immediately began researching music programs in San Antonio, and they stumbled upon a local nonprofit organization called Network for Young Artists. NYA gave young singers and musicians a chance to perform at local events around the city and sometimes even further afield. They had a humble studio downtown where kids could drop in, choose and rehearse songs, take voice lessons, or practice dancing or an instrument. It was a safe haven for young people—like me—that had a musical calling and wanted to perform. It sounded perfect.

Before long, my parents took me to NYA's studio and met the organization's founder, a man named Terry Lowry, whom everyone called Coach because he had worked as a coach at a low-income school in San Antonio for years. He was a kind man with salt-and-pepper hair and sparkling blue eyes behind his glasses; he spoke excellent Spanish. My parents took a shine to him right away. They asked Coach questions about how his program worked and whether it would be a good fit for me. He was so warm, with a kindhearted spirit, almost like Santa Claus. He explained the goal of the organization, which was to help kids gain confidence through music. Knowing how shy I was, my parents thought this sounded like just what I needed. Staying out of trouble and doing well in school was also a requirement to be in NYA, and although I didn't have any problems in these areas, my parents figured it couldn't hurt to have me in an environment where such positives were encouraged. They instantly felt at home with Coach and asked him what they'd need to do to get me involved in his program. He said that for starters, he'd love to hear me sing.

I spent a few days preparing a song, and then my parents took me to meet Coach and sing for him. I felt terribly shy and nervous, but I did the best I could. Coach was happy with what he heard. He welcomed me into his program with open arms. He told my parents that I would have to work on my shyness but that he saw something in me. Right then and there, Coach gave me the ultimate gift—a chance.

My parents signed me up, and I became an official student. I met the staff and some other students. I was timid and nervous at first, but NYA would soon become my second home. Right away I began practicing at the studio to prepare for my first-ever public performance. Again, Coach told me that I was a great singer, but I would have to work on my shyness, because he couldn't let me perform if I was shy like that. I loved NYA so much and really wanted to be one of the kids who performed, so I listened to everything he said and practiced my little heart out. I think being around this new group of people who were supportive and just as passionate about music as I was definitely helped me to feel more comfortable with myself. Along with Mrs. Merrill, Coach was important in my journey to get where I am today.

They helped me to become confident, made me feel like I already had the ability within me to shine, and gave me the strength to start performing in public.

The weekend of my first NYA performance, my mom helped me with my outfit, hair, and makeup. I wore a red sleeveless Tommy Hilfiger shirt, bright white pants, and tennis shoes, and put my hair up in a ponytail. We met Coach and the rest of the NYA group at the Market Square downtown, right outside our city's staple Mexican restaurants, Mi Tierra and La Margarita. The courtyard would be our stage.

My aunts, uncles, cousins, grandparents—everyone was there. They didn't know what to expect, and although they had caught some of my mini-performances for my parents over the years, they certainly didn't know that I could sing the way that I did. Of course, my parents and brother were there, too. I'd been practicing "What Dreams Are Made Of," a song from *The Lizzie McGuire Movie.* I had been obsessed with the *Lizzie McGuire* TV show and had watched the movie over and over again. Along with music, I was also influenced by so many films. I guess you could say I was drawn to the greatness that is entertainment. It filled me up like nothing else ever did.

As usual, the San Antonio heat was thick with humidity. I waited with my family as the other kids from NYA performed. My stomach was so full of butterflies that it ached. My parents were right there with me, encouraging me and trying to calm me down, but my nerves were getting the best of me. I stared out at the crowd—there were about fifty people walking around the square, plus the audience that had gathered, including my family and the other kids' families. That was a lot of people. How would they react to me? Would they like me?

It was finally my turn. Coach got on the microphone and introduced me. I heard his voice in my head: If I wanted to perform, I had to push through my fear. Coach believed in me, and he was right there. My parents believed in me, and they were there, too. Feeling all of their love and support surrounding and protecting me, I took a deep breath. *Here I go,* I thought.

I walked up to where Coach was standing at the center of the square. He handed me the mic with a big smile. It felt big and heavy in my hand, which was already a little sweaty. A floor fan whizzed behind me, circulating the hot air. I held tight to the mic. I gave a quick introduction—something along the lines of "Hi, I'm Ally. I'm nine years old and I will be singing 'What Dreams Are Made Of' by Hilary Duff." I talked fast and my voice was shaky. I rocked a little from side to side, full of nervous wiggles. But then the music came on.

Holding the microphone in my right hand, I took a deep breath and then started singing and moving to the music. My mom's friend had helped choreograph this "dance break," and I did the steps as best as I could, even though the result was pretty funny. As I sang, an indescribable feeling came over me. I was still nervous, but it was as if I had gained superpowers, and I was able to push through and sing.

To my surprise, the audience and my family went crazy. They actually loved me! My family smothered me in hugs, and with so many compliments, I felt like Lizzie McGuire at the end of the movie, when she conquered the stage, and found herself while she was performing. People in the audience whom I'd never met or seen before came up to me, too, saying how great and talented I was. It was unreal—after I'd nearly been derailed by all of those nerves, it had turned out that I'd had nothing to worry about. People actually liked me. And I had created that connection with my voice. I fell in love with performing right then and there.

Even with the success of that first NYA performance, early on, as a performer, I still battled my shyness. Sometimes it got the best of me onstage. At either my second or third performance, I was at one of the Market Square stages, where the kids involved with NYA often performed. On this particular day, Mrs. Merrill came to see me. She had never seen me sing outside of school, by myself, so I wanted to do an extra good job for her. I could feel her and my parents watching me as I walked onstage. As with my earlier performances, I had practiced long and hard, under Coach's guidance, and at home with the help of my dad. But I was still very nervous. And then as I was singing "Dreaming of You" by my absolute favorite singer, Selena, my voice cracked in the middle of the song. I was mortified. I managed to keep singing, but I wanted to sink under the stage and disappear. Trapped under all of those stares, I suddenly felt so self-conscious. I couldn't stop the tears that built up in my eyes. By the time I finished the final verse and walked offstage, I was completely crying. I felt so small and embarrassed.

Mrs. Merrill hurried over to me right away, ready to dry my tears. "Ally, you were amazing!" she said.

And somehow she made me feel that I had done a good job, even though I'd had that one little mistake in there. She had that power to fill you up with good feelings about yourself, even on the days that weren't going so well. I was so blessed to have her as my teacher. She was an angel.

Even though I'd had a rocky show that day, I didn't want to stop. I loved singing too much, because of the beautiful, indescribable feeling it gave me. It was magic. From that day on, I began singing anywhere that would have me. Of course I still performed at school, my brother's sports events, and family gatherings. For the next few years, rain or shine, all year round, I also sang at charity events, talent shows, restaurants, festivals, Fiesta events, the River Walk, carnivals, banquet halls, baseball and football games, malls, theme parks, galas, barbecues, birthday parties, and even Walmart. Plus, many of my performances were back at the Market Square.

Looking back at this time, I can see that the best thing about performing so often, and usually for very supportive local audiences, was that it was a safe way for me both to get better and to learn to roll with all of the uncertainties that go along with putting on a live show. I was becoming a pro before I even really understood what that meant. As I was finding out in those early days, when you go out onstage, you have to be ready for anything. You don't always do as well as you did during practice. Sometimes there are technical difficulties. Sure, I had rough days. There were moments when I forgot the words to a song. There were times when I became so self-conscious that I was crying by the time I left the stage at the end of the performance. These setbacks were discouraging. But my parents kept working with me, giving me feedback and pushing me to be better. And I just had to keep trying, through the good days and the bad.

One of the most important choices a performer can make is the song she's going to sing, and they were always brainstorming with me about new songs to learn and add to my list. Coach had a catalogue of karaoke CDs with hundreds of songs on them. So when we'd decided on a new song, we'd start by asking him if he had the music for it. If he didn't, my dad was always taking me to Walmart or Target to look for our own karaoke CDs, which were great for providing backing music and lyrics. While I was learning a song, my parents always helped me and gave me advice. All of this practice also helped me to get over my shyness and begin to grow into who I am today, as a performer and an artist.

In those early years, the songs I performed varied in styles and genres. Of course, my number one was Selena, so I loved to sing her songs, like "No Me Queda Más" and "Como la Flor." One of my go-to songs became "I Will Survive," first recorded by Gloria Gaynor. I gave my rendition lots of soul and attitude, and it always got the crowd going wild and cheering me on. At this point, I began to truly come into my own and discover my confidence and the persona I would adopt onstage. As I've already mentioned, my parents raised me on the classics, and so I had a great appreciation for the greats. I sang "At Last," most famously recorded by Etta James, countless times. They also got me into popular music from the seventies and eighties, and another one of my favorite early songs was "Last Dance" by Donna Summer. I regularly performed both of those. I also loved the music that was coming out at the time—one of my favorite songs was "Sk8ter Boi" by Avril Lavigne, so I had to perform it. The album, Let Go, was one of the first albums I ever bought.

Sometimes my performances felt natural and I was in my element on the stage, and the crowd went wild for me. Then there were times when I made mistakes. I was so young, and I always just wanted to do my best.

One hot spring day, when I was about ten years old, I was singing at a festival called the Oyster Bake, singing "If I Can't Have You" by Yvonne Elliman. And then just like that, I forgot the second verse. I was way past the early days when this would have reduced me to tears. By now I was quick on my feet, even when there were many eyes watching my every move. I drew on my stage smarts now, going into emergency mode. I acted like my mic went out, during the length of the verse I'd forgotten. I mouthed the "words" and tapped my mic as if it wasn't working. Then as soon as it was time for the chorus after the second verse, which of course I remembered, I jumped back in, as if my mic had suddenly come back on.

The audio guy was freaking out, unable to figure out what had gone wrong (because nothing had), and I felt so bad for him. But I was thankful that my little act had worked, and the audience believed my mic really did go out, instead of me forgetting the words. *Thank God!* I thought.

Later, when I was offstage and far from the audience, I confessed to my family what had really happened. Of course, it seemed hilarious in retrospect. And, if I do say so myself, it was pretty impressive that I'd come up with something so last-minute that had actually worked. My parents and I still love to laugh about this story.

My parents were all about supporting my passion for music in whatever way they could. They decided that piano lessons would be a great way to expand my musical abilities, and since I loved music, they figured I'd be a natural. Once I started, it's true that I caught on fast, though not in the way I was supposed to. From my first lesson, my teacher was happy with the fact that I could play whatever she taught me. And then one day she started to catch on.

My piano teacher would play a song and then ask me to give it a try. While looking at the piano book, I played the same tune, as easily as could be.

"Okay, let me hear you play this," my teacher said.

She pointed to another song in the piano book. I looked at the notes as if I knew what to do, then played the first song again. The teacher studied my face, then played something else.

"Can you play that?"

And I did, perfectly. My teacher realized that I couldn't read the notes, but I could play the piano by ear. Music was definitely my element. But with my schedule as busy as it was, my parents had been selective about my activities. After a while, they decided not to keep up my piano lessons. But I know that foundation has helped my music, even if I was trying to get around learning the notes by playing by ear. And this is another of our favorite stories, as a family, to this day.

I have many wonderful onstage memories from these years, and it was a time of discovering who I was as a performer. I loved feeling the magic of connecting to the audience and making people smile or even cry. I loved to sing songs with soul, and again, I attribute that to the classic music my parents raised me on. I worked incredibly hard for a kid, but my parents were very supportive, whether they were driving me to a show and helping me to get ready for my performance or we were simply practicing around the house.

As I grew older, my parents and I continued to work hard to pursue my dreams. My dad continued to help me with my vocals. My mom helped me with my outfits. We had become a good team, and we continued to do our thing.

My parents were incredibly patient and they always seemed to have energy for me, even though my dad was busy with his job and my mom volunteered at my school. And they were both also very involved with my brother, who was super active in sports. They drove me all around, because my shows were literally all over the city, and Mom would pack plenty of snacks for us: fruit, potato chips, and my mom's delicious sandwiches—roast beef, peanut butter and jelly, and turkey.

One of our favorite things was to put Fritos inside our roast beef sandwiches. My dad always carried his fruit punch Gatorade. We'd find a place to eat our lunches and snacks together, or sometimes we'd snack in the car as we hurried from one venue to another. I can't tell you exactly how many shows I did over the years. It definitely was in the hundreds, and my parents came to every single one.

Before long, I started singing "The Star-Spangled Banner" at basketball, baseball, and football games. My brother Brandon was involved in these sports, and sometimes I sang at the opening of his games. My parents were as supportive of Brandon as they were of me, so if we weren't at one of my performances, we were often sitting in the stands of one of his sporting events, rooting for him and his teammates.

What really made me smile and kept me hooked on singing, even during the years when I was still learning the ropes and sometimes had mishaps, was the way it drew people to share pieces of themselves with me. It was as if seeing me open up onstage inspired them to do the same. As much as I loved to sing, I also loved talking to the strangers who would come up to me afterward—moms, dads, aunts, uncles, grandparents, little girls, little boys. They would say how good my performance was or how beautiful my voice was or how my voice had moved them. I was in awe that they liked me, and I always felt this powerful love for them, because the music had created a connection between us. I was just so happy that I could make people happy. I still am in awe at how music brings people together, instantly touching the spirit and adding so much magic to the world. It's truly a gift from God.

Not that my parents and I worked on my singing all of the time. Often we'd eat Tex-Mex at my favorite restaurants like Blanco Café, where they even know us by name. I love their enchiladas, rice and beans, and tacos. I could eat that every day for the rest of my life. I still go to those spots when I'm home today. It's so nice to have those pieces of my personal history that I can always return to, instantly making me feel at home when I set foot inside. Really, is there anything better than having a great meal with people you love? Some of my favorite memories are of eating and talking about life with my beautiful family and friends at these favorite places of mine.

One thing my parents did have was belief, which they instilled in me. And we had each other. It quickly became clear that my other great love was music, and that I had such a strong love for the stage. My parents took my passion seriously and encouraged my dream of music.

As performing around San Antonio became a regular part of my life, we began to meet other parents who'd made changes to their own lives in pursuit of their children's dreams. My parents saw them for the valuable resources they were, and they always asked a lot of questions. They also began to research everything associated with building a music career in order to figure out how to best support me. My parents saw my dream and talent as a gift from God. They were energized by their belief in the power of my voice and the good it could do in the world. But looking back, I know it was hard on them. Every spare minute they had went to us kids.

There was another challenge for my parents. My mom was in a great deal of pain. She was born with scoliosis, which means she has an S curve in her spine. Her back hurt her all the time. Car rides, stadium seats, and the constant travel that went into building my career, even just in my hometown, were very painful for her. When I think back on it now, I want to cry, because she kept going, encouraging me, giving up her own interests for mine, and pushing through sometimes excruciating agony so I could keep pursuing my dreams. This would go on for years and years.

It was made all the worse in the late spring of 2003, when we were involved in a terrible car accident on the freeway in San Antonio. My mom had noticed that another driver seemed intent on merging into her lane, so she'd sped up a little, but the other woman still didn't see our car. She ended up hitting us so hard that we spun around and crashed into the median. In order to avoid losing control, my mom held onto the steering wheel so hard that she came away with carpal tunnel syndrome. This mental and physical strength on her part probably saved our lives, because it kept us from flipping over onto the car's roof. Even so, the car was totaled so badly that the engine was almost completely through the steering wheel. My mom turned around, terrified, to look in the backseat and see if I was okay. Miraculously, my side of the car was the only place that hadn't been dented in, even though it should have been. My mom had to climb out the passenger window to open my door for me. I was hysterical. It was one of the scariest things I've ever experienced, and I think that experience is partly why I've never gotten my driver's license. To this day, I can still smell the smoke from the crash.

My mom has always said there was a guardian angel with us in our car that day. And while it's true that it was a miracle we were able to escape from the crash without any physical injuries, it did increase my mom's back pain. When she was younger, she'd had two steel rods surgically inserted into her back to try to fix the way her spine was severely curved from her scoliosis. Something about the impact made her back far worse than it had been, and it would continue to cause her more and more pain in the years to come. Still, she always put me first and was selfless in the way she gave of her time and energy to help me with my singing.

The more I sang and made music, the more I didn't want to do anything else. Music filled me with this special joy, and even today, it still feels like it's my everything, my great love. I think childhood is the perfect place where our passions and callings begin, even if most people don't know exactly what their life purpose is as a kid. If you don't know what your calling is, it's worth thinking back to who you were and what you loved as a child. Were you naturally drawn to sports, or maybe toward setting up a little business in the form of a lemonade stand or lawn-mowing service? Did you dream up stories or love to try making things with your hands? It doesn't matter what age you are; it's never too late to find and pursue what's in your heart. It might be working with children or animals, designing buildings, becoming an athlete, coaching or teaching others—it could be a million different things. It seems we live our best lives when we live out the best version of what God made us to be. It sure isn't easy, but I suppose life never is, right? It takes a lot of hard work, honing ourselves, growing our faith, and devoting ourselves to the work that goes into the constant improvement needed to be the absolute best. That said, a life of meaning is worth all of that effort. But first we have to believe we were meant for greatness. All of us—you and me. *Believe* is one of my favorite words.

It felt like I had already done so much with my singing—and for someone my age, I had. Little did I know, though, that my musical journey was just getting started. So many incredible things waited ahead. Difficult days were coming as well, but at least I had my family and my faith, and now I knew what my true passion was—and with that knowledge, I was on my way to something greater.

FIVE

Be You

I was twelve years old, and music filled my life.

For three years, I'd been performing regularly around my city and the surrounding areas. During the school year, I had shows almost every weekend, and in the summer, I was always singing somewhere. Of course sometimes I just wanted to be a normal kid. There were times when I wanted to take a long enough break and go on vacation with my family, or to be with my friends after school or on the weekends. I grew up with some amazing kids from elementary school and our church, some of whom are friends of mine to this day. When we would get together, we loved to eat pizza, watch movies, have dance parties, bake, and talk about boys. They also thought my music was exciting, and sometimes they would come to one of my shows.

While my parents expected me to take my singing seriously because of how much energy we were putting into it as a family, they also wanted me to have fun and relax sometimes. They never pressured me to do more than I felt up for. My parents really believed in me and supported me at every show I ever did. They were there to smile, clap, and root for their little girl. Rain or Texas shine.

About this time, my friend Clarissa was competing in a talent search at a mall. We'd always done shows together, and her mom, Gilda, was such a sweet mom and a beautiful soul—she loved my singing, especially when I sang "On My Knees" by Jaci Velasquez. And she used to go on shopping trips with my mom to get stage outfits for me. Clarissa tried to convince me to sign up for the competition as well. "Ally, you should do it, too. Please!" she said.

I talked to my parents, but they were skeptical. I didn't end up auditioning, but we promised to go and support Clarissa. The talent search was being held at one of our local malls, North Star, where we went all the time. When we arrived, it felt like just another normal day.

The event was in an open space in the center of the mall. Kids and teenagers were getting ready for what they believed to be their shot at fame. When I found my friend in the crowd with her mom Gilda, Clarissa was nervous, and she asked me again to join her.

"Won't you sing, too?" she said. "It would make me feel so much better if you did."

There was a long table covered in a black cloth where a few judges were sitting. A woman asked my parents if I was going to audition, but we politely said that I was just there for my friend. I stood with my parents and Gilda as my friend sang her song in front of the judges. She did a beautiful job, and she advanced to the next round.

I don't remember how it happened exactly—maybe someone talked my parents into it or Clarissa convinced me—but somehow I ended up singing, too. I hadn't prepared a song, but I decided to sing one of my favorites. Because I had been performing for years, it had definitely become easier for me to sing on the spot.

Well, little did I know it at the time, but this was another of those moments that changed my life forever. As I've learned from experience, sometimes they're not planned or the result of your efforts. But instead, they happen just because you showed up. In my case, not only did I show up that day for my friend, but I'd been showing up for my music for years. I know that if I hadn't been performing for that long, I wouldn't have been prepared to sing on the spot that day, and I certainly wouldn't have been prepared for what was to come.

I was in front of the judges, singing "On My Knees." This song had meant so much to me, as it had carried me through so many pivotal moments since I was a little girl. To this day, it reminds me of the power of prayer, and it helps me to reconnect to my faith.

As I finished singing, the judges seemed to be very impressed. I noticed that the woman who'd asked me if I was going to audition was getting a little teary-eyed. Another judge asked me to sign up for the next round, but my parents respectfully declined.

We were about to go home, but then the woman who'd gotten teary-eyed during my song came over to talk to us, pulling us to the side, away from the other judges and contestants.

"Hi, my name is Dana Barron," she said, telling us how she was there that day only as a favor for a friend. "I don't have any affiliation with this organization, so I have no ties to this. Now, I never, ever do this, but you gave me chills, Ally."

She gave me a long look, her face full of lingering emotion. "You were incredible," she continued. "Now, again, I never do this, and you're going to think that I'm crazy. But I would love to take you guys to Los Angeles and introduce you to some casting directors and agents."

My heart started racing, and I'm sure a huge smile was spreading across my face. But my parents were exchanging serious looks, trying to process what she had just offered.

"I know it sounds strange, but your daughter is amazing," Dana said. "I would love to help her get with a good agency. I'm not going to charge money or anything like that. I promise, this is not a scam. Ally has such a talent, and I would love to help in any way that I can. If you could get to LA, I'm going to be filming in a few weeks and would love to bring you on the set."

I couldn't believe that I'd just been offered such an incredible opportunity, out of the blue. Especially at only twelve years old! Agents?

Casting directors? LA? That sounded like my ultimate dream come true.

My parents were grateful but taken aback enough to be a little tongue-tied.

"Thank you so much, Dana," my mom said. "We don't know what to say. And I'm so sorry to interrupt with this, and excuse me for asking . . . but you look really familiar."

Dana smiled bashfully.

"Well, I am an actress," she replied. "You might have seen me when I was younger. I was Audrey in the original *National Lampoon's Vacation* movie."

We gasped. Our family were big fans of all of the *National Lampoon's* movies. In particular, *National Lampoon's Vacation* was a cult classic in our home. And we watched *National Lampoon's Christmas Vacation* at least once every year. My dad was a big fan of Chevy Chase, the main actor in the movie. Though the Christmas movie wasn't the film that Dana had appeared in, the franchise felt like a part of our family, and now by extension, so did Dana.

"I also played in *Beverly Hills, 90210,* as Jason's girlfriend," Dana added.

My parents immediately knew who she was and recognized her from both of these projects. I was freaking out. It was such a cool moment, to meet a real actress right here in my hometown of San Antonio. The connection may have seemed minor, but it was enough to overcome my parents' suspicion. From the first moment she'd approached us, Dana was so kind and seemed genuine. But knowing she had real Hollywood credentials fully eased their minds.

"Again, no strings attached," Dana said. "I'd love to help you navigate through this business because there's a lot of crazy stuff out there, and you have to be careful."

Then she turned and addressed me directly. "I can help you, if you take this seriously," she said.

This was a lot to take in. As always, my parents wanted to do what was best for me and our whole family. While this had the potential to be a major opportunity for me, it would also mean a significant expenditure of money and energy. Opening the door to Hollywood was exciting but also a little terrifying. They needed some time to think about it.

Still, we were extremely flattered that Dana had spoken so highly of my voice and delivery, and we were grateful that she had gone out of her way to make a connection with us. We thanked Dana as she gave my parents her contact information, and I gave her the biggest, brightest hug before I walked away, hand in hand with my parents.

After praying about Dana's offer, my parents decided to take the next careful step. My parents had good friends in Lake Arrowhead, just a few hours outside of LA, and we'd been planning to go visit them anyhow. Maybe we could combine the two trips and see where our time in LA might lead. A few days later, I was in the kitchen with them when my dad made the call.

He got Dana's voice mail and left a message. They half thought that she might not ever call us back. Even though she was obviously a very thoughtful, genuine person, we knew how busy she was with her career. It was pretty incredible that she'd even considered taking the time to help me. We would have understood completely if it was just too much for her to actually do.

But she returned our call, and she was as gracious as ever.

"I'm so glad you called me," she said. "My husband and I were just talking about your daughter. She's amazing."

Dana again extended an invitation for us to come out to Los Angeles over the coming summer so she could take me around town. When we told her that we might be coming to LA for a family trip, she told us that she'd check her schedule and free up time for us the week that we would be there. I couldn't believe it—this was really happening.

Of course our entire family would be going, so I ran to find my brother.

"Bobo, we're going to LA!" I screamed.

Just a few weeks later, we took a Southwest flight to Los Angeles, California. My heart felt like it might jump out of my chest. I looked out the window of the airplane, dreaming of the possibilities that might lie ahead for me. After years of performing around San Antonio, I was actually going to the City of Angels, where the entertainment industry was based and so many artists saw their dreams become reality. It nearly felt like I had made it already.

We landed at LAX, picked up a rental car, and drove to our hotel. We were on a very tight family budget, but I didn't care. All that mattered was that we were really there.

Dana was above and beyond gracious to me. She took a week of her time to take me around to meet acting agents, casting directors, producers, and writers. We even went to the Nickelodeon offices. I was interviewed by everyone she had me meet with, and I always sang for them. Although I was confident when it came to singing live, this was a new type of opportunity with way higher stakes. I was pretty nervous, but all that practice had made me much better at managing my nerves. It also helped that everyone seemed to like me, and after my first few meetings, I was starting to get the hang of this new adventure.

Dana also invited our family onto the set of a film in which she was appearing, *Saving Angelo,* which was so unbelievably thrilling. My first ever movie set. I felt like the coolest kid on the planet. These were the moments I had dreamed of, and now it was actually happening. We met actors and actresses and got to see what a film set was like. The biggest-name actor, who was playing the dad, was Kevin Bacon. I'd loved him in the movie *My Dog Skip,* where he'd also played the dad, and I'd admired him ever since. He was the nicest man—just lovely to me and my family. I still have a copy of the photo I took with him. I was wonderstruck and my parents were amazed because he was one of their favorite actors.

In addition to all of the opportunities she opened up for me, Dana was a wonderful mentor. She gave me invaluable advice about how to carry myself and behave in the industry. "Ally, you need to take this seriously," she said. "I don't want you to ever be late."

Of course, this was in keeping with how my parents had raised me, but it definitely had extra weight coming from someone who'd achieved so much. This was my first entrée to LA and Hollywood, and I will always be thankful to Dana for giving us our introduction to the entertainment industry. Not only did Dana provide me with an opportunity that changed my life, but even more than that, she believed in me. She was the first professional in the industry to do so, and she in turn helped me to believe in myself.

This belief was important—because if I was going to make it in the entertainment industry, I was going to need every ounce of confidence I could muster and all of the loyal backers I could find. Something I learned early on, during this time, was the importance of having people believe in you. I had my parents, my brother, and so many other amazing people in my family and our local community. But Dana was the first one beyond our little inner circle, so her support meant even more to me. Not everyone has that kind of support, and I'm most grateful to have had it.

Some people have a much harder time finding a supportive group. But one trick that can really help you to do so is to start out by supporting others. Not only will you feel good about helping someone with their own dreams, but you'll start to build your own community of like-minded dreamers, which will go far over the years it often takes to get anywhere in life. You don't have to grow up being the star of your school, your team, your family, or your city to reach your goals. Sure, some people fly high fast, and at a young age, but more often, it takes years of working hard to reach any level of success. Of course, having talent is great and helpful, but you have to find the courage to use it. Then there are people who work hard to master skills and keep trying even in the face of obstacles.

Even with all of the positive elements I've described, I've also had my fair share of setbacks. Times when I've had to keep getting up over and over again, with a smile on my face and a determination in my heart to keep going. Through these, I've built my faith in God—and that has been the key part for me.

So don't be discouraged, if you, too, want to become a singer or an athlete or a designer or anything else that takes talent and hard work, but you don't win competitions or have people coming up to you with words of admiration yet. Many people eventually become successful because even on their darkest days, they love what they do and they don't stop trying or believing, no matter how many times they get knocked down. That was me.

Although the first producer Dana took us to see wasn't looking for artists as young as me, we also had a connection to an LA music producer who was my dad's client at the insurance company where he worked. After hearing my dad talk about my singing, this man offered to have a meeting with me if we were ever in LA. On our trip to see Dana, I was supposed to sing for him, but he had to go out of town at the last minute. He felt so bad about this that he arranged for me to meet with a friend of his who was also a producer. When we went to see that person and sing for him, he was blown away by my voice and couldn't believe I was only twelve. The next day, he had me record a song in the studio, to see how I would do with original music. Again, he was really impressed. He signed me to what's called a production deal, where we would record music, trying to see if any record labels would pick me up and offer me a deal.

My parents had diligently studied the entertainment industry. They were always doing whatever they could to help me, and sometimes it paid off, which was amazing. But the kind of powerful connections Dana had were suddenly opening up a whole new world of opportunity for me. At the end of our LA trip, Dana took me to audition for a big talent agency for kids, Coast to Coast, where I met one of the agents. She was friendly and asked me to read two sides, which are scenes from a script. I went outside and practiced for a few minutes, then came back in and read for her. I was nervous, of course, as it was not only my first audition but also one with great significance. Still, I took my dad's words to heart—he was always reminding me to just have fun, and in this moment, I let myself do just that. The woman seemed impressed and said that I was very natural. She told me that I had done an excellent job and she was happy to have met with me. Her feedback gave me the biggest smile.

Dana and I left the building before she told me what she thought. "Great job, Ally!" she said. "That went amazing!"

After all that she had done for me, I was so happy that I had been able to live up to her expectations and make a good impression. And soon enough, to my family's great joy, I got the fantastic news that Coast to Coast was going to sign me!

My family and I were amazed at how God had opened this door through Dana. It wasn't something we ever could have orchestrated on our own, not from our little corner of the world in San Antonio. Yes, I had worked hard, but this moment had taken more than just hard work. It had required the kind of connections that may have seemed accidental but were really meant to be—God was preparing the way.

Even when doors were opening and I was so excited to rush through them and see where I could take my music, sometimes it was hard to know what to do. We lived in San Antonio. Our entire world was there—my dad's job, our school and friends and church, our extended family and our cats. But everyone we'd met during the trip told us that we needed to be in LA.

My parents faced some big decisions. Looking back, I now know that there was much more to figure out than a twelve-year-old could have possibly comprehended. First, they had to think about the impact on our family. They were wary about making such a huge change in our family's life, and they wanted to make sure my brother, who was still in high school, was okay with our moving forward. If we did this, I and at least one of our parents would have to go to California and start spending a great deal of time there. Brandon would have to stay behind and finish school. We'd have to live in two cities. Our close family unit would be divided for sometimes months at a time, and I'd need to be homeschooled. My parents would have to switch off, which would be challenging because of my dad's job and my mom's back problems.

My mom's back issues made it difficult for her to move around, let alone travel. Her condition was getting worse. To help my mom, I tried to take on more responsibilities. I learned to make break-fast and helped her carry the laundry basket, fold clothes, clean the house, and grocery shop. Some days her pain was manageable, but other days it was so crippling that I had to help her to even walk. There is no heartache like seeing your mom in pain, and I would se-cretly cry in my room. I wondered how she would possibly be able to travel so much, if we went back and forth to LA. There was also the money. It was so expensive to live in California. My parents prayed a lot about what God wanted and what would be best, not just for me but for all of us.

Brandon was actually starting his last year of high school, and while he was already super independent, my parents didn't pretend that having our family divided was going to be easy on any of us. There was a lot at stake—our finances, our living situation, my school-ing, my dad's career. We'd need to alter our whole lives to make this work. And of course there were no guarantees that any of it would land me a music career. It was a lot to consider.

But my parents knew I wanted nothing more in life than to chase my dream, and they believed my talent was a gift from God. They were also aware that opportunities like this didn't come along every day. When Dana had singled me out, we had been graced with a one-in-a-million connection with an industry insider. They knew in their hearts they couldn't pass up this once in a lifetime opportunity.

I was on pins and needles during this whole time. I wanted so badly to go to LA, but I also wanted what was best for our family. I felt guilty about anything that might put an extra strain on my mom's back. It was a lot of responsibility. As always, my parents reassured me.

"Mama, we're gonna try to figure it out," they said, giving me a kiss on my forehead.

Somehow, though, my parents figured it out. We would bounce back and forth between Los Angeles and San Antonio, and my parents would switch off, taking turns bringing me out.

And so it began.

I was in sixth grade and started homeschooling through an online program. For the first few months, my mom and I went out to LA first, because it was hard for my dad to get time off from work. We would be staying in the Oakwood Apartments, just up the street from Hollywood. We were told this was the place to stay if you had a dream of being a successful actress or singer. It was the be-all and end-all of apartments for young up-and-comers. Hilary Duff and Dakota Fanning were just two of countless celebrities who had stayed there when they were first trying to break in. It was overwhelming in the best possible sense—I was living in the same place that some of my favorite actors and actresses had stayed, and hopefully this would just be the first of many ways in which I would follow in their footsteps.

But when we moved in, suddenly we were in a different world. My excitement drained quickly as I studied the other kids. I was nothing like them. I didn't look like them. I had crooked teeth. They had flawless smiles. I had conquered my stage fright, but I was still painfully shy, especially around new people my own age. They carried themselves with confidence and ease, seemingly with all the friends in the world. I had no friends in this new city, just my mom.

For the last three years, I'd been hustling and singing around San Antonio wherever I could and attracting a small following in the process. But now suddenly I'd entered a whole new world, filled with many other extremely talented people, many of whom were LA veterans. I immediately felt very small, a little tadpole in a big pond; at the age of twelve, I was completely out of place for the first time in my life.

Well, in Southern California, and especially in the entertainment industry, it's difficult not to be constantly comparing yourself to other people—especially when you're going up against them at auditions. And so these feelings of inadequacy and competition get enormously inflated. So much about show business can be superficial—about what people look like on the outside, instead of who they are on the inside. And when you have only a few minutes to make an impression at a meeting or audition, it can be difficult to show your true heart.

Then there was the issue of money—mainly that everyone around me seemed to have so much of it. These kids dressed like models who'd just stepped out of a magazine, with the latest styles from the hottest brands, purchased with seemingly unlimited funds. Meanwhile, my mom was a master at putting together cute outfits for me to wear to performances and auditions, but we were definitely on a tight budget, so we spent hours at the mall, scouring the discount racks. My mom was resourceful as well as creative, using coupons whenever she could. Everything we bought was intentional, and Mom carefully considered every purchase. I was so grateful for her, but I was also aware that our circumstances were different from those of the other girls I met at Oakwood and out at auditions. This gap only added to my insecurities.

Every girl in the entertainment industry needed some sort of look to stand out, and Mom worked tirelessly to get that for me. She had a great eye for style and would research what pop artists were wearing at the time. She would watch the Fashion Channel and entertainment news shows and study magazines for inspiration. Gwen Stefani, Jennifer Lopez, Carrie Underwood, and Beyoncé were often her muses. It was amazing what she was able to do with items from the sales rack at Ross, Marshalls, Forever 21, and sometimes Bebe.

My mom would diligently try to craft a look for me that was striking but within our budget, and this took hours to do. Sometimes she'd have to sit down for a break because of the severity of the pain she suffered from her scoliosis. I hated these moments and felt so guilty about putting her in this position. With tears in my eyes, I'd beg her to stop for the day, telling her that what I already had was great. But then she'd insist on continuing to work. That's how much it meant to her to help me.

Even with my mom's efforts, though, I felt like I looked different—not only in what I wore but also everything about me. Growing up in San Antonio, I'd been surrounded by the rich Mexican heritage of the city. But at that time, in those apartments, I was surrounded by mostly Caucasians for the first time. This was at a time when there wasn't as much wide-stream diversity in our industry as there is now. I had a dream of representing my culture in entertainment. I am very proud of my Mexican American heritage, but feeling and looking like an outsider in this new world wasn't easy.

For the most part, I didn't experience any overt racism, but there were moments when people tried making me feel "less than." One time when my mom and I walked into a high-end store in Beverly Hills to look around and dream, the employees were clearly looking down at us. It felt terrible to me, but my mom never let it get to her. She was a strong woman, confident in who she was. It made me even prouder of her. And though I didn't like the feeling I got from the looks, I followed her example and never allowed myself to feel ashamed. We were proud Hispanic women. I know that came from our family roots and upbringing in San Antonio, where we celebrate where we come from and who we are. I wasn't ever ashamed of my heritage in LA, but I definitely had many moments of feeling unsure of myself.

We were no longer in our beloved, charming Great State of Texas. Instead, it was another universe. Nobody said "y'all." The food was also different—no Tex-Mex anywhere. In addition, the people in LA weren't as friendly as the people back home in Texas—at least the people we had experienced at that point. And don't even get me started about the traffic.

The result of all this was that the shyness that I'd struggled with in the past returned and kept me from approaching other kids at Oakwood and potentially making new friends. I felt so different from them, and I floundered, as my insecurities and loneliness grew. There was one young actress living at Oakwood who was like the princess of the place. She'd already appeared in a movie, and so we kids looked at her like she'd made it. She was friends with all of the other cool kids in the building, and I would watch them longingly, wishing to be included, but feeling way too scared to try. Once I was sitting in the lobby of the main building when she sat down next to me and said hello. I thought I was going to have a heart attack. I managed to squeak out a timid "Hi." I definitely wasn't able to come out of my shell enough to connect with her. And although she was nice to me during that conversation, she never approached me again.

One night, all of this bubbled up to the surface. Here I was, living at this apartment complex where many of my favorite stars had caught their break. But I didn't feel on the verge of success. I felt alone— overwhelmed and out of place. My excitement about making it in LA was long gone. My emotions overtook me, and I was crying my eyes out, lying in my bed. My mom heard me, came in. She sat down and started to comfort me.

"Oh, Mama! What's the matter?" she said.

"Mom, I'm just not good enough," I said, tears streaking my cheeks. "I'm not cool. I'm not that pretty. I don't look like any of those girls. I don't have friends. I will never be what they are. I will never fit in with them. I will never be good enough!"

My mom, fighting back her own tears, gave me the biggest hug and held me tightly. "Oh, Mama," she said. "You are good enough. You are more than good enough. You are so special. I wish you could see what I see in you. I promise, you will get through this. Everything will change one day. We are going to get through this together, and don't think for one second that you aren't beautiful. You are beautiful, not only on the outside but also on the inside. You are the most beautiful girl in the world."

She lay with me that night, never leaving my side, and we both cried ourselves to sleep. I'll never forget that night.

My mom has since told me that this was one of the most heart-wrenching nights she'd ever experienced. Her heart broke in half. There is nothing worse than witnessing your child feeling like she isn't good enough. But my mom and I got through it together.

The next day, an inspiration arose within me. Words came to my mind like a letter to myself. I quickly wrote them down; it seemed that the words were just flowing out of my body. Beauty from ashes—because of that heartbreaking experience, I wrote my very first song. It was called "Be You," and this is the chorus:

Don't you dare turn into someone else
You know that that's not you
Do you really wanna be like that?
So go ahead and be yourself
If they don't like you
Surely someone else will
So go ahead and be you.

Writing that song did wonders for me, most important because I began to believe the words. I began to have hope. I began to feel confidence. I began to be me, not the me I thought I should be when I looked at other girls around me, but the real me.

When I wrote down those words at the age of twelve, my strength returned, and I was able to get back up and keep pushing forward toward my dreams. I hope these words can help you, too. I also want to encourage you, when you struggle, to find what works best for you so you don't quit. But, instead, you get back up and go ahead with your path, and you be you. Maybe you would also be helped by writing down your feelings. Maybe you need to go for a long walk or talk to a dear friend. Or pray. Or get up and dance around to an empowering song. Whatever it takes, believe me, there is a way to climb out of the darkness and begin reaching for the light.

What I couldn't have guessed then was that I'd need these same words, not just during this time of my life, but later on, after I'd found all of the success I'd ever hoped for, at a time when it looked like everything on the outside was wonderful. But inside, I was struggling.

SIX

Talent, Hard Work, or Both

It's tough not to get emotional when I think of everything my mom and dad did for me in the early years of my career. My mom didn't have to work as hard as she did to find clothes for me. She should've spent some money on herself, but she loved me enough to care that much even about something as small as my outfits and accessories. So every free penny went to that.

I'm sure Mom struggled with her own emotions and culture shock, being away from her husband, son, and home. She'd never lived anywhere but San Antonio, and suddenly she was navigating not just a whole new city, but also the entertainment industry. She didn't have friends in the city of LA either, and she even put her health second for me, pushing herself to do more than she probably should have and intensifying the pain in her back.

I'll never, ever be able to thank her for the number of sacrifices she made for me. She is truly the strongest woman I know, a role model of unconditional love and support. Even with her scoliosis, she kept at it, pressing on through the pain because she believed in me and my dream. My mom and dad are my true heroes. They both had to be very creative to make it so that I could stay and work in Los Angeles during those years.

Whenever we hit an obstacle, they helped me to find a solution. My first online homeschool program was pretty tough and clearly wasn't working for me. I liked working in my pajamas, but being on the computer so much of the day gave me horrible headaches. And I couldn't check in with my teacher when I was confused or had questions. There was a messenger service for communication between us, but I couldn't talk directly to anyone.

My parents researched our options, eventually enrolling me in City of Angels School, a program right in the center of Hollywood. I had an in-person session every Friday with my teacher, Mrs. Escobar. She was a young, sweet Latin American woman who made me feel safe and connected. Now if I had questions about my work or problems with anything, Mrs. Escobar was there to support me. It felt as if I had my own terrific tutor. I did that for a year or two, and it was a great experience. It worked with my schedule, and there were usually a few kids my age there at the same time as me. So in between tests, we'd hang out and get to know each other a little bit.

I had transitioned from the City of Angels program to homeschooling with my mom. From ninth grade to senior year, I helped to choose my own curriculum. My mom and I went to a large homeschool library in San Antonio that housed a wide variety of curriculums. We spent a lot of time asking questions and researching before choosing what we thought would be best for me. I took all the main subjects, including math, science, and English. I loved English and excelled in it. I did well in math, too, but I had to work much harder to get good grades in that subject.

While homeschooling worked with my schedule, sometimes I felt lonely and missed my friends from home. My mom did her best to help me spend time with kids my own age whenever she could. If she saw a chance for me to connect socially, such as at a dance studio or once a week at school, she would encourage me to put myself out there and interact with others. Eventually I made a few friends in town. I grew a little more comfortable with LA, although it never felt like home, at least not back then.

As soon as I'd arrived in LA, Coast to Coast started sending me out on auditions for TV shows, movies, commercials—many different kinds of parts. If my agent sent the lines ahead of time, I always prepared carefully, and in the morning before my audition I would take extra time to dress in a cute outfit and do my hair. Often, I would come close to getting the part. The casting directors would bring me in for a callback, but I never landed the role. Although my main focus was on my singing, I had also begun taking acting lessons at age nine, and acting still remains a dream of mine, so that sometimes felt frustrating. But even at the time, I could tell it was a wonderful experience. They sent me to meet with many producers, helped me sign up for more acting lessons, and taught me how to behave in front of a camera, which would definitely come in handy years later, even though I didn't know it then. All of this helped to build my confidence and gave me a sense of purpose, like there was a reason for me to be in LA.

In the end, I stayed with Coast to Coast for a couple of years. Through the music producer I'd met on my first trip to LA with Dana, I'd been given my first opportunities to break into the music world. It became obvious that with the amount of work and dedication required to get anywhere in acting and music, I couldn't really do both. And of course, music was always my first love. This was reinforced when I went out for the Broadway play *Thirteen*. Even though I didn't get cast, the casting directors and producers said I blew them away with my rendition of "Let's Hear It for the Boy." This was amazing feedback because it had been a strenuous audition. They had a clear message for me: "Wow, you need to be singing."

And so that's where I put my focus. In Los Angeles, I got my first real professional experience in the studio and began to record music. Even though I had a lot of performing experience, I had only been in a recording studio a few times in San Antonio when I was younger, for a children's album that I'd recorded with my uncle Conrad, who was a firefighter, and once when I'd auditioned for this producer.

Now I was shown how to use a recording microphone and how to develop my voice. I was given the chance to play with a piece of music and to be creative with the tones or notes. I discovered how to record harmonies. I met local songwriters and recorded songs that they'd written. Even though I was much younger than most of the people I was working with, they always expressed admiration for my talent and treated me with respect. This was where I was meant to be. I felt free to be myself and to do what I loved. I was creating music, *my* music. It was the most amazing feeling in the world.

My mom tirelessly drove me back and forth between our apartment and the studio, and sometimes we'd be there until nighttime. She never liked driving in LA, and I hated when she drove in traffic, because she found it so stressful and became very frantic. After the terrible accident we'd had when I was nine, I still sometimes got nervous in the car myself. I'm only half joking when I say that, of all the things we got through in those days, surviving LA traffic with Mom behind the wheel just might have been one of the hardest! After a few months, my dad was able to join us for a little while. It was wonderful to have him there. It felt so much more complete. (And he took over the driving, which we were all happy about.)

Through a nonprofit program called P.A.C.E. (Promoting Academics thru Creative Expression), I gave some performances at area middle schools and high schools. My mom dressed me in cute little outfits, and my dad printed out flyers for me at Kinko's, with my name and Myspace page on there—shout-out to Myspace!

One day I was in the auditorium at one of the schools where I was due to sing, and I looked up and saw my dad handing out my flyers to the students, working so hard for me. It's one of the sweetest memories I have of him. My parents never did anything halfway. They put their full heart and effort into everything, and that included promoting me—not because it was their dream, but because it was mine.

No matter how many times I went onstage by myself, I always got a case of nerves beforehand. But once I walked out there, I was filled with confidence and a sense of being exactly where I was meant to be, and I instantly dove into my performance. Given that most of the students at these school shows were my age or older, I didn't know what to expect. I was nervous about being judged by kids my age, especially because I often performed my original songs. When I think about it now, I am proud of myself for being brave enough to go out and perform music the audience didn't know, especially for kids so close to my age. It could easily have gone so wrong, as teenagers can be painfully honest. You never know how you're going to be received. If they don't like you, they will let you know. But despite my fear, I went out there and did what I loved most. And again and again, I got the biggest thrill—the kids actually liked me! I loved who I was onstage. It was like I transformed into a different character. I felt almost like a superhero putting on her cape every time I stepped in front of the mic. After the show, they'd come up and ask for my autograph or a picture—sometimes hundreds of kids, and I'd be there signing flyers for hours. I spent time talking to all of them, asking about school and their lives, trying to get to know them, once again feeling the powerful connection of music. While in my personal life I could be shy, after shows I felt comfortable talking to the students. Those encounters reminded me of what I had to offer. After all, I could see it plain as day in the faces of those kids. Once I put myself out there and gave it my best, my true self began to shine. And I became more confident about putting myself out there in other areas of my life as well.

After we'd lived at Oakwood for a while, my parents tried to save money. There was a period of time where we stayed at a hotel in Marina del Ray—my dad, my mom, and me. For breakfast, we went downstairs and ate as many free waffles as we could stuff in. Looking back, it seems like it must have been so hard, but I guess when you're in it, you adapt pretty quickly. Still, it must have been very challenging for my parents. They definitely had to juggle to make it work.

We lived in a series of apartments around the city, sometimes getting a better deal for moving a little farther outside of LA, like when we lived in Sherman Oaks, which is in the San Fernando Valley. Rent was just one expense of many. My parents would ask around to see if anyone we knew had any furniture that they were getting rid of, and when we still needed things, we'd scour yard sales and Craigslist for bargains. When that *still* didn't give us everything, we'd go to the local thrift store and spend as little as possible on just the bare minimum to furnish our new apartment. Sometimes I would sleep on the couch. Or my dad slept on the couch. A few times, we had nothing more than air mattresses. One apartment had silverfish and other bugs. I was freaked out by the insects, and nothing my parents tried could make me feel better. I hated it there and felt miserable because this was nothing like home—our real home. I was homesick and missed all of my friends, my family, and my cats back in Texas. But I couldn't give up my dream, not when we'd come this far.

Every day we looked for ways to save money. My mom always had coupons. We took many trips to the 99 Cents Only store. Almost every day for breakfast, my dad and I would walk to McDonald's and order the breakfast platter or Egg McMuffins. We'd go to Subway, order the five-dollar foot-long, and split it among the three of us. Or we went to Panda Express and shared one big plate. At El Pollo Loco, the three of us would share a chicken, rice, and bean bowl, with one burrito on the side. We definitely loved a value menu—and good thing, too.

Eventually we moved to another apartment in Culver City. That was the best one so far. It had two bedrooms, which felt big compared to the places we'd stayed before. But it still wasn't home. All of those hard times made a lasting impression on me, filling me with even more gratitude for where I am today. As difficult as the situation was at the time, those silverfish and air mattress moments were crucial to strengthening my resolve and shaping me into the woman I've become. I never take where I am for granted, and I always remember the sacrifices my family made to give me a shot at success. The hard times are part of the beauty of my story, just like your hard times are an important part of the tapestry of your life experiences. And as humans, we can always connect over our struggles. Everyone is fighting their own battles and has a story, no matter how perfect they may look on the outside. I've learned that not only from my own story, but also from watching my mom and others close to me. Even if your life isn't where you want it to be right now, don't worry, you're making stories to look back on that will one day show you just how far you've come.

Although we never missed a Christmas in San Antonio, that first holiday season in LA was hard. We didn't want to be that far from home during our favorite time of the year. But at that moment, we needed to be in LA. I was so lonely, being away from home. Seeing how much my family believed in me, I knew home was wherever we were together. And yet we were incredibly happy when it was time to go back for Christmas, with its abundance of traditional foods, loud and joyous celebration, festive decorations, and most important, our dozens of family members.

A year passed and then another, with us living between two states and trying to make something happen for my career. Then at the age of fourteen, I had a meeting with a producer. His name was Larrance Dopson. He was part of a team of producers, musicians, and songwriters called 1500 or Nothin'. My parents and I met up with him outside a small studio in Inglewood. My dad told Larrance about me, my performance background, my vocal and acting lessons, my original songs, and my big dreams. Larrance listened closely to everything my dad said, and then my dad insisted that I sing for Larrance on the spot. I sometimes got annoyed when my dad did this to me, but in that moment, I was so grateful that he did, because it ended up helping me so much. I went ahead and sang. And right then and there, Larrance said he was blown away by my voice and agreed to work with me.

Finally, here was the kind of a breakthrough we'd been hoping for and working toward for two years. Now, at the time, 1500 or Nothin' was working with some of the biggest artists in the business, including Jay-Z, Snoop Dogg, and Rihanna. They were successful well-known producers, plus they were phenomenal musicians. Larrance's sister Alexandria, known as Alex, was a great songwriter. Larrance, basically on a handshake, signed me, and he and his family took me under their wing. I especially appreciated that they were a family organization, made up of brothers, sisters, cousins, and friends all working hard together to create amazing music. That was exactly how I'd always worked toward my own musical dreams, and now to have that kind of crew also behind me was spectacular.

Larrance was another person who changed everything for me simply by believing in me, by having the conviction to get behind me and my voice. As soon as they were on board, 1500 or Nothin' took the time to really invest in me. I returned the favor by working hard for them.

Larrance has a big personality and quickly showed me just how talented a producer and musician he is. He can play anything on the keys and can even produce a whole song in just a few minutes. Meanwhile, Alex and I were fast friends, and she became like a big sister to me. I spent a lot of time talking to her about my feelings, and she always listened when I confided in her. We would hang out, go to the beach together, and go shopping. She also helped me in my writing. Sometimes we would write together, or she would write songs for me. She was always patient with me and took the time to explain why she had chosen one word or phrase over another. I definitely improved so much in my songwriting because of her mentorship.

The Dopsons got me started in the studio. Our first few sessions were at their home studio, in the bedroom of their apartment, but they had enough equipment in there to lay down some serious tracks.

During one session, the microphone and booth were actually in a closet, but I loved every minute of working with them, no matter where we were. After that, most of the time, I recorded in their studio in the heart of Inglewood, spending hours and hours there. It was a single, cozy studio, and a cool, homey place. This is where everyone would record. There were inspirational quotes on the walls, sayings like *Music Heals*. The studio had one booth and a board and microphones—everything they needed to make it work. I'd show up in sweatpants or shorts—though of course my mom always made sure I still looked good, even in casual and comfy clothes—and put the focus where it belonged in such moments, on singing my heart out.

One of my favorite songs that I've recorded, "Right There," was done at the Dopsons' studio. It's an acoustic mid-tempo song, with a message about how you're always going to be there for someone you love. We had been recording together for a while at this point, and they had seen how hard I worked and how much of my heart I put into everything I did. They had expressed how proud they were of me. The intent was to use the songs we were recording to land management and a record deal for me. They believed in me so much that they helped me to make a music video for "Right There" happen. The budget was understandably tight, but we had so much fun pulling it all together—we were at the beach, riding bikes and laughing. Plus, even a small video shoot meant a crew and extras, and all of them were there, working together, because of my song. I loved the end result because it represented where I was at the time. I was so excited. And I felt like I was finally really gaining some momentum—anything seemed possible.

Another person in the 1500 or Nothin' camp was a songwriter named James Fauntleroy, a person I'd been dying to meet. He was one of my favorite songwriters, and one of the biggest at the time, so this was a huge deal. As soon as he heard me sing, he also believed in me at such a young age. It was like a dream that I was working with him. Larrance and Alex would always talk about how amazing and talented James was, and sometimes I got a little shy when he would come around. But even though I wasn't a signed artist, he always took me seriously and gave very generously of his time. He even wrote a song for me called "Think About You." All these years later, I remain incredibly grateful to him, and the 1500 or Nothin' family will always be a part of mine. Plus, his stamp of approval helped me to take myself seriously as an artist.

Even with the expert mentoring of the 1500 or Nothin' crew when it came to my music, my parents knew they had to guide the business end of my career. They made it a goal to become fully educated about the music industry in order to help protect me. It was tricky finding management because I was so young and unknown. I point out to any parent of a child or teenager aspiring to be a singer or actor: educate yourself like my parents did. Never leave your kids alone. Be extremely careful who you trust. And always be involved, even if it annoys people a little. And, of course, always be kind and polite.

Each of these people who gave of their time and their wisdom during the early days of my career were essential to getting me here. Because of my faith, I see God in everything when it comes to the people who have been brought into my life, the doors that have opened, and the guidance I've received, both from external sources and my own inner voice. Believe me, it wasn't always easy to keep the faith, but when you keep God in your heart, His righteousness and His love, He'll watch over you.

Yet even though God did put generous, talented people in my path who helped me on my journey, six years eventually passed. We'd tried so hard and done everything we could think to do, sacrificing for our goals, bouncing across the country, and missing our family and friends back home. But I hadn't "made it" like we'd hoped when my parents first decided to live part-time in LA and part-time in San Antonio.

By the time I reached my eighteenth birthday, my brother had long graduated from high school and started his life as an adult. Meanwhile I kept performing and recording and improving, but a breakthrough in my career hadn't happened yet. For these six years, I had never stopped working toward my dream. Sure, there were times when I wanted to just be a normal teenager, but they never lasted long. I imagine it was trying for my parents, too, but God always sent a little hope to keep us going. He gave me a song when I was at my lowest. He sent people along who believed in me, taught me more, invested their time and expertise in me, and helped make me better as an artist and young woman.

And of course, most important, He'd given me wonderful parents who were always there for me, holding me all night when I cried, passing out flyers at school performances instead of going on vacations, sacrificing years of their own plans, including when they sold the piece of land they'd bought in San Antonio to build their dream home in order to help finance everything it took to keep us with one foot in LA and one in San Antonio. And somehow they kept our family as close as it had always been—that's a true miracle right there.

Among the most beautiful gifts my parents have ever given me are the values that are at the heart of who I am. For my eighteenth birthday I asked my parents for a very special ring, which they were happy to give me. It reads TRUE LOVE WAITS. It symbolizes the choice I've made to save myself for marriage, a commitment I have maintained to this day, even in an industry where such values are not generally celebrated, and I've sometimes been judged and made fun of. But I've just held my head high and remained true to who I am and what I believe in. I would never judge someone for their values or the life they choose to live. It's a delicate subject to talk about, because it's so personal to me, but I felt it was important to share, because I'm proud of myself for honoring this promise I've made to God. And my parents are very proud of me, too. I can't wait to one day walk down the aisle and give myself away on my wedding night. For now, I will have to patiently wait.

Turning eighteen marked a big shift in my life. At the end of these six years we'd spent living between LA and my hometown, we returned to San Antonio until I finished high school. Now I went to work with local math and English teachers. I looked forward to meeting with them, and we developed such close friendships that they introduced me to their families and made me feel special in so many small ways. They each helped me to become better, sharper, and smarter. I still thrived in English, and math continued to be a challenge, but my teachers rooted for me and became role models and sources of encouragement. They always supported my music career and accommodated my schedule if I needed to travel. They also prayed for me, for which I was very thankful.

At times it was hard to miss out on the experiences that most kids had, like school dances, graduation, and the normal celebrations and events that happened during high school. So when my friends Olivia and Madi invited me to their prom, I was thrilled. We rode in a limo, danced at the prom, then had a pajama party and ate ice cream late into the night. I'm so grateful they included me, because I wouldn't have had that experience otherwise. My mom also tried to balance supporting my dream and giving me what most of my peers were experiencing. When I finished my schooling, she took me to JCPenney to get my senior pictures taken. How sweet is that?

As I reached the end of high school and faced the idea of being a real adult, I had no clue what that would look like for me. My diploma arrived in the mail one day, and even though I hadn't had a graduation ceremony, I saw this as the rite of passage that it was. I knew it was time to get serious about the future. I began studying for my SATs.

During these years, I'd been growing up and learning what plans God had for me, discovering how to take my talent and refine it, and determining who I wanted to be as a person.

No matter how old you are, I want to encourage you to be you, the very best version of yourself. The road of life is full of both wonderful and challenging times, but being yourself will always make the good times sweeter and help you to stay grounded during the dark moments.

I was trying to hold on to who I knew myself to be, even during this major transition time when there were so many question marks. What I didn't know yet was that something was right around the corner for me—something that I had never expected or planned for, but that would once again change my life forever.

SEVEN

Destiny When You Don't Expect It

Have you ever prayed that God would open or close a door? I did, and crazily enough, it led to one of the biggest opportunities that has ever come my way. Believe me, I had never planned to get my big break on television, let alone in a televised singing competition. As I look back now, it's amazing to see the dots connect in ways that only God can orchestrate. After all of those years we'd tried to make it in LA, my rise to success actually started in our little family room in our house in San Antonio.

In 2011, my dad and I had spent many of our evenings watching the first season of *The X Factor*. Immediately, we were hooked. It was a competition reality show where people auditioned in front of famous judges Simon Cowell, L.A. Reid, Paula Abdul, and Nicole Scherzinger. The show had a lot of hype because Simon had just announced he was leaving *American Idol* after nine years. It was a huge moment in television. Now Simon had brought *The X Factor* from England—where the show had led to the creation of the biggest boy band in the world at that time, One Direction. Plus, it was the only show that awarded five million dollars to the winner. All of this added up to maximum hype, and I always loved to watch people chasing their dreams and singing their hearts out.

I already loved Simon and had watched every episode of *American Idol* with my family since it began in 2002. We would have viewing parties, just the four of us, and my parents and I always looked forward to hearing his comments to the singers. Simon somehow always seemed to be able to tell when someone was special. He had a gift for it. He predicted Carrie Underwood would become the bestselling *American Idol* winner. He believed strongly in Kelly Clarkson when she was on the show. I greatly respected him, and deep down I even dared to dream: *One day, I hope I can sing for him.*

What my dad and I liked about Simon's new show was that you didn't just have to be a solo artist. You could be in a group or be a rapper, and you could be of any age—a young girl or an older woman all had a shot at the prize. The show seemed to celebrate diversity.

When contestants made it to the next round, right after getting their yeses from the judges, they would move on to a boot camp. If they made it past these intense rounds, the contestants were separated into four categories—Groups, Girls, Boys, and Over Thirties. They were then flown to their mentors' lavish homes, where they sang their heart out in the hope of making it to the live shows. After they sang, the judges made their final picks.

It was a unique show, unlike anything we'd ever seen. We enjoyed seeing such refreshing talent and found it fun to watch the contestants go through the whole process. But while I thought it was a cool concept for a TV show, I never considered auditioning for it myself.

After all, at the time, my path seemed to be leading me toward a career in music, even if it was happening more gradually than I'd expected. For six years, I'd been working hard to build a little following, and I was praying to get discovered through my recordings and performances. I'd even made many YouTube videos of me singing cover songs, to try to be creative there. I'd done all of this in the hopes of one day getting a real record deal. And while I hadn't had anything definite happen in this direction, I still felt confident that all of my efforts were adding up to a body of work I could be proud of, which would eventually get me signed. But honestly, it was unclear what the next step would be for me.

Not long after my high school graduation, my mom heard on the radio that *The X Factor* was coming to Austin to hold auditions. She excitedly mentioned this to me. I didn't think I ever wanted to audition for a reality TV show. I was scared for so many reasons. I was afraid of the unknown and unfamiliar. I did not want to get lost in the shuffle. There were no guarantees. I was terrified of failing on national TV. The thought of going through all the necessary steps and then ending up right where I'd started seemed awful. Plus, I had already been involved in the industry.

But I had been feeling recently like something had to change. My mom's back was getting worse than ever. My dad's job wasn't flexible enough for him to travel with me, so we were taking a break back home in San Antonio while figuring out what to do next. I'd turned eighteen the summer before. I felt at a crossroads and had so much to think about. How were we going to make it work? Should I go to college? Get a job? I wasn't ready to stop pursuing my dreams. But I had no idea what I was going to do to further them at this point. All I'd ever wanted was to do music, but suddenly I had heavy decisions to make—adult decisions. I wasn't twelve anymore. And that's why I had begun studying for my SATs, just in case. I held on to God's promise, and one of my favorite Bible verses: *For I know the plans I have for you," declares the Lord, "plans to prosper you and not to harm you, plans to give you hope and a future* (Jeremiah 29:11).

In the midst of all this, Mom started telling me that I needed to give *The X Factor* a shot.

"Mama," she said, "you really should audition for this show. What do you have to lose?"

"No, Mom," I immediately replied. "I don't want to go through a reality show. I don't want to be just another contestant, lost in the shuffle. It's scary."

I was not at all feeling this idea of auditioning. Like most eighteen-year-olds, I thought I knew what was best. But for some reason, my mom persisted. She felt so strongly about it. For the next few weeks, I dodged any conversation that had to do with the show. It was a firm no from me. Not happening. No way. Absolutely not. Ironically, one afternoon I even received a spam mass email from *The X Factor,* inviting me to audition. I hit delete.

Then my mom finally convinced me. It was May 12, 2012. I remember the day so clearly. My parents were going to Costco. I always enjoyed running errands with them and helping with the groceries. While my favorite store was our local supermarket, H-E-B, my second favorite was Costco. We went there so often that the employees knew us by name. We joked that we could have "lunch" because of all the free samples of food they gave out. We would literally get full on samples, laughing at ourselves the whole time. Because we had spent so much time together and had weathered so many ups and downs, my parents really were my best friends.

On this particular day, I wanted to join them like normal, but my mom insisted that I stay home and submit my audition video online. I didn't want to do it. It was the last thing on earth that I wanted to do. I even argued with her to let me go with them. But of course she won that battle, and I ended up staying home. I was so mad.

I'm really gonna do this? This wasn't the plan, I thought after they left. Then I realized that if I submitted the audition, my mom would stop talking about it and we could all move on. *What could possibly come of it, right?* So I set up my computer and watched this prerecorded video from Simon. He asked several questions, one of them being "Tell me why you have the X Factor." This made me laugh. *I can't believe I'm doing this.*

But I filmed my answers and my songs, anyway. It took several tries to come up with something I was happy with. Though I didn't think this little recorded audition would accomplish anything, I still wanted to give it my best.

The show allowed contestants two minutes to sing whatever they wanted. I chose to do a mash-up of two songs, "Beautiful" by Christina Aguilera and "Lovin' You" by Minnie Riperton. Even though I didn't want to do the audition, I found myself spending almost three hours on it. At one point I was so frustrated, I just grunted, spun around in my little pink chair in my bedroom, and put my head in my hands.

Finally I gave myself a pep talk, returned to my computer screen, sang the songs with all of my might, and got ready to hit the send button. I was tired by now, but I gave all that I had left to give. Then I said a prayer that would change my life forever: "God," I prayed, "I don't want to do this show. I really don't want to do this. If you want to close the door, by all means please close it!"

I prayed as if telling God what to do. But a few seconds later, with a tender and gentle voice, I added, "But if this is what you want for me, if this is Your will, please open it."

After that deep prayer, I pressed send.

A few minutes later, a confirmation email arrived, letting me know I had reached the point of no return. My audition submission was confirmed. It was too late to take it back, too late to make changes, and too late to question the process. It was up to God now.

When my parents got home, I told them that I'd submitted my audition. They were surprised that one, I actually had done it, and two, I hadn't reviewed the song I was going to sing with them, especially for such a big audition. I always rehearsed songs with my dad. Still, they were happy. I was happy, too—that we could now continue on with normal life.

Only six days later, on May 18, 2012, I received an unexpected email that would change my world. It was titled "*X Factor* Audition." My heart stopped; I froze. I jumped up. This was real. There it was, the reply I had thought would never come.

After staring at the subject of the email for a few moments, I gained the courage to open it. It said, "Hey Ally, give me a call as soon as possible. I have a question about your *X Factor* online audition. Thank you."

The email was from a producer named Maggie.

I ran to find my parents. My mom was in her room. I showed her the email, and she was filled with such excitement that she could hardly contain it. Then I ran outside to find my dad, who was working in the yard.

I screamed at the top of my lungs: "Daaaaad!!!"

"I'm busy. Can it wait?" he said.

But then I told him the news. He covered his mouth and barely could get any words out.

Together we called Maggie to find out what she wanted. She didn't have a question. Instead, she had incredible news: I had been chosen to audition in front of the judges in Austin!

The judges were Simon and L.A. Reid, plus the two new judges Britney Spears and Demi Lovato. I could hardly believe it.

My brother walked in the door from work just then, and I ran into his arms, bursting with my news. He was the happiest I'd ever seen him. We all screamed and celebrated together as a family—just like we did everything.

It took a while for the reality to set in. This was really going to happen. And to think that I almost didn't enter because I wanted to go to Costco with my parents. Sometimes our small choices define us in the biggest ways.

Soon after I learned I was going to the live *X Factor* auditions, I had a dream about it. I dreamed that while I was singing, the whole arena gave me a standing ovation, and I got four yeses from the judges. While I was standing on that stage, I felt this light shine on me. There was an overwhelming presence in the room that is hard to describe. It was celestial, and I knew angels surrounded me. I woke up and started crying.

The day before my audition, my cousin BJ and my aunts came to our house and helped me to pick out the songs that I'd sing. It was down to "I Still Believe" by Mariah Carey, "Lovin' You" by Minnie Riperton, and "On My Knees" by Jaci Velasquez. I sang each one to them, ending with "On My Knees." There was no question in all of our hearts that it was the right choice.

Later that evening, my mom, dad, brother, and I drove to Austin, where we were spending the night at one of my aunt's houses. Before the night was over, I said a prayer with my family that it would all go well. Then I laid my head down to sleep.

The next morning, we got up early and ate breakfast together. This was the big day! Then while the rest of my family finished getting ready, my dad and I headed out to the arena.

On the morning of May 25, 2012, my dad and I arrived early at the Frank Erwin Center, where the auditions were being held. We took a walk around the block.

"Mama, you're going to be amazing," he said. "No matter what happens, just know how proud of you we are. God is going to take care of you. We are going to be right there cheering you on. You are a star, our shining star. We believe in you. Never forget that. I know they are going to love you. You are not alone up there. You've got this."

Pep talks were his specialty, and this was a special one. I saw tears in his eyes. I gave him a big hug and thanked him. Tears ran down my face, and I hugged him even tighter. He then said a prayer, and we were off to check in. I loved having my family there to support me.

It was a long day. I tried to stay focused while I waited, but I had so many nerves buzzing around inside of me, my mind was racing. And then it was time to do my interviews for the package they would put together to introduce contestants to viewers at home.

I answered their questions about whether I wanted a clothing and perfume line. But mostly I told them about my family, my hometown, being born a preemie, my love of music, my mom's scoliosis, and how amazing my parents were. Then I waited for what seemed like an eternity to go up on that stage and audition. I was the most nervous I'd ever had been in my life. My dad said in all the years he'd watched me get ready to sing, he had never seen me so nervous.

And then it got worse. After killing time all day, my time slot was close. And I felt this weird fluttery sensation at the corner of my eye. Oh no, one of my false eyelashes had come off! I started freaking out. How could I go onstage with one eyelash on and one off? I'd look like a lunatic. Everyone would make fun of me. One of our family friends hurried over.

"It's okay," she said. "I have eyelash glue!"

I could feel the clock ticking down inside of me, and my hands shook with panic even as she successfully helped me to glue back on my lashes. I blinked my eyes, checking if my lashes were secure, and everything was fixed. Thank God.

Then just before my name was called, my family and friends gathered around me in a big circle. There were about fifteen of us, and they laid hands on me and prayed. As they prayed, I felt a calm come over me. I had to remember, whatever happened, it was His will. All I had left to do was to go out and do what I loved, right then and there. I was actually going to sing in front of Simon, *the* Simon Cowell, whom I'd admired for so many years. All I could do was to give my heart, through the music, and so I would.

They called me up to the stage. I was still extremely nervous; my hands were shaking, my heart pounding. But I walked onto that stage, and that's when the light switched on inside of me.

"Hello, Austin, Texas!" I shouted joyfully as I walked to my mark.

I saw the judges there in real life, all looking at me—Simon Cowell, L.A. Reid, Britney Spears, and Demi Lovato. It felt like I'd stepped inside of the most amazing, unbelievable dream. They said, "Hello. How are you?" Then, they asked me a round of questions, including: "What's your name? Where are you from? What are you going to sing?" "'On My Knees' by Jaci Velasquez," I said. I was emotional, and Simon lovingly acknowledged it. I could not believe I was speaking to Simon and the judges. Somebody pinch me. I took a breath, carrying the prayers and support of my family with me. The music came on. Here was the moment. And then suddenly I felt a force move through me like I'd never felt before. I just started singing "On My Knees," the song that had carried me through so many moments of my life, not to the judges, not to my family, not to myself, but to God.

During my audition, the music stopped, but the Holy Spirit had filled me with such an amazing feeling that I didn't even truly realize what had happened. I just kept singing to Him in front of everyone. It was one of the best moments of my life. I'll never forget that feeling. Then Simon brought me back to the room by making a funny joke for me to stop singing, but there was nothing unkind in his voice. He was wonderful. They all were. I heard roaring cheers from the crowd. And then the judges poured out a series of heart-stopping comments. Britney said I could sing on Broadway. Demi said that my voice blew her away, and it was so special, so beautiful. L.A. said that I was very good and that I looked good. I couldn't believe Simon's words. He said: "I have a feeling we're looking at a future star. You have an aura about you."

I immediately started crying after Simon told me those unbelievable words. The judges gave me four yeses—Britney said, "easy breezy yes," and then Simon said, "easy easy breezy yes." My dream was coming true. It was actually coming true! I ran off the stage, crying, into my family's arms.

I couldn't believe they all loved me.

My parents were crying, along with the rest of my family. At that point, this was the greatest day of my life. It was what some people would describe as a mountaintop moment. I had been given an open door and I'd passed through it. God was moving me forward. I felt incredible, full of light. There would definitely be more mountaintops ahead for me, but I didn't know then that I would have to walk through some deep, dark valleys to get there.

Nothing else mattered just then. For this moment, life was perfect. I walked offstage with four yeses! My family crowded around me, screaming and crying. I felt invincible.

My parents and I were soaring with joy and couldn't believe it. But as I filled out the necessary paperwork I'd been given by the producers, it began to feel real. The next round in the competition would be boot camp. I had no idea when that would be, so when we returned to San Antonio, I prepared myself by launching my own kind of a personal boot camp, singing every day, learning new songs, and taking vocal lessons and dance classes.

It was late July, a few weeks after my nineteenth birthday, and two months after my audition in front of Simon, L.A., Britney, and Demi. I got the call I'd been waiting for—the information on the next round. I was told to pack my bags because I was going to Miami for boot camp!

In the second season of *The X Factor,* which was the season I competed in, contestants who were successfully selected at the end of each round would progress on to the next one. This was how the producers would refine the contestants each week, until a small number eventually moved on to the live television finals. During boot camp, the judges collaborated and chose twenty-four acts, which were spread throughout six categories. They did this by having us sing alone and also with other contestants until they'd heard enough to make their choices. My goal going into the boot camp rounds was to be one of the twenty-four acts that would make it to the next part of the competition, which would take place at the judges' houses.

Of course my family and I were excited, but there were also a lot of nerves. I had no idea what to expect. And there was one big catch: since I was a legal adult, I could not bring my parents with me to Miami. I had to go by myself. At this point, I did everything with them, just as I had for my entire life, and especially for the past six years. Now after all of that time, suddenly I'd be without them.

My parents can't go with me? I've never even been on a plane by myself, let alone traveled to an entirely different part of the country, I thought with both sadness and fear.

But it had to be done, if I wanted this chance to further my future. I had to be brave, trust God, and go. So that's what I did.

I had no idea what I was walking into, so I had to be as prepared as possible. I did the Insanity workout every day before boot camp, and I was in the best shape of my life. I learned a bunch of songs beforehand, just in case there was a chance they'd throw new songs at me. All I knew was I'd be at boot camp for three days before we progressed to a round of competitions in the judges' homes—if I made it through that far. That was a scary thought.

Since the process was a weeklong, we had to find enough killer outfits. My mom and I went on several shopping trips, and she worked extra hard, spending hours at Urban Outfitters. Once again, despite her back pain, she kept pushing through for me. I could tell her suffering was getting worse. She'd have to rest for longer than before, and I could tell by the look on her face how excruciating all this was for her. One day, seeing her attempts to hold it together and be cheerful, I felt so horrible, I started tearing up.

"Let's stop and go home," I told her.

"No, Mama, I can do it," she said. "I just need to make sure you're okay and have your outfits so you don't worry about them once you're there. God will take care of me. I love you."

We'd gone on many trips in pursuit of my dreams over the years, but this time I was going alone, and my mom wanted to prepare me as much as she could. Gratitude for my mom washed over me.

After she bought everything we needed for my outfits, we went home and put them all together. The night before it was time to leave, we packed. As always, my mom went above and beyond, organizing the outfits for each day, including the clothes, shoes, socks, hats, and jewelry. She then took a picture of each outfit before putting it into its own plastic bag so it would be easy to pull out the perfect look each the morning, no matter how busy I was.

"Okay, Mama, I organized the outfits for each day, and you have extras just in case," she said as we put the clothes in the suitcase.

"Thank you, Mom. I'll never be able to say it enough," I said, hugging her and wiping away tears. "God bless the mom that you are. I love you with all of my heart."

My dad, mom, and brother gathered around to pray for me that night. They squeezed my hands hard as my dad prayed: "Lord, we give this to You. Please give Ally insurmountable strength that only comes from You. Bless her every move. Let her feel Your presence around her. Please don't let her feel alone. We are there with her in spirit. Thank you for this opportunity, for this very moment. We know You have given her a real gift. And above all, we know she has the biggest heart for You. Her intentions are pure. She loves to sing to bring happiness to people. That's all she wants to do. We will think about her every single second, but we trust You with our baby girl. We know she's in Your hands. It is Your will, Father. We bless her, in the name of Jesus."

This was one of the most tender moments we've had together as a family. We let out our fair share of tears, gave each other the tightest hugs, and finally, went to sleep.

Morning arrived. The house was quiet. I could feel the emotion in the air. I didn't want to do this alone, and my parents longed to go with me, but the time had come for me to make my own way. Right then and there, I had to become a real grown-up. This was it. When I came home, I'd either return as a contestant going to the live shows on *The X Factor* or with great disappointment. I'd practiced and prepared to the best of my ability. Now all that I could do was give it to God. There was no other choice. This is where our faith really had to kick in.

My parents came inside the airport with me, and we could hardly stand to part ways.

"We love you, Mama," my mom said, holding me close. "We are proud of you no matter what—so proud you don't even know. Call us whenever you can. We will be praying for you like crazy. We will be there in spirit. You are not alone, and God is with you. We love you with all of our hearts and souls. God bless you out there, Mama. Go and shine your bright light."

We said our final goodbyes, gathering into the biggest embrace in history. And then I pulled myself away and headed to my gate. Right before boarding the plane, I said a deep prayer to God: "Please be with me, Lord. Please bless me. I want this more than anything. Help me to be brave, help me not to be lonely, help me to make friends, help me to be myself, and help me to be the best I could ever be."

Before I knew it, the plane was landing in Miami. After I pulled my luggage off the baggage claim conveyor belt, I saw the other contestants and the people who'd come to pick us up. I was really nervous, but the others were already talking to each other, and they seemed friendly. I'd never been to Miami. Let's just say, it wasn't the sunny Florida I'd expected—it was raining.

For the first time in my life, my family wasn't there for me. In a great coincidence, at the airport, I had befriended one of the other contestants—a young boy—and his mother. We were happy to be reunited at boot camp, and it was nice to be able to sit next to them. When I met the other contestants, I was super nervous. These were people I didn't know, from all different backgrounds, and they were my competition, so I didn't know how they would treat me. But most of them were very kind. And it helped to realize they were all going through their own version of the same thing.

We piled into a van, making friendly small talk and starting to get to know one another. I looked out at the city as we drove by. It felt like a different country altogether, with its tropical-scented air that smelled and felt so different from San Antonio or LA. I saw Cuban restaurants and tall buildings throughout the city. We passed people playing live music on the streets. It seemed a lively city with a vibrant culture, even in the rain. And beyond the metropolitan area, there were beautiful white sandy beaches.

The van pulled up to a stop at the Fontainebleau Miami Beach, the most luxurious hotel I'd ever seen. I carried my suitcases down the long walk to the front desk, taking it all in. The hotel grounds seemed to stretch for miles; it was massive! There were lounges, bars, restaurants, shops, an outdoor pool, and rows of sparkling chandeliers. The walls were a glistening white, and I could see the beach outside, only steps away. The hotel had its own distinctive, glamorous scent. Everything was stunning.

After I checked in and took my room keys, I hurried up to my room and let myself inside. The room was beautiful, and like a little kid, I excitedly jumped on the bed. It was so soft and bouncy, it felt like a cloud. There was a shower and a gorgeous tub with crisp white towels that felt incredibly soft to the touch. I couldn't believe I was really here. After looking around for a moment, I called my parents. They'd been waiting to hear from me and both got on the line right away.

"Hi, Mom and Dad, I made it to Miami!"

"Hi, Mama! How are you? Are you okay? How is it over there? We miss you."

"I miss you guys terribly. It is so weird without y'all. But I am so excited to be here."

I told them about my arrival and described how gorgeous the hotel was.

"Thank God you are okay. Take it all in, Mama. We love you, and we believe in you so much," my dad said.

"Go out there and kill it, Mama. And be careful, my sweet baby girl. You are going to shine. We believe!" Mom added.

They said a prayer for me; then we hung up. I laid out my clothes for the next day, marveling once again at how sweet it was that my mom had thoughtfully picked them out for me and then packed them together in their own bags, each marked for a specific day. Then I headed to bed. Boot camp started in the morning, and I needed all the rest I could get. I was praying so hard that God would be with me and calm me down. I kept thinking of the cameras, the scenarios, the contestants, the unknown. Nothing was sure. The reality of being on this show was starting to set in, and I let all of my fears out by putting it all in God's hands.

The next morning I woke up, did my hair and makeup, prayed with my parents over the phone again, and put on my clothes for the day. My mom had put together an outfit that was sure to stand out—a lime-green neon shirt, gray sequin shorts, socks and heels. Right before *The X Factor,* I had taken vocal lessons, and I had recorded the exercises on my phone, so I could use the warm-ups before shows. So I also took time to warm up my voice. As I finished getting ready, I tried to prepare my mind, focus, and breathe in every minute of this dream experience.

I turned my focus toward walking steadily to the pickup area outside the lobby. All of the contestants were gathered around. The producers gathered us up and took us to the venue where we would be filming. My heart was pounding so fast. They led us to the stage, and *bam,* it all sunk in! I saw bright lights, cameras, and a large screen behind us that had a big X across it. I really was here on the show. There was no going back now.

The boot camp had officially begun.

Over a hundred of us contestants flooded the stage, where we would all remain while each contestant sang. Our names were called at random, so I had no idea when I would go—talk about nerve-racking! As I waited, I tried to do everything in my power to be ready. And of course I prayed.

Then a girl ahead of me sang the exact same song that I'd planned to sing. I was thrown for a loop, but I couldn't let this bother me. I knew I just had to go out there and give it my best.

Finally I heard, "Ally Brooke!"

It was go time.

"What song are you going to sing, Ally?" the judges asked me.

"I'm singing 'Somebody That I Used to Know' by Gotye."

The other contestants let out a big *ooooooh* because the other girl had just sung this song. That added to my nerves, but I focused and prepared to give it my absolute best. At least my version was in a different style—more of a pop version. I sang the song with attitude and tried to make it my own. The judges seemed to like my performance, but I couldn't be too sure.

Then it was back to waiting. The other contestants and I were there for hours while we watched the rest of the auditions happen. Then that night the staff gathered us around them to let us know our fate. My stomach felt all twisted up in knots, and I prayed my heart out while I waited to hear my name. There it was! My name was called and I was on to the next round. My first step away from home had been successful.

Though the next day never made it onto the show, the contestants were instructed to perform in groups of five. This was intense. We joined a group of strangers, worked together to learn our parts and harmonies, and hoped that we did well. My group was given the song "Ain't No Mountain High Enough" to sing. We sounded great and performed really well together, and I had a good feeling that we were one of the best groups of the day. Little did I know how significant this moment would be for me.

My hunch was right. The judges loved our audition, and it put me through to the next round. By now I was feeling more hopeful that I'd make it to the next round.

With the second day completed, I was back to singing on my own. This was a battle round. It was the final day of boot camp. For this stage of the competition, I'd sing against another girl. If I was chosen to move on, I'd advance to the judge's home. That was where I would sing in front of one of the judges, plus a mystery celebrity guest. That performance would be the final stop before the live television rounds.

The song "Knockin' on Heaven's Door" was assigned to us. Before I went on, our vocal teacher pulled me aside.

"Ally, I need to tell you something," she said. "You're one that the judges are watching. I'm not supposed to tell you this, but they have their eye on you. Simon is watching you like a hawk. You're killing it out there, so go out there and show them who you are. I'm rooting for you, sweetie. Good luck."

I'd been feeling good about my performances, but these words from one of the show's insiders gave me an incredible boost of confidence and confirmed that I really was on the right track. All I needed to do was to go out there and be true to myself, so I did. I kept in mind that at one point in the process, Britney Spears had called me spunky. Britney was one of my biggest inspirations and pop icons, and I couldn't believe I'd been singing right in front of her. This was my final chance. I went for it and put it all out on the table. I held nothing back and sang my heart out.

All of us sat and waited anxiously, knowing that soon we would know if this was the end of the road or if we were advancing on to these next, exciting possibilities. I called my mom and dad to ask them to pray for me. Then the waiting continued. I was so anxious to know what would happen that I could barely sit still. It was painfully long.

We were divided into large groups to learn our fate. Finally the moment had arrived. I felt like the judges liked my singing, so I thought I had a chance.

"I want so badly to get to the judges' homes," I had said in my interview earlier in the taping. But only God knew what was in store.

Then I heard the words "A lot of you really deserved to go further. I'm really sorry. Thank you very much indeed."

I did not make it through.

My body went numb. My heart fell. That was it. The door had closed. Even though I'd started out not wanting to do this at all and I'd told God I would be okay if He closed the door, now a huge wave of disappointment consumed me. This opportunity that I'd put so much hope in was now over. It was done. My dream had hit its biggest roadblock. I'd be heading back to San Antonio, and I had no idea what I was going to do with the rest of my life.

All at once, the concerns I'd been putting off before embarking on this *X Factor* journey came rushing back, on a deeper level. I tried to wrap my brain around returning to my life in San Antonio, to SAT prep, and to college. Was this a closed door on my entire singing career? I wasn't sure, because it felt like I had put everything I had into this one chance. Now it was over.

I couldn't stop myself from crying, and the cameras recorded every second of my devastation. I felt heartbroken and exposed.

"How do you feel, Ally?" a producer asked me on-camera.

With a big red nose and tears covering my face, I told him, "I guess I wasn't what they were looking for."

The pain and disappointment were just agonizing. I felt the shame of rejection, and all of those things I had told myself over the years about not being good enough came rushing back.

I kept on crying, and I called my parents while I was waiting for the producers to help us with our final exit. As soon as I told them the devastating news, they started crying, too. They couldn't believe it, after I'd called them every day with the latest exciting story about how well it had been going. "This doesn't seem right," they both said. "Something seems wrong."

I had no idea what would occur next. I was crying so hard, and I couldn't stop. All of a sudden, out of nowhere, one of the producers shouted: "Can I have your attention for a second?"

What's going on?

"The judges asked me to call the following people back to the stage."

I quickly told my parents that I had to go but I would call them back later. Of course, I was pleading in my head that one of those lucky names would be mine.

Name after name was called out, but I didn't hear mine. Then the heart-stopping moment: "Ally Brooke." I'd never felt more excited in my life. My head spun. *Did the judges make a mistake? Would I have to sing again?* I noticed there were some rappers gathered here, too. *Would I have to rap? What was about to happen?* This was such an emotional roller coaster.

I dried my tears and found myself standing in a group of contestants back on that by-now-familiar *X Factor* stage.

Simon moved me around a bit, changing where I was standing, and I found myself with a group of some of the other girls. As we stood on that stage, Simon began speaking to us. For some reason, we reached out and held hands. There were five of us together. Then Simon said the words that changed life as we knew it. Forever.

"You are all . . . as you are . . . invited to the judges' homes."

I let out the biggest scream of my life and jumped so high. I'm not gonna lie: I ugly cried in that moment. It was like nothing I had ever experienced before. It was as if I went from thinking I'd lost everything to realizing I had won it all.

They explained that we were now a group. It hit me that I was on to the next round. I had never been more grateful for a second chance.

When the cameras stopped rolling, I went up to the judges and gave them big hugs.

Simon said something to me then that I didn't anticipate would end up haunting me. "Ally," he said, looking me in the eyes, "you are the glue that holds this group together."

"Wow," I said, looking at the four girls off in the distance. "Thank you, sir. Thank you."

That was a hefty thing for him to say to me. It felt like he had crowned me right there, bestowing this great responsibility on me. I vowed right then to prove myself worthy.

I called my parents from the bathroom and shared everything that had happened, and how I was in a group now. They were relieved to hear from me, because they'd been so worried about me, and they'd felt terrible that they weren't there to console me.

"Are you okay, Mama?" my mom asked.

"Yes," I said. "You wanna know why I'm okay? It's because they put me in a group! I made it to the next round in a group with five girls!"

We were all so excited. But I was still processing what had happened as I talked with them. My thoughts and emotions kept fluctuating. I'd always performed on my own, but suddenly I was in a group with a bunch of strangers. This was a lot to take in. In one day, my plans had dramatically changed. I had spent a decade already, since I was nine years old, working my butt off to become a solo artist. It was what I'd wanted, the goal I'd pursued so passionately, the thing my parents had sacrificed so much of their lives for. Yet at the same time, I was grateful for another chance.

My parents listened, and then my mom said wise words that stayed with me: "Mama, Simon is amazing at what he does. He is a gifted man. If he sees something, listen to him. He has launched unbelievable careers. Carrie, Kelly, and he even formed One Direction, the biggest boy band in the world. He has a real instinct, Ally."

And wow, was my mom right.

After the five of us girls returned from sharing the news with our families, we came back together and gathered for more proper introductions. After celebrating for a short time and getting to know one another a little better, we were led to a room in the auditorium. We were chatting, trying to get comfortable. Looking at their faces and taking in their personalities, I saw an interesting and unique mix of girls. We were a diverse group, from all over the country. They were from everywhere, from Miami to California, and they were fourteen and fifteen. They were all much younger than I was.

In the past, I'd found it easier to collaborate and identify with musicians that were older than me. The other girls in the group were a bit younger, and I hoped we'd all get along and mix well. Somehow, I hoped to be able to be what Simon had said, the glue that would hold us together.

"You need a name for your group," one of the producers had told us.

We sat in the room and got down to brainstorming names. I tried breaking the ice by making a joke. Joking, with a smile, I said something like, "How about the Tree Growers?"

At first they thought I was serious. But when I told them I was joking, we all started laughing.

At least I wasn't the only one who couldn't come up with a name—none of us could. We sat in that room, throwing out ideas, but nothing seemed right. Since the other girls were all under the age of eighteen, their parents had been at boot camp all week and eventually were allowed to join us. Seeing those parents walk in, I instantly realized how much better I'd feel if my mom and dad had been there, too. We were so close, and their absence was like a hole in my heart. The other parents weighed in on ideas, but still everything fell flat. For a while, the producers simply called us "Girl Group" until we could land on a name.

Next, the girls and I started rehearsing together, and my hope grew for what the future could bring. We were working long, hard hours to perform for one of the judges and a mystery guest judge. While we rehearsed, we met with a group of brothers who had released successful cover videos on YouTube. They coached us as we went through various songs every day. We had two or three days to rehearse, not very long considering the fact that we'd met just a couple of days earlier. It would be a quite an achievement if we could nail a song and make it through to the live rounds. We needed a song that would showcase what we could do and would be impressive for our judge and his mystery guest. We didn't know who our judge was yet, and we were excited to find out.

Finally, after trying song after song, our judge picked two songs for us to perform. One was "I Wanna Dance with Somebody" and the other was a song called "Impossible."

After some long nights of rehearsing, and trying to get to know each other, we felt ready. The producers had also given us a new name: Lylas, which stood for "Love You Like a Sister."

The time had come to perform. It was a beautiful sunny Florida day, and along with all of the other competing groups, we were off to our judge's house. We pulled up on a yacht to this magnificent property right on the water. Our judge's home was on Star Island, the legendary part of Miami, where all of the A-listers and the most successful artists, actors, and entertainers in the world lived. It was a true dream home, and the sun was shining, the water sparkling. Though Miami was hot and we were performing outside, I was determined that wasn't going to affect me. This was a grand moment that almost hadn't happened. We walked out to his backyard and saw our judge and his mystery guest—it was Simon and Marc Anthony!

We all screamed and clapped when we saw them. Marc Anthony is a legend, a phenomenal artist. He's one of the greatest Latin artists. He inspired me and helped to pave the way for someone like me to even be here. I couldn't believe he was in front of me, though I tried not to let his presence distract me. We had spent hours working hard, preparing for our turn. We waited for the other groups to perform their first songs. At last, at the end of the day, our turn came. We were the last ones to sing. It had already been a crazy long day. It was our final moment to show the judges what we were made of. I led us in prayer before we went on. We held hands and took a deep breath. I knew this was our one shot, and we had to make it count.

We started with "I Wanna Dance with Somebody" and even had some cute choreography to go along with it. I loved our version of the song because it had some nice harmonies. It never aired on the show, but I thought we did a great job.

Then we did our second song, "Impossible." In that moment everything changed. For this one, we sat on stools and sang our hearts out. And then toward the end, on our final notes, we stood up, put our hands in the air, and belted our last words. I could feel the power of us singing together; it ran through all of us. I knew in that moment that something special had happened. We had an electricity that I'll never forget.

Simon would be the one to tell us the next day.

The next morning felt weighted as we headed to Simon's house. We had so much on our minds, and all we wanted was to excel. I wanted this so badly for us. In my opinion, we were undeniably amazing, and we were too good to pass up. We prayed again, and I left it in God's hands. This decision meant go home or move forward to the final part of the show, the live portion. After we arrived, I walked with the other girls to where Simon was seated on a sofa outside by the water.

Simon started talking, and my heart pounded almost as loudly as his voice. I heard him talking, but all I remember him saying was "clearly one great group," and then those three magic words: "You are through."

We had actually made it to the live rounds! We burst with joy and tears. It was a one-in-a-million chance, and we were that one. I could not believe it.

In that moment, my life changed again. I knew from watching the exposure the first season gave contestants that doors opened for the artists who made it to the live performances. Nothing would be the same—no matter the final outcome. I called my mom with the cameras rolling and shouted, "Mom, we made it to the live shows!"

It was finally time to go home, and I was surprised to learn I'd be flying first-class on American Airlines. It felt like a movie.

"Ms. Hernandez, let me know how I can help you," said the flight attendant.

Ms. Hernandez? Is that me? Wow. It is! I thought with a smile. I called my parents before takeoff and whispered to them that I was in first class. We were all freaking out. I couldn't believe the legroom. I snapped a picture of my feet, dangling, because they didn't reach the floor of the plane. I sent the photo to my parents, which of course made them laugh.

During the flight, I ordered pasta, drank a few Cokes, ate some snacks (and stashed some in my purse). At the end of the meal, the flight attendant gave me amazingly delicious warm chocolate chip cookies. They were the best I'd ever had. I looked out that little window, played music on my iPod, and let my dreams soar even higher than we were flying.

Once home, I ran into my family's arms, but we celebrated quietly. Everything had to be kept secret. For the rest of the summer, we patiently waited for September to arrive. Then fall came, and when my audition aired, as you already know, I faced the humiliation of the false image they'd created of me. The cruel words online afterward were like physical blows that brought a crushing end to what had been such an amazing few months. I wondered how I could ever face the producers, the other contestants? How could I pull it together to perform in the live shows after this? I was scared that I would be judged, based on my audition. I had two choices: let this knock me down for good or get back up again.

EIGHT

The Show Must Go On

woke up the morning after the airing of my *X Factor* audition with red, swollen eyes and the worst migraine. It all came rushing back. The nightmare of witnessing my TV portrayal the night before. The feeling of being betrayed and misrepresented and having no power to defend myself. The nasty online comments from people who didn't know the real me.

I didn't want any of it to be true. But it was. I snuggled down into my childhood bed, Bobbi beside me, as always, but she could provide me with only so much comfort. I broke into tears all over again. I'd gone into the *X Factor* taping with such high hopes of setting a positive example in areas I cared about deeply—as a preemie who'd gone on to thrive, as a proud Latina from San Antonio with a deep love for my culture, and as a devoted daughter who was so grateful to my mom for all she'd done to get me to this moment in my career, even while dealing with the excruciating pain from her scoliosis—not to mention the chance to finally share my voice with the world. I'd been so proud, thinking that's exactly what I'd done. But what millions of people had watched, as my television debut, had been totally different from what I had experienced and projected. The version of Ally that they'd met had been edited to the point that it looked like I'd given an alternate audition.

I couldn't find the will to get up and start my day. I tried to tell myself that maybe I was being too hard on myself, and it hadn't been as bad as I was making it out to be. Maybe some people had enjoyed my performance and liked me as a person. Looking for any reason to feel hopeful, I flipped open my laptop and went to a YouTube clip of my audition. I scrolled through the comments until I couldn't take it anymore. They were so mean—about my personality, about everything. It was too much. A wave of nausea rushed over me, and I leaped out of bed and ran to the bathroom to throw up.

The way I'd been portrayed in the audition wasn't me. But everyone thought it was. I was angry and hurt. But I didn't even know who to be mad at, because I didn't really understand how the production worked. So all of those bad feelings festered inside of me. Now that I'd witnessed just how vicious the online cruelty toward me had been, I couldn't unsee it. Negative comment after nasty dig played over and over in my mind, touching on my deepest fears and insecurities. Family friends checked in with calls and messages of support, but I couldn't really hear them. All I could think to do was to quit and hide myself away from the world with Bobbi, who always looked at me in the sweetest way, like she knew exactly what I was feeling.

As usual, my parents were right there for me. My mom knocked on my door to check on me, with a bouquet of flowers her best friend had brought over to lift my spirits.

"Ally, this isn't the end of your story," Mom reminded me.

But as much as my mom was trying to put on a brave face for me, she was almost as upset as I was. It hurt her so much to see people misunderstand me and be mean to me, and she was crying on and off that morning while gratefully receiving prayers and encouragement from her friends. Later in the day, my parents tried to cheer me up by getting me out of the house for enchiladas. My dad and I would often go eat tacos together at different spots we loved around town, and just talk and enjoy being together. But even this familiar ritual didn't put a dent in my sadness now. My parents could see how down I was, and they never stopped giving me pep talks, for as long as I needed them. They insisted I was stronger than I felt right now. I would overcome this.

"We know who you are," my dad said. "We all know—your family and friends, everyone at church. We all know you are not the person the show portrayed you to be. You will let them see who you really are."

Yes, that was exactly what I wanted. My dad's words gave me strength, as I also gained power when we spent time at our church with our dear friends. I cared deeply, and I hoped that through my voice, I could help to make a positive impact on the world. Slowly their belief in me sank in. I had a choice to make. Yes, I felt embarrassed, but this was just something that had been done to me by people who obviously didn't know the first thing about me. It was not a reflection of who I was as an artist or as a human being. In the end, it was up to me to express my true self. To get up and keep pushing myself, keep trying. And that's just what I'd do—no one else was going to have the last say in my story. I was going to prove to them who I really was.

God had allowed this door to open. If He didn't think I was strong enough to walk through it, He would have closed it. I vowed to trust Him now more than ever. I vowed to keep doing my best and focus on staying true to who I was. My time at home with those who knew my true heart and talent gave me a much-needed recharge of my confidence. After a few days, I had recovered enough to return to my normal role in our family, going out of my way to encourage my parents and to try to make them feel better. I was still the same girl I'd been.

When the time arrived for me to travel to LA for the live shows, I was excited to return to the city where I had fought to make it as a performer for six long years, now with a spot on a popular TV show and the chance to possibly win it all. No matter what happened, I had made good use of my singing talent and had earned a huge opportunity to gain even more experience and exposure.

But I was scared. Once again I had to go alone because I was a legal adult, and the producers wouldn't allow my parents to accompany me. Even though I'd gotten through this same fear before in Miami, it was still only my second time away from my family. And now I had the added anxiety of worrying about how I would be portrayed. But every time I grew afraid, I thought about the progress I was making toward achieving my dreams. Once again my parents helped me pack, which was like a way of taking their love and support with me. And then it was time to go.

The show put us up at the Sheraton Hotel, right beside Universal Studios. I was thrilled to have my own room. I still remember the scent when I walked into the space and breathed deep—this would be my own little sanctuary, whatever came next. And as an added treat, I could order room service whenever I wished.

The Universal CityWalk was a short stroll from our hotel and had a long strip of shops and restaurants. Often we contestants from the show would all hang out and eat at the Hard Rock Cafe after rehearsals. It was exciting to be there together, getting to know one another and feeling the exhilaration of chasing our dreams, surrounded by tourists who had come from around the world to see how Hollywood magic was made. It was so wild that just a few years earlier, when I'd been living in LA at twelve years old, my dad would sometimes splurge and take me to Universal Studios for the day, to have fun, like all of the other kids my age, so I didn't feel left out. We were on such a tight budget that my dad would stop at the Carl's Jr. right by the park and buy two burgers, which he'd tuck into his backpack for our lunch, along with Doritos and Gatorade. Fast-forward to now—it was amazing to think of how far I'd come.

There were sixteen acts competing, with the number dropping each week until the finale, when the final three would compete and the winner would be announced. Most of each day was devoted to rehearsal. We practiced for hours. No matter how much time we spent running through the first song, it felt like the time was flying by. Suddenly we were due to take the stage for our first live performance as a group. It wasn't our best. In fact, it was pretty bad. But apparently America could see through our nerves and newness, and we made it through to the next round. And the next. We were finding our footing together and working as a group. We were continuing to rise on the show.

The pressure of the countdown to the next night of filming was constant. Every minute was filled with the stress of something new. Just when we thought we'd nailed a number, the show would surprise us somehow—our song would change, our wardrobe would be revamped. From the beginning, I was really struggling. It wasn't what I'd expected at all. The insult that was hardest to swallow was that our vocal coach did not give me many singing parts—only a single line here and there. When I tried to speak up for myself, the vocal coach didn't want to hear it, and she pushed back on me, hard. "You should be grateful that you're here," she said. "It shouldn't be about parts."

I was grateful. But getting spoken to like that in front of everyone embarrassed me. I knew I could do so much more if I was only given an opportunity. I felt humiliated and worthless. And I internalized the situation and started to believe that I wasn't good enough. It was really hard to feel so insecure, when we were a newly formed unit, trying to find our collective identity. Or having our identity found for us.

I didn't have much say over any aspect of our transformation. Not how to dress, how to wear my hair, or how to do my makeup. I couldn't even wear eyelashes, which was one of my favorite parts of getting made up. It probably seems like a small thing, but it was a big deal to me. I had just turned nineteen, and after six years of being responsible for every detail in my look—with help from my mom, of course—I was now in the position of being dictated to. If I wanted a certain lipstick, that would be a battle. Really, I didn't even get to choose my lipstick color? I felt frustrated and powerless to change my circumstances, especially because I really hated any kind of confrontation, and so even small asks were difficult for me. So most of the time, I was too scared to make a request.

I'd definitely always been a people pleaser. I try to make everyone happy whenever possible, even if my own contentment suffers. It was a big deal for me to speak up for something I wanted, whether it was as significant an issue as a vocal part or as minor a one as a lipstick color. I would get so nervous that my heart would pound in my chest. But it never seemed to matter how much courage I gathered, the answer was always no. When I heard this negative response, again and again, on matters big and small, it began to make me question my judgment. *Was I wrong about what looked best on me? About what was cool? About my voice? About who I was, even?*

I was already under so much pressure to learn the songs, deliver during performances, and be a team player that it didn't feel worth the fight to push back. And I was too overwhelmed by doing it all alone. Although I was technically an adult, I can see now that I was quite sheltered, from having been homeschooled and spending most of my adolescence in a small supportive bubble of our friends, family, and some people I had become close to while working with them.

What really got to me was that I wasn't allowed to contribute when it came to the musical decisions we were making—which meant everything to me. Singing was the great love of my life, and if I couldn't give my all when it came to that, then how could I be happy? Again, I began to doubt that I really knew what was best when it came to my voice and my delivery style. Going into the *X Factor* audition, I had been quite confident about my singing and what I had to offer, having honed my skills and resilience during six years of performing everywhere I could, working with established songwriters and producers. I hadn't had a breakout hit, but I knew I could find a place for myself within the industry. Suddenly I wasn't allowed to be me. I detested the feeling. I began to wonder who I even was anymore, and if there was a place for me—on the show, in the group, within the music world. And all of this was happening with the cameras rolling all around us, during what was supposed to be the best, most exhilarating, time of my life.

After all, this was what I had dreamt of for so long, what my family had sacrificed so much for, and it was nothing like what I'd thought it would be. I didn't feel represented. I had a tough time standing up for myself, and when I overcame my shyness and dared to try, I caved quickly. On top of that, I desperately missed my family and wished my parents could be there all of the time, not just for the few quick visits they made during the weeks we taped the show. I called them every day—multiple times a day—and they always listened and did their best to give me advice and keep my spirits up. When I asked about things back in San Antonio, they told me everything was great. With our long shoot days and busy schedule, I was too cocooned in the world of the show to push for more details—and maybe I needed the fantasy of the perfect oasis of home life, waiting for me to return to soon.

They kept it upbeat. Talking to my parents always cheered me up and reminded me of the values I cared about—to be punctual, to be kind, to be a leader, to be generous in my attempts to lift up the other girls. I tried to remain grateful, even as I prayed that things would change.

It can be tough to know when to make waves and when to go with the flow, especially when you're young. When do you sacrifice your own wants for others, and when do you stand up for yourself? This was a skill I would learn the hard way, over and over again. For now, as the oldest girl in the group, whom Simon had called "the glue," I was trying my best to be a leader and a team player—qualities my parents had always encouraged me to foster.

It was close to Thanksgiving. We had managed to avoid being eliminated. As the number of contestants dwindled, even a normal day of rehearsing and filming was getting more and more exciting—but also the pressure was on. The longer we stayed on the show, the closer we came to the finale. I still wasn't getting good vocal parts, and personally, I was demoralized. But even so, I was trying to be happy for our group, and I was excited about the success and love we were receiving. It was a balancing act, between my personal experience and emotions, and the excitement of the huge opportunity we had in front of us.

Then during a break, I happened to hop on Facebook to catch up with my home life and noticed a post from my aunt that stopped me cold. It said something like: "Friends, can you please pray for my father-in-law? It's not looking good for him. We don't think he has much time."

I stared at the words and for a moment couldn't take them in. My aunt's stepdad was my Grandpa Paul. I had just talked to my parents the day before, and when I'd asked them how everything was at home, they hadn't mentioned anything about Grandpa Paul's being sick. How could this be possible? I was in such shock, I crouched down, curled myself up in a ball against the onslaught of pain, and began to sob. When I had calmed down enough to form words, I called my mom, fighting through my tears to speak.

"Mom, what is going on? I saw this Facebook post. What is happening? I don't know what's happening." I was so upset, I just kept repeating myself. Nothing made any sense.

"Mama, we didn't want to worry you, because we know you're out there, and you're on the show," she said. "A lot is going on for you. We didn't want to tell you until we had to."

"Why, why? Why didn't you tell me?"

I could feel her trying to comfort me with her voice across the miles. But the shock felt so raw and painful, I broke down. I'd had no idea that my grandpa was suffering. He'd had health problems for a while, culminating in heart surgery earlier that year, but I didn't know anything was wrong right now. To find out on social media that he was declining fast was awful. It made me feel like I'd been too distracted by the show. This right here was what mattered—family, health, love, being there for one another.

My mom felt terrible; I could hear it in her tone. "We love you, and I'm so sorry that you had to see that and find out this way. But . . ."

I could hear her tears. "Your grandpa is not doing well. And we don't know how much time he has left."

I couldn't quite take this in. The show was so demanding, and I already felt emotionally drained from the long, exhausting hours, the hard work, and my personal frustrations. Now to hear this about my grandpa was absolutely devastating. I didn't want to get off the phone with my mom because that was my lifeline to home, to my grandpa. We finally had to hang up, because I had to do my best to pull myself together for my duties on the show.

Every moment leading up to our next live taping was crucial. But as I stood outside our rehearsal room, taking deep shuddering breaths, I couldn't stop crying, no matter how hard I tried. Pulling myself together, I reminded myself that I wanted to be the kind of dedicated professional who always showed up. The other girls were depending on me. I couldn't let them down. It took all of this and my most fervent prayers to get through that long brutal day.

Later that night I finally got to be alone and speak to my grandpa. We had been moved to a mansion near the studio where we filmed, and my room had a balcony. I leaned against the railing and tried to be my best self. Through tear after tear, I was careful to say everything I wished to express, even if words could never get across all that I felt for my dear grandpa. I tried with everything inside of me to speak to him from my heart: "I love you so much, Grandpa. Thank you for being the most incredible man."

I thanked him for coming into my grandma's life and taking such good care of her. He gave my grandma a tender, beautifully pure love. He was more than wonderful to her. He would do anything for her. He loved me and his family with all of his might. I promised to work hard for him and to take care of Grandma. I was crying and couldn't stop. "Grandpa, you were everything to me," I concluded. "And you are my heart."

My grandpa had always been funny and full of life, joking around, smiling, and laughing. I could hear from his voice how weak he was. But he still made sure I knew he was unbelievably proud of me. He was so happy for me. As much as I wanted to go home, he told me that he wanted me to stay on the show. I already knew from my grandma that while he was in the hospital, he'd always tell the nurses about me and my singing. He would tell them to watch me on *X Factor* and brag that I was his granddaughter. That meant the world to me, of course. But I heard the change in him, and I can't tell you how much it hurt me. He took deep breaths, trying to get the words out. I kept telling him how much I loved him.

"I love you, mija." Then his last words to me were, "Everything's gonna be okay."

A day or two later, one of the assistant producers pulled me aside and asked if I'd come with her. I followed her to a room and was surprised to see my mom and dad sitting there.

I'll never forget their faces. Instantly I knew they'd flown to me for one reason.

"Is this about Grandpa, Daddy?" I could barely get the words out.

My dad's face said it all. He started crying. "Yes, Mama."

The assistant closed the door, leaving me alone with my mom and dad. They wrapped me up in their arms, but grief and pain overwhelmed me, and I was inconsolable. I was only nineteen, and I'd never lost anyone to death except my dad's mom, who had passed when I was very young. Plus, I'd been so close to my grandpa. I couldn't process the loss. Or speak.

I cried and cried. I couldn't do rehearsals. I couldn't do anything. We had to perform the next night, but how was I going to sing when it seemed I didn't even have the strength to stand?

Everyone on the show came up to give their condolences. I was so grateful to feel such overwhelming support. One of the hosts that season was Khloé Kardashian. Radiating warmth, she pulled me aside, giving me a big hug, and I cried in her arms. "I am so sorry for your loss," she said. "I lost my dad when I was very young. Even to this day, it's still hard. But I'm here for you, and I'm praying for you and your family. One thing that I'll tell you is don't let anybody tell you how to grieve. If you want to cry, cry. If you want to try to be happy, be happy. But you grieve in the way that you grieve."

I thought it was so incredible that she was willing to be vulnerable with me about her own loss, and I deeply appreciated her generosity of spirit. I held on to her words and her kindness as I did my best to pull it together for the long night ahead.

Then my grandma called. When I heard her voice, I fell apart all over again. I told her how sorry I was, and that I didn't think I could perform.

"Mija, you go out there," she said. "That's what Grandpa would want you to do. He was so proud of you, Mama. The proudest grandpa in the world. And he loves you with all of his heart. We all love you."

Even to this day, I don't know how I had the strength to get through that night. All that can be explained is that it was with the tremendous support of my family and loved ones, including my grandpa. I know he was with me that day. And I know God gave me the strength when I had none.

As if orchestrated by God (which, of course, I know it was), during our live performance in the fifth week of the show, on November 28, 2012, we happened to be singing a song about strength, Kelly Clarkson's "Stronger." Leading into our performance, the producers always screened what was called a package, updating the audience on our journey. This time it included video of my telling my grandma and grandpa that I'd made it onto *The X Factor,* and of me vowing to dedicate the night's performance to my grandpa. By the grace of God, and with Grandpa looking down on me, I sang my heart out, with the words taking on a whole new meaning as we belted out that rousing chorus, "What doesn't kill you makes you stronger / Stand a little taller." That night Simon said that my grandpa would be incredibly proud of me. I was able to really believe him. And again we were safe from elimination.

NINE

Knocked Down, Getting Back Up

I had dug deep and done my best for our group, and for myself. But once the performance was over, I wanted nothing more than to get home right away. The problem was, we were on a tight schedule for the show and last-minute flights were expensive, but I didn't care. I knew I needed to be with my family more than anything. And then a producer came up and pulled me aside. "Simon is going to cover your flight to San Antonio and back, so you can go to your grandpa's funeral," she said.

I was deeply moved by Simon's amazing act of kindness, and it remains one of the nicest things that anyone has ever done for me. With the support of Simon and the producers, I flew to San Antonio, even though it would mean missing rehearsal. I was able to spare only two days from the demands of the show, but it felt so comforting to step off the plane in my hometown. I immediately went over to my grandma's house, where my entire family had gathered to comfort her and be together. We circled up. We cried, we laughed, we remembered, we processed our feelings of loss. Everyone was, of course, proud of me for how far I'd gone on *The X Factor*, but our focus now was on our family. We leaned on one another in our time of tears and deepest sorrow. This was exactly what we needed, to grieve and to say goodbye to Grandpa together.

On the day of Grandpa Paul's funeral, I was devastated, but I kept my focus on my grandma—our whole family did. Out of all of us, she had suffered the biggest loss and was experiencing the most agonizing heartbreak. We were all mourning, but we were also trying to stay strong for her. We did everything we could to comfort her. And when it got too hard, Grandpa's words never left me: "Everything's gonna be okay."

I would need such reassurance in the weeks ahead, and not just as I underwent the slow and painful process of mourning. The loss of my grandpa didn't feel real. It still doesn't. I know in my head that he passed away. But in my heart, it almost feels like he will return some-day. I suppose that's how grief is—we don't always have the tools to comprehend our loss, and it's just so incredibly painful. Although my family is doing a lot better, more than seven years later, we will always miss him. Thankfully, in the worst early days, I had our family, and we had our shared love and support to lean on. And music is such a source of therapy for me, helping me to release my pain. And I know I will see him again one day in Heaven.

As we advanced on the show, episode after episode, an incredible momentum was building—we were becoming something, and I could feel it. I wasn't the only one. We exploded on social media. People on the streets started to recognize us. This girl group thing was actually . . . working. After learning that Bruno Mars's sisters actually already were a singing group called the Lylas, we'd gone through a few different possibilities. And then, with the help of our fans online, it was decided that we would officially be called Fifth Harmony. We finally had a name! And we had fans who cared! Our potential seemed endless. I was kind of in disbelief. But more than anything else, I was thrilled.

Behind the scenes, I was still struggling to figure out how I fit in. For our performance in the semifinals, we would redo the song

"Impossible," which had made such a great impression on Simon and Marc Anthony when we'd sung for them at Simon's Miami house, what felt like lifetimes ago. Now Simon had specific notes for us going into our performance:

Simon wanted two of the girls, who were Latin, to sing their verses in Spanish.

The first chance I had to speak with a producer, I asked, "Can I please sing Spanish as well, because I'm also Latin?"

The answer was no.

Normally, I would have taken that as the final word from on high, no matter how disappointed I was. But this was different. I thought about my family and how important it would be to them that I had proudly represented our Mexican culture. Sometimes it's actually easier for us to be strong for the people we love than it is for us to stand up for ourselves. After all that my family had sacrificed for me and all the love and care they had put into supporting me, during the long years it had taken me to get this far, I was determined to do something for them, and to honor them.

I also thought back to how I'd often drawn on the example of my hero, Selena, and how I could do so again now. Like me, she hadn't been raised speaking Spanish, but she'd learned to speak it later and had done so in interviews and other areas of her life. She'd sung in Spanish, and she'd always been outspoken in her pride about her heritage.

This issue was too vital not to fight for my voice to be heard. I pushed back, asking for someone on the show to please stand up for me, because having the chance to sing in Spanish was so important to me. But again, the answer was a strong no.

As we rehearsed and got ready for the next taping, I couldn't stop wrestling internally with what was right. I prayed about it. I practiced the Spanish lyrics in case I found the courage to sing them on TV. I was conflicted. My family and I had just lost my grandfather, and I knew in my heart that my grandpa would have wanted me to sing in

Spanish, too. He would have wanted me to represent who I am on the show for all of America to see, and not to let anyone tell me what to do or who to be (or not to be). It's what my whole family would want for me.

And it was what *I* wanted for me. The fact that I don't speak fluent Spanish has always been a major insecurity of mine. Sometimes I've worried: *Am I really Mexican if I don't speak Spanish? Do people think I'm a fake?* A lot of personal identity issues come up for me around this topic, and it has always really bothered me when people have made a comment or teased me about it. What they might not understand is that when my parents were growing up in Texas, they got in trouble for speaking Spanish among themselves, because the teachers couldn't understand them. They literally had their hands slapped with rulers if they said a word in their native tongues. It's so sad to picture this. It was a different time, and my parents and aunts and uncles internalized that treatment. They wanted to protect their kids, and they felt like they were doing so by not teaching us Spanish, beyond food words and a little slang.

Even so, they raised us to be proud Mexican Americans. And I've always tried to defend my heritage whenever someone has questioned me about not speaking Spanish. I'm hoping those who read my story will finally understand why I can't speak Spanish. Maybe my story will help other people like me, and my cousins, to not feel as insecure. I know who I am. And I'm unbelievably proud to be Hispanic. That's what matters. Of course, it is my dream to learn Spanish. I will work to do so, and I encourage anyone who is a part of our culture to do the same. For now I feel thankful to be able to at least sing in our beautiful language and to have been embraced by the Latin community, exactly as I am.

All of this was on my mind as we went into the taping of the semifinals.

Just then we were cued to go onstage, and I went through with my plan. I felt so proud as the Spanish words flew from my heart and my mouth. This was huge for me. I'd stayed true to myself during a challenging moment, when it would have been easier to fall back and just go along with what I'd been told to do.

Soon after, I got a much-needed affirmation to be myself from a fan who came to the Loews Hotel in Hollywood, where we were staying for the finale. It was exciting to walk into the lobby and, for the first time, to find our supporters—now known as Harmonizers—gathered to try to see us. It was so amazing, hearing some of them shout, "Ally! Ally!"

A girl who was probably just a few years older than me, with one of her arms in a cast, had waited downstairs until she had the chance to speak to me. Seeing me, she smiled shyly. I met her with a wide smile of my own and went right over to talk to her.

"Ally, I want to say, I'm a huge fan of the group," she said. "You are so powerful, strong, and beautiful together. I know that you auditioned with 'On My Knees' by Jaci Velasquez. I love that song, and I love that you love God, and you're open about your faith online. I want to say thank you so much for inspiring me to hold on to my faith and to be proud and to keep on trusting God in my life, because I am going through a lot right now."

"Wow, thank you so much," I said. "That means a lot to me."

I felt myself light up from my core. I'd been feeling insecure within the group, but here was proof that I was being seen not just for my singing, but for what I hoped to represent. I was helping people, and that was all I had ever wanted to do. Even though in some moments I felt frustrated, like I wasn't really coming across to the audience as I would have liked to, it was intensely gratifying to know that I actually was being appreciated on a deeper, more soulful level.

In the end, we took third place at the finale. My parents, of course, were in the audience on my big night. They'd also organized a viewing party at our church, Oak Hills, which had been attended by hundreds of people, who cheered us on, voted for us, and left special messages for me, along with my family and other loved ones.

Though we did not win, I was so proud of how far we'd come, and I felt confident we'd only just begun. And by that, I mean I knew there was a great chance we would get signed to a record label. The fan base was too strong to ignore.

We did not have to wait long for our next big step. We were at the wrap party for the show when we heard: we'd been signed by Simon's and L.A. Reid's labels. It was incredible!

I'd spent all of those years working hard toward a solo career, giving up so many aspects of what should have been my normal teenage life. Instead I'd practiced and worked hard, performing wherever the door opened, from high schools, baseball games, and barbecues to little music festivals and recording studios in San Antonio and LA. Sure, this girl group wasn't a part of my plan, but I knew we could be great together. I saw something special in us. I was overjoyed and grateful and determined to work just as hard for our collective good. It also meant a lot to me when at the end of the show, the producers apologized to my parents for how they had edited my audition, saying they felt bad about their decision, especially knowing how sweet I was, and knowing who I really was, versus how my audition had presented me.

Looking back, I see how God brought the pieces together that I didn't even know to ask for. It wasn't my plan to go on the show. And it wasn't my plan to be in a group. But God was guiding me in a way that wasn't on the map I'd drawn. In the process, He was refining me. And He was making me so much stronger than I'd even known that I would need to be.

From the embarrassment I felt after my audition aired to my grandpa's death, I'd discovered that sometimes our hardest days are those that define us the most. As difficult as challenges can be, these dark times help us grow and gift us with perspective. All of which enables us to have greater compassion, to be better daughters, sisters, humans. If we really dig in and ask ourselves, with honesty: *What did I learn from these hardships? How was I able to grow? How can I live more boldly, yet humbly, because of them?* If we really take the time to process our grief, our answers will refine us further. Little did I know, I would need all of this wisdom, because I had even more hard lessons and growth ahead of me.

It felt amazing when I returned to San Antonio, after our *X Factor* season ended in December 2012. I felt the love from my hometown. It was incredible to have people recognize me when I went out, saying that they loved me, they loved Fifth Harmony, and they'd voted for us. That was such a special feeling, and something I had dreamed about as a little girl.

My family always grounds me, especially in my hometown. This time back in Texas provided perspective, including the reality that my grandpa was gone, as much as I struggled to accept it, and that my life had changed forever. From the highs of becoming a contestant on *The X Factor* and being chosen for a fan-favorite girl group that had landed a record deal, to the lows of feeling powerless about the editing of my audition and the insecurities the show had launched within me—and of course my grief over the loss of Grandpa Paul—the past few months had been draining on all levels.

Now winter brought a breather. We gathered at my aunt's house as usual, ate all of our favorite Christmas foods, laughed together, and told stories about Grandpa Paul. I enjoyed quiet hours cuddling with my cat Bobbi and watching Christmas movies on the couch. I also spent time with Grandma, appreciating her all the more. It was the perfect gift—the chance for me to rest and savor all that it means to be home at Christmastime. As usual, my parents went all out celebrating our favorite holiday. Mom picked her theme for our inside Christmas tree, and my dad, aka Clark Griswold, outlined the exterior in lights until our house looked like it could be on its own reality competition show.

While we decorated and cooked, I was saddened to notice that my mom's back was getting worse, and she had to stop and rest more often because it hurt. My mom was in the process of searching for the right doctor to perform a risky operation, one that could hopefully reverse her scoliosis and help her to live pain-free. I knew that she'd been caught in a frustrating cycle of hope and disappointment for several years now. Every time she dared to think her prayers had been answered and she'd found the right surgeon, there was some reason why the doctor or timing just didn't work out. Of course, seeing her suffer upset me terribly. I wondered what could be done for her, and until we could locate the right person to perform the procedure she needed, I tried to help out even more than usual.

Being able to assist my mom was one of many reasons I was glad for this time at home. I immediately felt uplifted by the chance to just be with my family. And I savored the break, knowing that I was about to be very busy.

——

TEN

Losing Your Voice

In January 2013, the official announcement was made that we had signed our record deal with Simon's Syco Music and L.A. Reid's Epic Records. After the deal was finalized, the five of us were called back to Los Angeles, where we were put up—guess where? The Oakwood Apartments, where I'd stayed with my mom when I was twelve years old. It was such a full-circle experience—a true mix of returning to my roots and starting over with fresh success. Thinking about how shy and unsure of myself I'd been when we'd first lived there, I saw how far I'd come, even if my confidence had taken a recent hit. I hoped that being back in the city where I had originally gone to pursue a music career, and now with a record deal, would help me to believe in myself and my talent again.

We were officially introduced to our core team—a manager, an agent, a lawyer, and those who would work with us at our two labels. The holiday breather had revitalized me, and I was full of energy and excitement as I prepared to dig into my new life. This was it—the breakthrough I'd been waiting for was finally happening. The only question was how it was going to work now that we were out in the real world.

First up, we had to find our sound and record the songs that would introduce us to the world. I was ready to start anew and leave the past of the show behind me. I was optimistic about this clean slate. It was so energizing, having this newfound attention, receiving records from different songwriters, producers. People who wanted to work with us! We all wanted to see where this new adventure would lead us. But what happened on the track that would become our first single, "Miss Movin' On," was unfortunately all too representative of my struggles during our first few years as a group. One by one, we went into the studio to record the whole song, each belting out all the verses and choruses, with all of our might. We were told the producer would listen, then decide which lines were best suited to which girls. The track would be edited and mixed accordingly, and we would hear the finished product later. As always, I did my best and tried to stay optimistic and upbeat.

After the producer finished the song, we were called in for the playback. As I listened to the track, I felt my face draining of color. Verse after verse, I kept listening for myself, but by the time the song had ended, I was crushed. This was our first single—our first chance to show the world we were more than just a reality TV group—and I'd only been given one line on the bridge, and one ad lib.

Everyone seemed very excited about the song. But inside I was frozen. I couldn't tell them how I really felt. Overall, I was a team player—just as my parents had raised me to be—way more likely to compromise on what I wanted than to risk making others unhappy. Rather than trusting myself that the breakdown of the song actually was unfair and a missed opportunity to showcase my voice, I gave in to my doubts. These decisions had been made by some of the top producers in the industry. I couldn't fight them or even stand up to them.

Even though I didn't feel able to express my feelings out loud, I definitely had them. Angry thoughts crept up to the forefront of my mind: *Why am I getting only one line?*

I tried to give myself a pep talk, like my parents would have done if they'd been there. I wanted to be happy and grateful. I reminded my-self that thousands and thousands of girls would've loved to be in my shoes. I reminded myself to have faith and believe God had brought me here for a purpose—that this was His plan. But I also knew that sometimes God wants us to grow and become braver, instead of just asking Him to solve everything for us.

I was sure I had recorded some great parts. If I'd done a bad job, someone would've told me. Still, again, the negative voices inside my head were much louder than the positive ones: *After how many times my ideas and contributions have been shot down, can I really trust my own instincts about my delivery, my voice, my anything? Am I enough? Am I good at all?*

I thought I'd put such doubts behind me. But as I was learning, it's incredibly challenging when the issues we thought we'd overcome return to hurt us all over again—and from what I've seen, they often do. In this situation, it wrecked me, and I didn't know how to move forward. I started to pick apart my every decision up until that point, second-guessing myself: *Maybe I should have demanded more time in the studio. Maybe I shouldn't have left the room until I felt satisfied. Maybe I should have asked more questions.*

We were busy getting ready to launch our first single, "Miss Movin' On." In my heart, I knew it was time to speak up. I'd known it since I'd first heard the track. But back then, I was trying to find my voice again, to get back to the confident young performer I'd once been. I was scared I wouldn't come up with the right words, or they would land wrong and make it worse.

Finally I couldn't stand feeling so disappointed and upset any-more. A few days after first hearing the song, I gathered my courage and called our manager. As I listened to the phone ring, it felt like my heart was beating everywhere in my body. I could step onto a stage in front of a live camera feed that would broadcast me into the homes of millions of people, no problem. But trying to tell someone I was unhappy—that was terrifying.

I stayed focused on what I needed to say, and as soon as I got the chance, I blurted it out: "I should not have only one little line," I told her. I had been left with one token line and one tiny ad lib. "Miss Movin' On" was our first release, and I wanted to be represented fairly.

"I'll call and see if anything can be done, Ally," our manager assured me.

As we ended our talk, I was still praying that something could be done for me. I was actually feeling hopeful and a little proud of myself. Even though I'd wanted to avoid any conflict, I'd stood up for myself with our manager. Even better, maybe a solution could be found.

When she called back later that day, I answered quickly, hoping her words would be those I had prayed to hear.

"I'm so sorry, but it's too late," she said. "The song is locked."

As I already knew, when a song is locked, it has gone to mix and cannot be changed. There was nothing anyone could do for me now.

This was our first release, and it felt like another embarrassing start for me. I was nervous that our fans would see me as nothing more than being in the background.

Alone in my apartment, I cried my eyes out. I was tired of these long days of hard work, while feeling underutilized and increasingly unsure. I couldn't shake the feeling that I had no worth. Also, my parents and my entire family and everyone who'd believed in me back in San Antonio were getting totally amped up for the release of our single. They couldn't talk about anything else. My mom kept telling me how excited she was to hear me on the local radio station for the first time. I knew she was just proud of me, but it made me feel sick, thinking how I had let her—and everyone else—down by not securing more lines for myself on the song.

Finally, at the last minute, I admitted what was going on behind the scenes. But, as I'd feared, my family was now upset for me. That's why I hadn't wanted to say anything. Normally, I would have tried to make them feel better, but I was so disappointed, I had no strength. All I could do was cry and tell them: "I tried to talk to our manager. I did everything I could to get my voice represented on that song."

When I thought about how crushed my parents were, the pressure weighed me down, and I felt like I'd embarrassed my family. Over the phone and by text, they told me to remain strong and continue to bring my best every day, no matter what. My parents also offered to talk to our manager for me, but I wanted to stand up for myself. And it was too late. Nothing could be done.

The pain of what had happened on the show came flooding back, but this felt even worse—it was our first single. On the one hand, I had this success, and it was being celebrated. We got to make our first music video and there was a ton of promo and press—all of which was incredible. But at the same time, I couldn't fully enjoy it because I knew deep down that I wasn't being represented, and behind my smile and laugh as I helped with promotion, I felt humiliated and like an outsider. Away from my family, back in LA and on the road, I tried to keep everything buried deep down inside of me. All I wanted was to be recognized for my talent and for being a part of an amazing group.

During this time, we were ecstatic to learn we'd be working with a producer who had been responsible for so many of the hits by One Direction. Having been formed on *The X Factor* in the UK, One Direction felt like an amazing example for us to look up to, as they were currently on fire and dominating the music world. He had helped to launch One Direction into a crazy stratosphere of success, and now, hopefully, he could do the same for us.

During our early recording sessions, we were already collaborating with some of the best talent in songwriting and producing, people who'd worked with everyone from Rihanna to Beyoncé and who'd created huge pop records. It was amazing, collaborating with the writers behind some of my favorite songs. We girls tried to write for a hot second, but with so many of us in the room, there were too many different opinions, and we got down only a few tracks. Plus, our record labels wanted us to work with the biggest songwriters, who already had hits. They were brought in, working closely with us and other top producers to figure out our perfect sound.

I'd thought that once we were signed, I'd finally get a chance to be creative and show my talent in a way I hadn't felt able to during the rush and grind of the weekly show. Instead I was trying to find my identity again, and this time in a new environment. I was also struggling to overcome my lingering insecurities, especially after what had happened with "Miss Movin' On." I'd been recording and performing for years in Los Angeles and San Antonio, but now I faced a totally new challenge. While I had my own vision for what the group could be, the reality of finding a balance together was much harder than I'd expected. It was different from anything I had experienced before and proved to involve a huge learning curve for me.

We worked on recording music, most days, for several weeks. The studio where our producer worked was located in his house in Calabasas, a neighborhood on the edge of Los Angeles. The atmosphere was relaxed, and it felt so serene to be out in the woods. We'd make snacks or order food. Sometimes we cooked meals together or would go out for ice cream or lunch. The studio was located in a beautiful house, bordered by greenery, and I found myself turning to nature—soaking up the beauty, listening to music, praying, trying to hold on to my gratitude.

Fortunately, my main form of personal expression has always been through music, and there were moments when I had the chance to pour everything I was feeling into my vocals. One night, after a long day of waiting around, I was finally called into the vocal booth around two in the morning to record "Who Are You," a beautiful ballad. I was exhausted because we had been there all day and it was late at night. Maybe being so tired worked in my favor, because instead of overthinking, I just let go, allowing the music to move me and pull all of my emotion out of my body and into my voice. As I was recording,

I could feel something bigger than me channeling through me, and I belted my heart out, at the top of my lungs. It felt so powerful that tears formed in my eyes. When I was done, there was a moment of silence in the studio. Everyone in the room was floored. When I heard the edit, I felt so proud. I was ecstatic with my part, and how at the end of the song, I was able to give a really powerful, emotional performance and hit these huge high notes that would go on to be a fan favorite. To this day, this gorgeous ballad remains one of my favorite songs that we ever recorded.

The experience was great for my confidence, and it helped me to push myself further on our next few songs. On "Don't Wanna Dance Alone," I was able to secure a great bridge for myself and a big high note at the end. I took along this ember of belief in myself when we went to another studio to work with other producers and record "Leave My Heart Out of This." On this particular song, I had a really big ad lib, which would lead me to start being known by fans as the "Ad Lib Queen." On "Better Together," I finally had the chorus, which felt absolutely incredible and gave me hope for the future. Even with the blow to my confidence that our single caused overall, these meaningful accomplishments added up enough to keep me going. And it's a good thing, too, because we were in greater and greater demand.

Everyone on our team knew how important it was for us to get out and interact with the public as much as possible. We sang everywhere we could, debuting our first single on the *Today* show in mid-July. We did multiple pop-up shows in New York in a single day. We were also known for our covers of songs by other artists, and I'll admit we killed it on many of them. That summer, we launched Harmonize America, our first promotional tour, performing in shopping malls across the US. That's when we had our very first tour bus. It was so exciting for us all. We had worked incredibly hard that summer, to the point of exhaustion, but it seemed to be paying off. To see the fans that showed up was incredible. There were so many.

We did other fun appearances, too. A highlight was when we were invited to the grand opening of Topshop LA, the new Southern California outpost of the beloved UK store and fashion label. A camera crew came along, interviewing us, filming us meeting fans. We had fans. It was all happening. That summer, we would even win our first VMA for "Miss Movin' On."

I was floored by how many people showed up to watch us perform and to take pictures with us at our meet-and-greets in different cities. At every appearance, our crowds grew bigger and bigger. We did signings after our shows and connected with so many kids. I was happy that we had the chance to let our young fans get to know us in a more intimate way in the smaller venues we played. Many of them were very sweet and open about how much they loved us and how much they loved me, too. They nicknamed me the "sunshine" of our group, and I tried to live up to that honor and always be positive. Their words lifted me.

Between traveling in and out of LA to work on our music, the shopping mall tour, and several short club tours, we were constantly on the move. My dad always helped me to pack in those years. He was like a magician who somehow knew exactly how to fit everything into one suitcase. I tried on my own a few times, and my bag completely overflowed. My dad laughed when he saw the mess, but he always reassured me: "I got it, Mama, don't worry." And then he would put everything together for me, and it would all fit, pristine and perfect. He also somehow managed to slide in under the weight limit, which was a big deal, because we had to pack a ton of stuff but we would get charged if it was overweight. He had a travel scale, and he was always triumphant when he showed me the final number—his skills were next level useful.

I was grateful to feel my mom and dad's presence in these small signs of their love, even though I was the only girl who didn't have a parent traveling with her often, because my mom's back prevented her from traveling, and my dad needed to be with her. They did visit me once or twice a year, and my dad even made everyone tacos during one of these stays. Now I was out on the road, far from home, my family, friends, pets, our church, and everything that felt safe and comfortable, and I struggled—especially as we were receiving external pressure about how to look and who to be, which only made me even more insecure. There were times I longed to push back, to have my voice heard within the larger ecosystem of our group. Unless it was an issue related to one of the things I held most dear—my family, my heritage, my faith—it seemed easier to just go along with what was happening and put the group first. But actually, the cost of backing down in such moments would prove to be higher than I knew at the time.

In part, I think I was still catching up with my new reality. I had dreamed of this life for as long as I'd known to have dreams—tour buses and stage lights and the chance to sing my heart out for excited fans. All of this magic was my everyday life. But in order to live out my fantasy, I was also going to have to get through some real challenges, unlike any I'd ever faced before. The thought was scary. I'd been so full of hope just a few months earlier, when I had thought I was about to be the happiest girl in the world. Now I was struggling to find myself. But you know what? I was still a part of something incredible and doing amazing things. I was able to meet people on the road, sing my heart out, and experience things most people don't ever get to.

Adding to my personal insecurities was the fact that around this time I'd decided to try a new look—bangs. When you're in a group, it's important for everyone to have their own style. Our then manager asked me if I was interested in getting bangs. I talked it over with my mom, who thought it could be a good change for me, and I was eager to be a team player when possible. So I agreed.

"Sure, why not try something new?" I said.

Now, some people look great with bangs. When I saw myself in the mirror, I took it in for a beat. I didn't necessarily love it, but I was trying to embrace a new look, and I even hoped it might help me to stand out, in a way. Instead, the girls in the group teased me a bit, not knowing just how sensitive I was about my bangs. I'd been homeschooled and spent most of my free time as a teen with my family and our church community, and these kinds of jokes were foreign to me. Even though I knew they were supposed to be funny, I didn't roll with them well.

There was a show on Nickelodeon called *Ned's Declassified School Survival Guide,* with a character called Coconut Head. Someone pointed to me in the poster we'd been photographed for right after my haircut and said, "Ally looks like Coconut Head with those bangs!" Everyone thought it was hilarious and started calling me Coconut Head.

I joke about it today, but at the time it was painful, opening up old wounds about not being pretty enough, at a time when I was already doubting myself. Even now I can't stand to look back at pictures of myself from these months, but when I do, I can now find a way to laugh. If I could go back in time, I'd make sure that my individuality didn't come from those horrible bangs. It would come from just being myself. Thankfully, bangs grow out, and I can mostly smile about the whole nightmare now. At the time, though, I was in it.

Still, there was much to be thankful for. Our velocity was incredible. That October, our video for "Miss Movin' On" earned more than 15 million views for an original song on YouTube, making us the first American *X Factor* alumni group to achieve this milestone.

That same month, Syco and Epic Records dropped "Better Together," our debut EP, which is a short album with about half as many songs as a full-length. It debuted at No. 6 on the Billboard 200, which was crazy. And of the six songs on the EP, including the second single, "Me & My Girls," I was thrilled that I'd actually landed more parts than I did on "Miss Movin' On," and some of them were really great. We were even able to co-write on three songs, on "Me & My Girls," "Who Are You," and the first track, "Don't Wanna Dance Alone," which we also released a Spanish version of, with all of us getting to take a verse. I loved it when I had a chance to show my range, to hit the high notes with a lot of power. I was so happy that people had a chance to finally see and hear what I could do. I wasn't completely, one hundred percent happy with the distribution on the EP, but I tried to focus on the positives. As we continued to tour and make direct contact with more of our fans, I was grateful for the increasing number of people I was meeting. I wanted more than anything for the group to take off, so I was happy that we were starting to gain some traction.

It was incredible to experience such rapid success. There hadn't been a breakout girl group in a decade. If I do say so myself, we were one of the first artists to break on social media. It became our best friend, and I credit it for helping us to launch our careers, along with our die-hard fan base. To be a part of this phenomenon, from the inside looking out, was just crazy. Sometimes I describe it as an out-of-body experience. I was completely aware that it was a rare opportunity, even as I lived it. But as we were under a lot of pressure and in the public eye, it also came with its challenges. So I was constantly on my knees, asking God to give me strength and to bless my efforts. Some days were better than others, and on those days, hope rose within me. But then I encountered rough patches again, which tried to steal that hope away. It was tough, juggling so many different personalities and opinions. The emotional blender continued for months. I tried to stay positive and give one hundred percent every minute of the day. That's all I could do, while praying the other stuff would work itself out.

ELEVEN

Dreams Become Reality

studied the Barbie's face and couldn't believe that I was seeing a rendering of my own features. Barbie had always had a special place in my heart, since she'd been my first friend when I was a little girl. From a young age, I was the biggest Barbie fan, and I'd had so many of the dolls, including the Holiday Barbie, plus the Barbie Dreamhouse and the Barbie car. I'd spent hours playing with her, both alone and with my mom and other friends my age.

And now, as part of our group's partnership with Mattel, the company had created a Barbie doll for each of us. It was a dream come true. The fact that we had joined forces with Mattel was announced along with their new brand anthem, "Anything Is Possible." This was such a positive, empowering message, which I was very proud to be a part of—I loved that we were being a positive example for so many kids. Plus, it was such an unbelievable honor, seeing myself as a Barbie.

Having Barbies made in our likeness was definitely a significant marker of the surreal level of success we'd now reached. We were getting the chance to perform for increasingly large and ecstatic crowds of fans, all over the United States. Plus, we were having the chance to start traveling outside the country, including to Canada, Puerto Rico, and Brazil. I'll never forget the first time we arrived in Brazil. We were met by a sea of passionate and beautiful fans. There was a barricade at the airport, separating us from them, because the crowds were so huge. As we were waving to them, all of the sudden, they broke through the barricades. I'd chosen to wear high heels and a heavy backpack. And boy, was that the wrong move on my end. I almost got trampled. They pulled my backpack, and I almost fell over. But our security guard Big Rob scooped me up and rescued me. He got me safely to the car. Thank God I was okay. That was an unbelievable feeling. We felt like the Beatles. And Brazil would soon become home to one of our biggest fan bases, ever.

All of this might have made it seem as if we'd already hit the top, but we still had a tremendous amount to prove. As I was learning, now that I was on the inside of the industry, pop artists are under extreme pressure to release a hit album, with a single that breaks out on the radio. We all felt how high the stakes were as we started working on our full-length album *Reflection*.

We were looking for songs when we were introduced to one of our artists and repertoire (A&R) reps. Basically, her role was to find new music for us. She believed in us one hundred percent, but she also pushed us to expand our music and our vision. She said whatever came to her mind, and she constantly encouraged us to add some edge to our sound. I remember her saying something like "You guys are so much more than squeaky-clean puppets. You have voices; you can sing. Your harmonies have grit and power. Let's step it up."

One day this A&R rep called. She insisted we come in right then, that same day, and record a new song. It was called "Boss." We rushed down to the studio, and she played it for us. I immediately loved the sound. We hadn't encountered anything like it in all of the music we'd heard so far, and we definitely had not released anything with so much edge. It was cowritten and produced by one of the top writers and producers in the game.

But was it *too* different? At first we weren't sure if it was going to be believable coming from us—some of the girls in the group still weren't even sixteen yet. But the music was infectious and the words were empowering. She encouraged us to have the confidence to choose the song, as a bold way to shift our image into the realm of really strong young women. Her words were the encouragement we needed, not just about choosing records, but about how much we could achieve—and how inspirational we could be—as a group. We all loved "Boss" and thought it could be an amazing game changer and help us step into our womanhood.

Almost immediately, we went in and started putting our voices down on the track. When I stepped into the vocal booth, I was again hit by nerves about what lines I'd be given—or not given. But this time, I tried not to let any negativity or my past experiences hinder me. I knew I had to push myself. If there was a time to show what I could do, it was now. I started singing, and I just let loose. I sang with poise, confidence, and soul. At one point, I was doing ad libs, and I released all of the attitude the song was making me feel, letting my voice roar. I belted this powerful high note at the end. It felt incredible. I left the booth with the biggest smile. When I saw the writers and the producers, their mouths were wide open. They clapped for me and shouted, "Woah, girl, you killed it. Yes, Queen!"

Right then and there, I knew I had killed it, and I beamed with pride. Even better, I was ecstatic to soon find out they'd be keeping what I'd done. My ability to silence my self-doubt and be my true self had paid off. Little by little, I felt more validation vocally. I still had some of the lesser parts on this record, but I was very happy that I secured the bridge, my high notes were kept, and I was able to close out the song with my final roars.

From "Miss Movin' On" to "Boss" we'd matured dramatically in our sound and vision. I felt like "Boss" was a positive shift. I loved the message about being an independent woman who was working hard and finding success on her own. I also embraced the more mature and sassy style and had fun with it. Being the oldest in the group, I might have been a bit more comfortable with the image change than the others, but it felt natural. I was excited for how it might be received.

We also had some bold choreography in the "Boss" video. A new choreography and creative direction team came in, who had worked with big names. Between them and our new A&R person, we were being propelled into another stratosphere. I loved the chance to work hard and up our game.

At this moment, I was feeling a little more confident with who I was within the group and the music business, even with all of its demands—at least for the most part. And my bangs had grown out. (Sometimes it's just the little things.) When I did doubt myself, I tried to just go with what was happening around me. Collectively, we were excited and also nervous, wondering how our fans and the industry would respond to our new direction. I hoped by taking this chance, we'd reach an even wider audience.

I couldn't believe it when I heard the release date for "Boss." It was coming out on my twenty-first birthday! Suddenly it was July 7, and I flew from celebrating my birthday weekend in Las Vegas to the *Today* show to perform our newest single. On the plane, I found myself thinking: *Whoa, it's all really happening. I'm going directly from living it up in Vegas to jet-setting to New York, where I'll be celebrating in the best way possible.*

As soon as I landed, even though I'd had no sleep, I was thrown right into performing live on the *Today* show's outdoor stage. We were all dressed in white, ready to introduce the world to a new side of our group. Even exhausted, I was energized by the excitement of it all.

Living up to our high hopes, "Boss" received a fantastic reception. It peaked at 43 on the Billboard Hot 100, got some radio play, and was eventually certified platinum in the United States. Our next single, "Sledgehammer," peaked at No. 40 on the Billboard Hot 100—our very first Top 40 entry. It was so exciting to reach these major milestones. Yes, there was still pressure from the label for that smash hit record, which we had yet to achieve, but this was definitely the beginning of a different era for us and the first of the leaps and bounds we would eventually make as a group. It was almost like the hit before the *real* hit, marking a noticeable rise in our level of success. Suddenly we were more popular, more in demand, and more on the move.

Not all responses were positive. Some people said we were pushing the envelope, and others were just plain critical. But for the most part, we got a lot of encouraging responses. Plus, by this point, I'd discovered that negative comments and opinions happen no matter what you do, especially in the entertainment industry. If you have much experience on social media, then you know that the more you put yourself out there, the more people can be cruel.

It wasn't the huge hit we needed, but it definitely brought us a lot of mostly positive attention. Our fans *loved* the change. They appreciated the hard work we'd put in to get here and were living for this new era in our sound and popularity. "Boss" was the start of that expansion, bringing brand-new audiences and a fresh group of fans. The public began seeing us as more than a manufactured girl group. We were a dynamic collective of talented women, demanding respect. The change had paid off. We were rising up. But closer to home, we were getting mixed signals about just how successful we were. The label said that we still didn't have the kind of hit we needed.

In the meantime, the year was winding down, and we recorded a cover of "All I Want for Christmas Is You" by Mariah Carey. Since Christmas is my favorite time of the year, I was so happy to do a song for the season. We even got to make a celebratory music video. Plus, it was amazing to be singing this particular song. Just like everyone else, I'd grown up with this as one of my favorite Christmas songs. I'd performed this one so many times during the holidays. So it felt special to be singing it again in an all new way. At the time that we put it out, we performed it live on the *Today* show. It was really wonderful to celebrate the Christmas season by singing such a holiday classic, and it made my favorite time of the year even more magical.

Then our manager gave us some phenomenal news: "Pack your bags, you're going to the White House!"

We all started screaming!

"Are you serious?" I shouted incredulously.

It almost sounded too good to be true. We'd been invited by President Barack and First Lady Michelle Obama to sing at the White House Christmas tree lighting. We were beyond excited for this incredible once-in-a-lifetime kind of an honor.

"And you can bring your parents!" she told us.

My excitement took a quick turn as I thought this through. My parents would be in awe with excitement if they could go, but there was a major problem. My mom's scoliosis, which had been getting worse ever since our car accident, had finally gotten so bad that traveling was near impossible. It was painful enough when she tried to complete simple tasks, like grocery shopping and laundry. Sitting for that long on a plane would be excruciating. I called my dad first, to share the incredible news and ask him what we should do.

"She just can't do something like that right now," Dad said sadly.

The severity of her physical challenges really struck me once more, and I felt so sad at the thought of her being left at home. We absolutely had to find a solution that would improve her quality of life, but so far we'd been unable. Mom was just as selfless as ever, and she insisted that my dad still attend with me and not miss such a monumental opportunity.

"It will make me so happy to imagine you two there at the White House, Mama," my mom said when we talked. "Please take Dad and enjoy every minute of it. This is beyond what we even dreamed or imagined."

I really missed my mom, and I wished with all of my heart that it could be different, but I couldn't pass up the gift of being an invited guest to the White House. And we all knew it would have caused my mom even more pain if my dad didn't go with me.

From the moment of our arrival in Washington, D.C., we were

in awe. The buildings and monuments were magnificent, and it really brought home the significance of what we were about to do. This was a show unlike any other we'd performed. We brought along our stylist, who set up at our hotel, which was stunning and felt like a Christmas wonderland. A car took us over for rehearsal the evening before, on December 4. The night was dark and cold, but it was magical to see the White House, in person, decorated for Christmas. When we pulled up for the first time, my jaw dropped. It was absolutely breathtaking, outside and in. I was struck by the magnitude of where we were, the legacy of this place, and its importance to the world. It was wild to realize that my voice had transported me here, against the odds. Seeing my dad's face was a beautiful moment. He loved history and he had never been to the White House before. We both teared up about how far we'd come.

The next day was the real thing. Our group was given a little tour of the White House. And then we lined up to greet the president and the first lady, who were so warm, charismatic, elegant, and gracious. It felt like a dream, meeting them. I couldn't believe that I was meeting the president of the United States of America and our wonderful First Lady! Then Michelle Obama, whom we'd name-checked as an icon of strong womanhood in the lyrics of our recent single, "Boss," absolutely floored us.

"I work out to 'Boss' every day!" she cheerfully admitted.

It was surreal to picture the first lady exercising to our song, with us singing about her. We were practically floating off the ground as our meeting with her and the president came to an end. Now it was time to go on. There was a huge crowd attending; not a seat was empty. And we were backed by the most perfect scene—straight out of a movie—in front of these giant Christmas trees. We saw President Obama and the first lady and their girls in the front row, smiling at us. I couldn't believe this was really happening. After we performed our songs, we were beaming. I took it all in. The tree was lit. I was so grateful to be there with my dad, as it was such a once-in-a-lifetime experience.

We met all kinds of people during the rehearsal and performance. Patti LaBelle, an icon in the history of music, was also singing. And with that powerhouse voice coming out of her, she is about as soulful as one can be. Her music is the bedrock of soul, and I had grown up listening to her music. I could not believe I was getting to meet her.

"You have been one of my great vocal inspirations," I told her. I thanked her for what she'd done for music, but I couldn't express all that I wished to say. Being the seasoned pro that she is, she was kind and gracious, and I took that interaction to heart.

As if meeting the Obamas weren't exciting enough, Tom Hanks and his wife, Rita Wilson, were there as well, and ever since I'd heard that they were going to be at the White House with us, I couldn't stop thinking about possibly meeting them. Growing up, I'd loved *The Polar Express* and *A League of Their Own,* and *Toy Story* was one of my favorite movies of all time—he was in too many great movies for me to even try to name them all. He was one of my favorite actors of all time. Plus, he and his wife just seemed like the kindest people. And I would be meeting them with my dad, who also was a huge fan, during an experience that I was making happen for him.

When we saw them, all I could do was hug my dad.

"I'm so nervous," I said. "I want to say hi, but I don't want to interrupt him."

"No, Mama, you go," my dad replied. "You say hi."

So I gathered all of my courage and made my way over to them. "Hi, Mr. Hanks, I'm a really big fan," I said. "I just want to say how much I love you and your movies. You're my favorite actor. You meant so much to me during my childhood, and your films have impacted my life forever. So I want to thank you."

"Oh my gosh, thank you so much, dear," Tom said with a huge smile, in that signature voice of his. "What is your name?"

"Ally," I said, still feeling shy, even though he couldn't have been nicer.

"Oh, Ally, it is a pleasure to meet you," he said.

He gave me the biggest hug, and I don't think I've ever smiled so hard in my life. My dad got to tell him how much he enjoyed his movies, and Mr. Hanks was incredibly gracious the whole time. It was beyond what I could ever have imagined.

"I love your movies so much!" I said to both of them, because Rita has been in many wonderful films that were my favorites, too. Among the ones I loved the most was *Sleepless in Seattle,* in which they had both starred. And of course, given how I feel about Christmas, I have a special place in my heart for her holiday movie *Jingle All the Way.* When I told her this, she laughed.

"I can't escape it every year," she said. "I'm happy that you love it. Thank you!"

She also gave me a big hug. She was so beautiful and wonderful to me, too. She was angelic.

To this day, that has remained one of my favorite "pinch me" moments. I hadn't even dared to dream it up, and I was sharing it with my dad.

Early in 2015, right after the holidays, we headed into the studio to find our next single. White House or not, we still hadn't had the breakout radio hit we were working toward, and so it felt like everything was riding on what we did (or didn't manage to do) next. And in our bid to project a more grown-up vibe, we sometimes disagreed about just how far was too far.

Around this time, our label gave us a song, possibly to be our next single. We had some serious questions about the song's theme, which was about a girl's walk of shame, home from a drunken one-night stand. Again, most of the girls in our group were still pretty young. It seemed way too adult for us. We let our management know we didn't feel comfortable with the lyrics, and they told the label.

The response was, basically: If we'd wanted to sign a Christian group, we would have signed a Christian group. We didn't sign a Christian group.

I knew this was a personal dig at me, since I was so vocal about my faith in the group. The tension made me nervous, but I didn't want the song to be our next single, and I wasn't backing down. Only the label wasn't folding, either. In the end, the other girls began changing their minds and saying that they didn't care and we should just do the song. I held my ground, asking if they truly felt comfortable. I made it clear that I didn't, even though I was older.

The label kept pushing, saying the lyrics didn't have to be about sex. They pitched us other possible scenarios—like it could be a walk of shame because we'd just rebelled against a teacher, and the video would show us strutting defiantly through the halls of a high school. They convinced us to at least try recording the song, with this new spin on the meaning. But I just did not think it was believable, and I was too far out of my comfort zone to go forward with the plan. Again, although I hate any kind of conflict and try to avoid it at all costs, I found the strength to stand up for myself and what I cared about.

"I'm not comfortable with this being our next single," I said to our manager.

I may have sounded strong on the outside. But at this moment in time, I was so torn up about the conflict and so stressed out about the song that I had many sleepless nights. We actually did record the song, but I still didn't feel right, and I definitely did not want it to be released. All of this made me feel so worried and overwhelmed and full of turmoil. *I might be alone in saying no,* I thought. I prayed that this stressful situation would resolve itself.

Finally our manager came to talk to us about the song. The anxiety was overwhelming, and as she sat us all down together tensions were high. "I called the label, and we're not doing that song," she said. "It's done. It's over."

God had answered my prayers. I couldn't imagine it having gone any other way, but there was a real chance that it could have. I was so beyond relieved, I started crying. *Thank God,* I thought. *Thank God.*

Fortunately, we were about to get the opportunity to record a song that we all absolutely loved, and which had hit potential we couldn't deny. We were in the studio with Stargate, a record-producing and songwriting team who'd worked with superstars like Rihanna and Sia. They had incredibly successful global records that included some of my favorite songs. These guys were the real deal, and we knew it as soon as we heard the track they had for us: "Worth It." It was absolutely undeniable, and it captured me immediately.

I went into that vocal session determined to do my best to try new things with my voice and put it all out there—all of my talent, all of my attitude. I was nervous at first, before we actually started recording, because I felt like I still had a lot to prove. But once I settled into the booth and got to know the guys, I relaxed and had fun. I loved working with them, because they were fun. The song had some playful lyrics that got a little flirty, and it also had a strong female power vibe overall, which was more in keeping with the direction we were trying to move the group. When we learned rapper Kid Ink would be guesting on the track, we were excited to hear how he could take it to the next level.

The stakes were high, and we were definitely putting our all into everything we tackled at this time. When we made the video for "Worth It," the shoot lasted almost twenty-four hours. I was completely drained by the time we wrapped. Even though I was still digging into our choreography in front of the cameras, really, I was a zombie. We all were. But it was absolutely worth it! (Pun intended.) The video for this song would become one of my favorite music videos we made, because in it, we were reversing the stereotypical gender roles, and we were strong, powerful females, who were taking over the world.

On March 2, 2015, we proudly released our new single. Once

again, we were nervous but hopeful. It was our third single from our debut album, *Reflection,* which had bop after bop. I had a great feeling about this song. I loved that we had again pushed boundaries and come up with a new image for ourselves. We would debut the song live the next night, on our latest tour. We decided to put it in the middle of our set, since we assumed it was unfamiliar to the crowd. The song opens with an undeniably catchy horn lick, and the instant it played, the crowd went wild. They already knew the song, and it had just dropped. We'd never had this experience before. Right then we knew something special had happened.

We were working so hard, with only a few days off here and there. In fact, I believe we traveled or worked 322 days that year—just like the year before, and the next two years. For the most part, we weren't flying first-class just yet or going high-end everywhere, like many people might have imagined. But we were living the dream, and I was more than willing to do the work to back it up. I was grateful and excited to be performing and discovering more Fifth Harmony fans all over the world.

Thankfully, during the time when we began traveling nonstop, we'd also had a valuable addition to our tour family, Will Bracey, who did so much more than his official role as our tour manager. He was with us before we blew up, and he always believed in us and supported us. He not only kept things running smoothly on the road, but he took care of all of us girls, and he really cared about all of us. He and I formed a strong friendship because we shared the same values and faith, and we both wanted to be a light in the industry. He soon felt like family. I was so glad to have him out with us. I knew I could trust him and depend on him, no matter what.

Then it all changed. After "Worth It" was released, *bam,* we took off like never before. It was if we'd suddenly gone from artists to superstars. That time was wild, and I loved it. So much was happening. We were playing the biggest radio shows, including Wango Tango, along with our favorite artists. Those shows were so hard to land, and when we finally booked them, it was a sign of just how big we were becoming. Our fan base had exploded. People were recognizing us more everywhere we went. We had fans lining up outside our hotels, our favorite artists knew our names and respected us, and we were performing at televised award shows. Everything had become so much more fast-paced and high-profile. More often than not, we began traveling and living better than we ever had before. We didn't know it yet, but our lives had changed forever.

"Worth It" reached No. 12, becoming our highest-charting single. That record blew up, and it had everyone dancing along with us. That same month, we won Favorite New Artist at the Nickelodeon Kids' Choice Awards, and a few months later, we were onstage for *Jimmy Kimmel Live!*, performing "Worth It" with Kid Ink—our first time on a late-night show, and it was just the beginning. At the Teen Choice Awards that August, we took home more awards, including Choice Summer Song ("Worth It") and Choice Music Group. Also, that spring had found us back in D.C. at the White House again, this time for the annual Easter Egg Roll—we were White House regulars!

The two summers before, we'd been touring shopping malls and gathering fans a few hundred people at a time, at more modest club tours across America. The summer of 2015, we launched a major undertaking, the Reflection Tour: sixty-three U.S. cities and six cities in Europe. This was our first major headlining concert tour. We went from playing smaller clubs to bigger theaters, and still, almost all of our dates sold out.

I tried to bring a little bit of home with me however I possibly could. One constant in my suitcase was a stuffed animal, Moose Moose, which my dad had brought back from a work trip for me when I was seven years old. He's been my baby and my best friend ever since, and he's comforted me through ups and downs and all kinds of heartache. I'm the type of person who finds a great deal of value in sentimental gifts, especially anything from my parents, and Moose Moose is the perfect example of that. Something about seeing his bright orange antlers poking out from amid the hotel bedding always lifted my spirits when I walked into my room at the end of a long night of being on.

My mom was so thoughtful, too, about finding me stylish backpacks that were perfect for carrying all of my essentials onto flights with me, including the super soft, perfectly sized travel blankets she was always sending me to keep me cozy on the road. It was very comforting to have a little bit of their love with me wherever I went. And before long, fans started noticing I always traveled with a blanket and giving them to me as gifts, which was sweet and thoughtful of them.

Fans might be surprised to know how many of these blankets my family still has and makes use of, not to mention the fan gifts my parents have lovingly packed away for safekeeping. Believe me, I appreciated each and every thoughtful gesture from people, including invaluable letters from the heart, incredible fan art, a variety of beautiful gifts, and so much more, especially when I was homesick. And yes, I cherish each and every one of my gifts and keep them safe. I display some of these amazing gifts and keep the letters in special boxes. Having such kind, generous fans all over the world began to make me feel like I was at home wherever in the world I was.

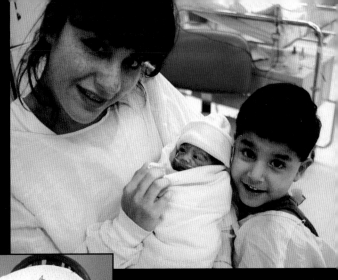

My mom and brother in the hospital right after I was born.

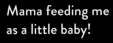

Mama feeding me as a little baby!

My brother and me with our Grandma Murray, who is now in Heaven. We love you with all of our hearts, Grandma. We will always miss you. You will forever be in our hearts.

With my beautiful mom in one of her favorite outfits to dress me in.
My mom always had style!

ne of the first times I enjoyed my
om's delicious food—it definitely

Putting on a big show. That might've
been my very first microphone!

My mom would set up photo shoots for our family so we could have these memories forever. At the time, my brother and I could barely sit still, so I'm surprised she managed to get such a serious shot! This is one of my favorite photos of us.

In my flowered dress in front of our house. I remember this dress was itchy, but it was so beautiful! My mom always dressed me so well.

With my childhood friend Erin. Love our matching haircuts!

There are so many strong women in my life who have taught me so much. Here I am with one of my favorite teachers, Mrs. Laureano. She had a big impact on me. She is now in Heaven. I love you, Mrs. Laureano.

My Mom visiting me at school. Isn't she gorgeous?

Hugs with Grandma during an Easter gathering.

I was obsessed with the 80s, and my mom threw me an 80s-themed birthday! That cake was so yummy.

Thanksgiving with Grandma. Holidays with the family, especially with Grandma, are some of my most treasured memories.

In the kitchen with Grandma at her house. Here she is making beans, fideo, tortillas, and pork chops. My favorite!

With my parents during my quick visit filming for *Dancing with the Stars*. My aunt made that banner for me! It is always amazing coming back home to my wonderful family and their love.

With my family backstage at a summer radio show I was performing at the AT&T Center. I got a visit from our Spurs mascot—the Coyote! My family and I were so excited.

Go Spurs go! Thanks, Coyote, for visiting me and giving me my very own Spurs jersey!

Fifth Harmony with Gucci Mane before going on *The Tonight Show with Jimmy Fallon* to perform "Down." Such an exciting night for all of us.

Hangin' out with The Rock and his daughter Simone after our debut performance at the People's Choice Awards. Meeting him such a highlight for me. It was an incredible night.

Backstage at *TRL* before our Fifth Harmony takeover in Times Square.

At the Teen Choice Awards in 2017. I loved this look. Photo by Frazer Harrison.

Posing with Suzette in front of a beautiful Selena mural in the Selena Museum's merchandise store. My dad, cousin, and I will always remember this special day. Thanks, Suzette!

An unforgettable evening with Gloria and Emilio Estefan, celebrating at Estefan Kitchen. Cheers! Thank you Gloria & Emilio!

Another amazing photo with Gloria Estefan from our wonderful dinner the night we met. I will never forget this night! I love you, Gloria.

With my dancers rehearsing for my ALMA Awards performance in 2018. "Vámonos," baby!

On a visit to Paris during my Low Key international promo tour. Paris is one of my favorite cities in the entire world. The Eiffel Tower is magical. Couldn't believe I had made it this far.

Riding the train to Paris! I was so excited!

At the Macy's Thanksgiving Day Parade in 2018, right before the parade began! I was so honored and happy to be a part of it!

Warming up before going to my float at the Macy's Thanksgiving Day Parade. I was beaming with excitement. This was one of my favorite outfits! I felt like a Christmas snow princess.

Backstage on *Dancing with the Stars* with Tom Bergeron, Tori Kelly, and James Van Der Beek. So many priceless memories with so many incredible souls.

Sasha and me during our last rehearsal in the *Dancing with the Stars* studio. I didn't want to leave. So many beautiful memories we shared. I'll always cherish Sasha and my *DWTS* family!

My parents and me backstage right before a taping of *Dancing with the Stars*. So many beautiful memories we shared!

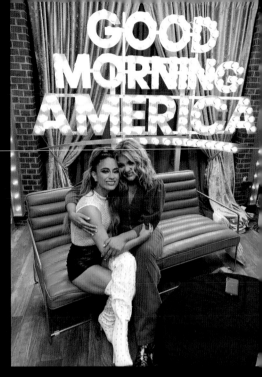

At my favorite place on earth—Disney World! We did an overnight shoot for Disney Week on *Dancing with the Stars*. The entire park was shut down for us to film in the early hours. It was a once-in-a-lifetime experience. I was in Heaven!

Saying goodbye to my dear friend Lauren Alaina at *GMA* right before we headed off to our homes for Thanksgiving. Friends forever!

Nickelodeon brought back my favorite childhood TV show, *All That*, last year and had me and Jonas Brothers as the first musical guest!

With my 1500 or Nothin' fam—Larrance Dopson and James Fauntleroy. We had such a great time filming for *Dancing with the Stars* at their 1500 Sound Academy. Love you guys!

With my manager Will. He's always been a rock for me. Look how far we've come together. God is so good. Love you, Will!

Sharing a laugh with my other manager, Charles, backstage for the ALMA Awards. This is one of my favorite photos of us. Thanks, Charles, for always having my back and for all you've done for me!

Filming my Time to Shine headlining solo tour announcement. I was announcing my New York and Los Angeles dates. My team made me a beautiful cake to celebrate! Definitely one of the best gifts ever!

Opening night in Chicago for my very first headlining solo tour—the Time to Shine Tour. It was such a special and magical day, one I'll cherish forever!

TWELVE

Answered Prayers

Reflection would be our first ever full-length album. It had taken a great deal of hard work in and out of the studio for months and months, digging deep the whole time, to really define our sound. I'd definitely gotten more parts on most of the songs, and while the distribution still wasn't exactly where I hoped it would eventually be, I felt it was starting to get better. But the best part was that when the album was released, it received an incredible reception. Fans loved it. Critics loved it. And it did really well, expanding our popularity by leaps and bounds. Now when we did appearances and signings in New York and elsewhere, we were mobbed by wildly excited fans. Since the beginning of the *X Factor* we were always met by excited fans, but now the crowds grew bigger and bigger. That album definitely kicked things up to the next level.

We didn't have much downtime once *Reflection* came out and "Worth It" took off. We were booked for back-to-back tours and had the chance to perform in high-powered lineups on some unbelievable radio shows. We were traveling all over, seeing many corners of the world for the first time in our lives.

As exciting as the happenings this year were, though, I had to face the fact that my mom's health was declining. She'd been deeply impacted by our car accident in 2003, and the fallout had only gotten worse since then. Her scoliosis had become more severe, so that she could no longer stand fully upright, and she was in terrible pain, to the point of sometimes being bedridden. Even simple tasks such as going to the grocery store often found her having to sit down and rest because the pain was too great. She could barely travel, and only as far as the Texas shows. It was next to impossible for her, but she still did it because she wanted to see me. I missed her terribly, and I was constantly worried about her.

When I would talk to her during this time, she was sometimes in so much pain that she would be crying, and saying she just wanted to find the right doctor to help her. During these years, my parents were constantly looking for the best specialist to perform the only surgery that might help her. They searched for doctors not just in San Antonio, but also in Austin and Dallas, and even as far away as Los Angeles. It was a very emotional process, because my mom would literally be putting her life in the hands of this doctor. And her surgery was especially complicated.

A few times she met with possible surgeons and prayed about whether they were the right choice for her, and it seemed like they might be. Just the thought of having found a solution filled us with so much happiness and hope. But then either they didn't feel able to do such a complex surgery or my mom didn't feel entirely comfortable with them for some reason, so there was this major letdown and the return to the search. They were beginning to despair that the perfect doctor might not exist after all. Given that my mom was in extreme pain throughout all of this, the stakes couldn't have been higher, and we were all trying our best to remain optimistic, even when things seemed dark.

All of this was even harder for me, because I worried that I was adding to the problem without meaning to, even though I would have given everything I had to lift my mother's suffering. My mom is empathetic and sensitive (that's where I get it from), and around this time, I began to fear that seeing me undergo such intense emotional ups and downs for the past two years was making her physically ill. When I felt sadness or frustration, I tried to hide it from her during our daily phone calls, but she could always tell what was really going on with me.

Finally, in 2015, Mom met with a doctor she thought might be able to help. He had worked with cases that were similar to hers, although none that were as severe, and she liked him right away. She asked if there was any way she could speak to one of his former patients who'd undergone a similar operation. She had an in-depth conversation with that woman, asking her lots of questions about her surgery, recovery, and life since the procedure. It was still a big decision, with a great deal of emotion attached to it, but Mom felt confident enough—for the first time in many years—to begin planning to have her surgery.

My fans found out about my mom's surgery, and in March of 2015, they started a GoFundMe account to help with the cost of her procedure. That was the most gracious act of kindness I have ever received. Even today I have a hard time articulating what it meant to me and my family. We all started crying when we found out, and my mom almost didn't accept the help. She felt grateful, yet extremely hesitant about receiving any money from my fans. But they insisted. They had already worked hard to raise the funds, and in the end, that money did help to pay for my mom's operation.

Overall, it was a mixed-up period. We'd had our biggest hit so far, which was continuing to break records. It had brought us a diverse fan base that ranged from tweens to adults to grandmas—and they were the best, most loyal fans ever. Our lives continued to change at a dizzying pace. People were recognizing us more everywhere we went. We had fans lining up outside our hotel. Our tour dates were mostly sold out. Paparazzi followed us. When we walked onstage, the audience screamed and went crazy. We were suddenly in demand for appearances on award and television shows. We received invitations to the hottest parties and met our favorite artists. It was hard to keep up—and we loved it. Fans started posting their own videos of their covers of "Worth It," which were fun to see. Some of these even went viral, including a remix of a version with *Bad Girls Club.* That took on a life of its own, and it was so hilarious, we would constantly watch it and laugh. We had crossed over into a new level of popularity, and the momentum continued to grow.

And on the home front, our prayers were answered. My mom had finally found the best doctor to try to fix her spine. In September 2015, after the summer Reflection Tour, I flew home to be with my mom for the surgery. Though we had great hope and faith, and my mom and dad had done as much research as they possibly could, the risks were high—there could be complications or an infection, or she could pass away while she was under. Her doctor also warned us that the surgery was dangerous, because it involved removing the two rods that she'd had inserted during a previous procedure, which had been contributing to her pain, and then breaking and resetting her spine, which housed so many nerves. There was also a possibility that Mom could end up paralyzed in the process. After all, her case was extremely severe. "I've worked with a lot of patients with scoliosis, but I've never seen anything like yours," her doctor had told her.

In the days leading up to the procedure, our family and friends prayed with all of our might. I knew my fans were praying, too, and that support brought me encouragement and strength. The night before Mom went to the hospital, my brother, dad, and I gathered around her and prayed over her, asking God to be with the doctors, putting His hands on theirs to guide them in their work and giving them the wisdom and focus to ensure the surgery would be successful. And we asked Him to put His hands on Mom's back, with His healing power, and to stay there with her throughout the procedure. With any surgical procedure, there's never a complete guarantee that everything will be okay, which was terrifying. We were well aware of all that could go wrong. Whenever these fears surfaced, nervous energy overtook me.

At the same time, I held on to my faith, and it brought me moments of peace and a certainty that all would be okay. My nerves had sapped my appetite, and I couldn't seem to eat dinner that night. When it was time to go to bed, I didn't want to leave my mom. I kept holding her tightly.

"Mama, I know you can't sleep," she said. "Don't worry, the Lord will be with me."

We were all too anxious to sleep. But I didn't want my mom to worry about me on top of everything else, so I finally went into my room. Of course Bobbi curled up next to me, offering her form of comfort. I cried and prayed until finally I prayed myself to sleep, and I somehow managed to get a few hours of rest. I even dreamed about Mom's surgery that night, I was so worried. And then it was time to wake up early and take her to the hospital. For an extra blessing, I put on one of the sterling silver James Avery rings she had given me, which had a dangly cross charm and always made me feel God was protecting us.

After Mom had been admitted, it was so upsetting to see her in her gown, lying in a hospital bed. This was really happening. I was already crying, and nothing had happened yet. I wished there was some other path forward, but I knew all of this had to happen. And while I would have loved to put myself in her place, I couldn't. I pulled her doctor aside.

"Please take care of my mom," I said with tears in my eyes. "That's all I ask, for you to be gentle with her and take care of her, Doctor, please."

"Don't worry," he said. "Your mom's going to be okay."

As my mom was given her initial anesthesia, I didn't want to let her go, because I didn't know if this was going to be my last conversation with her. My face was a mess of tears and my throat was clogged with emotion. Before they wheeled my mom into surgery, I wrapped my arms around her.

"Mom, I love you with all of my heart," I somehow managed to choke out through my racking sobs. "Thank you for everything you've done. You mean so much to me. And I'll be right here praying for you the whole time."

Then it was time to let go, even though it nearly broke my heart to be separated from her in her most challenging moment. As I followed my family out into the waiting room, I turned for one more look at my wonderful mother. The thought that it could be the last time I ever saw her alive was too much to bear, and I sobbed harder. And then we all waited.

And waited.

And waited.

The surgery lasted seven hours, but it felt even longer as we sat there together, praying, too worried to read magazines or watch TV. For a quick break and some fresh air, my aunt took me out for Mexican food at my favorite restaurant, Blanco Cafe. It was so nice of her, but I couldn't really eat. All I could do was focus on my mom. It almost felt like if I just kept my prayers on her at every moment, I could help make the outcome as positive as it could be. That whole day I couldn't think of anything but her.

Finally, when I was so exhausted from all of the anxiety and extreme emotion that I almost couldn't stand it anymore, the doctor came out. As he walked up to us, I prayed for the best news about my sweet mom. I tried to read his face. He told my dad, "The surgery was a success." My dad started crying. I started crying. Our prayers had been answered. This was the beginning of a new chapter in my mother's story, when she would finally be able to live her life with less pain.

But when I finally got to be with my mom in her hospital room, she was screaming in agony. It was horrible to see her suffering until the painkillers kicked in; that will always be one of the most painful memories of my life. I hadn't fully prepared myself for the reality of what she'd just been through. But I realized she'd had major surgery, and while it was an answer to our prayers, she was facing a long road of recovery. After nearly a month in the hospital, she moved to an in-patient rehab center for physical therapy, which she approached with her usual hard work and determination. I was sad to have to return to LA after a few days, but I kept in close contact and continued praying for her. Nothing made me happier than receiving videos from home, of my brave mom pushing herself to stand and walk. And when I saw a video of her being able to fully extend her spine—for the first time in years—I got emotional and started to cry. I had imagined this day and had prayed for it, but never knew if it would come. Her doctors had projected it would take eighteen to twenty-four months for her to be up and really moving again but miraculously she did it in two, amazing her doctors with her tenacity and perseverance. In November she was finally able to return home, although it would be several years before she could travel to see me. While she still has some nerve damage from the years before her surgery, and unfortunately, her spine isn't completely normal, she is so much better compared to where she was, which brings me pure joy. Our family was astonished. I did not know if finding a solution for her was ever possible, but with God, all things are possible. It is one of the miracles of God I have seen before my eyes, and it left me awe-inspired. The Lord does wonders. My mom is the strongest person I know and my ultimate hero. I will be forever grateful to the fans who supported my family through that difficult time.

When I returned to LA, the pace was immediately as fast and furious as it had ever been. It was amazing to have our *Reflection* album become a success, and to have "Worth It" be the breakthrough hit we'd needed. But the question remained, would that be our only hit? Would we be one and done? Would we ever be able to match or go beyond the success of "Worth It"? The next step we took seemed even more vital. Everyone seemed to want more Fifth Harmony as we continued to grow in popularity, and we were expected to begin work on our second studio album, which everyone was hoping would have an even bigger hit.

That October, we went back to the studio in Santa Monica to start work on what would become *7/27*. Now we had to find our new sound and capture it. There was so much going on. At this time, we had gotten new management and a new team to help us go further and manage our success and the situations now coming our way. We were starting our new era off fresh. This time in our lives was hectic. There were a lot of moving parts, and a lot of changes happening, but we were forced to push through the trials and moved forward, making a brand new start. The stakes were high, and it was stressful, balancing it all. At moments it got to be too much. Especially when I was faced with the more unjust aspects of the music business. During one listening session, someone at the label was trying to get me to do things I was extremely uncomfortable with, because I was not cool. The already searing pain of my insecurities took an even greater hit. I tried to awkwardly laugh the comment off. But there was no laughter from him. It was especially embarrassing because he was a very high-up executive, who carried our future in his hands. It made me feel humiliated.

Another time, I met with a record exec from a different label, who said he wanted to help me navigate the challenges within the group. I believed he really saw me for who I was in the group. I hoped he would share wisdom and direction with me as I navigated new challenges. Turns out, at our first meeting, he gave me a thong. "You would look really good in this," he said. I was deeply embarrassed and ashamed. On another night, he texted me to invite me to his hotel room. I never wrote him back. I had sought advice from, and been vulnerable with, this person, and to be let down in such a demeaning way only made me feel more frustrated, powerless, alone, and broken.

In times like these, I leaned on my faith to give me the strength to manage everything and take it all on.

Our label told us that "Work from Home" would be our next single, and it would feature Ty Dolla $ign. He was so great to work with—he was so kind and respectful to us all, including my parents, who were visiting at the time. He had the best manners, even holding doors for them when they saw him. He was one of my favorite people we'd ever worked with over the years.

When it came time to make the music video for "Work from Home," I tried to shake off my mix of emotions. It felt exciting to have our next album moving forward, and to be working on the video for our first single. Ironically, we hadn't thought that "Work from Home" would be our first single, but our label felt strongly that it was a hit. Of course we went along with them. Little did we know how right they would be. Fun fact: the song was originally called "Work." But we heard that Rihanna was coming out with a song called "Work," around the same time, and so we renamed our single "Work from Home." The video shoot itself was chaotic. The director had brought us this unique concept of having us be on a construction site, which had a lot of moving parts. Our wardrobe changed at the last minute. And we had to move between different setups and locations several times.

I was excited for the shoot. I hoped it would be fun. With new choreography and a statement video concept, it was time to start filming. I pushed myself a little outside my comfort zone, but I also had a lot of fun with it. We each had a guy as our partner, and we reversed the gender roles once again. We were females in charge. My partner was super sweet and respectful. Before we started filming, I was nervous. I wasn't supposed to be in the setup they ended up putting me in—at the last minute, they switched me with one of the other girls. But I adjusted and freestyled. When the camera rolled, I turned into a different person. I didn't shoot my solo scene until late, so it was a long day, and I was tired. But when I watched the video playback, I was surprised to find that I ended up loving my part for the video so much. It became one of my favorite moments in any one of our videos.

And of course, in a crazy turn of events, this song was our biggest hit to date. It became a bonafide megasmash. From the moment we pressed send and released that video, our lives really did change more than ever, all because of one song. It's that song that will be played forever and has broken records and hit amazing milestones. As of 2020, the video has been viewed more than two billion times on YouTube, with "Worth It" having been watched nearly as many times.

As big of a hit as it was, we also received some backlash, due to the lyrics being risqué. Looking back now, I think I should have probably said something and tried to change my own lyrics in the song, because they were a little daring—but I tried to make the best of it.

Throughout this time, my mom continued to make a remarkable recovery. That surgery changed the lives of all of my family, especially my mom. I believe this is just one of the many miracles I have seen from God. Everyone who loved me came together and supported us and prayed for my mom, just like so many had prayed for me when I was a baby. I have experienced firsthand the power of prayer and the power of God. God is real, and seeing Him work through the time of my mom's surgery and recovery helped strengthen my faith in such a powerful way.

THIRTEEN

Look at Us Now

With the dawn of 2016, we were also reaching new heights of success.

When you're on your way up and it's all happening so fast, it can be hard to have perspective on what will ultimately prove to be the biggest moments in your career, but it was clear we were crossing into a new realm now. We had already had several hits, won our share of awards, and attracted millions of devoted fans. In February, *Reflection* was certified gold, and we announced our second studio album, *7/27*. From the first days of our group on *The X Factor*, we had needed to prove ourselves every week to avoid being sent home. And ever since we'd graduated from the show, we'd been trying to prove ourselves by landing that undeniable hit or achieving some other milestone. Now it had become clear that we were the real deal, and we had achieved enough that we weren't ever going to get sent home. We'd made it.

When *7/27* was released in May 2016, it debuted at No. 4 on the Billboard 200. The lead single from that album, "Work from Home," featuring Ty Dolla $ign, peaked at No. 4 on the Hot 100, and it later won Best Collaboration at the VMAs.

The 7/27 tour was in full swing, and we were at the height of our success. We began to travel like high rollers, and we were welcomed by cheering fans in cities around the globe. I really loved being in a successful girl group, and so much about it was really fun. However, behind the scenes, my confidence was shaken by the frequent struggle to have my voice heard—literally and figuratively. I often hated my wardrobe during those years. I was trying to find myself, and trying to express yourself through your wardrobe in a group can be hard. It's a challenge to find what looks best on you, and what you feel confident in, because wardrobe is an expression of you. We had to look uniform, which I was game for. However, I had many let's just say terrible red carpet moments, and this only added to my insecurity within the group. I also felt that some of the stylists didn't take their time to dress me in the most flattering way. Making it worse, I was made fun of online for how I dressed, both in fan comments and articles. This was an even deeper blow to my confidence, especially when I was often getting teased for clothing choices that were out of my control. A lot of fans judged me online for my red carpet looks. I read so many comments, like: *The stylist did Ally wrong. The stylist just doesn't know how to dress Ally. Ally always has the worst outfits. Ally doesn't know how to dress for her body, poor girl.*

On one of our tours, I had a custom-made outfit that I was excited about it. But then, when I put it on, I was very unhappy about how it made my body look when I moved. I asked the stylist if there was any way of changing it, but it was too late. I ended up feeling really insecure about my body, and what I was going to look like. Her response was: "Well, go to the gym, if that's how you feel." When I look back at photos of myself in Fifth Harmony, I don't even recognize the girl there, because at the time I felt so insecure and unhappy.

All of this created a perfect storm. I felt overwhelmed and low, but I didn't know how to handle my emotions. Speaking up hadn't worked. And telling my parents didn't help, either; it only upset them. And so I started eating my feelings. One night I was so distraught that I took a large bag of Doritos to the back of the tour bus and ate the whole thing. Everything in my life was controlled from the outside. I craved whatever release I could find, and food offered a temporary escape. It was this one little corner of the world that I could control, even if it didn't shift anything else. I just wanted to feel better. I knew it wasn't healthy, but there was something soothing about indulging myself in this small way. Because my eating had an emotional root, I didn't want to acknowledge it, and so I tried to pretend nothing was wrong, even as I began to put on weight.

By the spring of 2016, it was hard to avoid the obvious, as I had gained twenty pounds since I'd started out in Fifth Harmony. I'm only five feet tall, and so on my small frame, it was noticeable. My parents tried talking to me about what was going on, but I think they understood that I was self-soothing with food because I was unhappy about things beyond my control. They didn't want to make it worse by embarrassing me. In "perfect timing" around then, we were supposed to shoot a video for our next single, "Flex," and it was decided we'd be at the beach, in bathing suits.

This was like being trapped in some kind of a nightmare. At this point, I was very body-conscious. Now I was going to have to wear a bathing suit in front of the whole world, and at the heaviest I'd ever been. I searched obsessively for something flattering, and finally I found an option that wasn't too bad. But I was still super self-conscious. It didn't help that in magazines and on TV, most of what was encouraged was to be thin. This caused me to not feel confident. I felt like I didn't look like the celebrities' body types, so I had low self-esteem.

From the moment we started production that day, I felt nervous and emotional, like I just wanted to dig a hole in the sand and hide myself away. As we went through hair and makeup and learned our marks, I couldn't shake the feeling that I was making a fool of myself and everyone would soon be laughing at me. Although this happened only a few years ago, at that time, there hadn't really been a body positivity movement that had caught on in the mainstream yet. It still seemed like only one body type was celebrated, and I felt like I did not meet those standards. I would later realize that my body wasn't the problem, it was the standards themselves. But at the time, I was self-conscious.

I kept asking people on the shoot: "Are you sure I don't look bad? Please tell me if I do. This is a music video. There's no way to Photoshop it."

"No, you look amazing!" the crew kept reassuring me.

But I didn't feel amazing—far from it. I was emotionally and physically exhausted, and my self-confidence was at an all-time low.

When it was my call time, I was driven to the location, a beautiful spot on Zuma Beach in Malibu. I kept myself covered until the last possible second while I had my hair and makeup touched up. When I was cued to drop my robe, I was so nervous that my hands were literally shaking. My heart was beating so hard, I felt sure people would be able to see it. Even though I was wearing a one-piece, it was still very revealing, and I felt naked. But even at my lowest, I was determined to do my best. I actually found the courage to speak up to the director. I requested we do more shots of me lying down on the sand, where the angle made me look leaner and more elongated, with no shots of me standing up.

I kept asking everyone around me about my appearance—I couldn't help myself. There were quite a few men on set that day, and they told me repeatedly that I looked amazing and I should feel it. I did in the end feel sexy and great, and I had a moment of feeling good about my body finally, which had always been very hard for me. When I watched the playback on the monitor, I was surprised and relieved to be happy about how I appeared in most of the shots. So slowly I started to become less self-conscious and more at ease. Of course, as always, I was really trying my best and giving it my all, which was a good distraction, too. By the time shooting was over for the day, I was feeling pretty good in my body, and I was definitely proud of myself for having made the most of a difficult situation.

And then, a few hours later, there was a social media post with paparazzi photos of us filming our music video. Some of the shots of me were *not* flattering. I was embarrassed. It was my worst fear come true—to be exposed in public and to be made fun of—and it was happening to me at a time when we had millions of followers. And then I got ripped apart.

I started to cry. I was humiliated. Reading some of the comments only made me feel worse:

Ally looks fat!

Ally has a refrigerator body!

She has no shape to her!

She has no curves!

Her body is not okay!

People were laughing at me and calling me all of these mean names. I was devastated, especially because they'd touched a nerve. My self-esteem plummeted even lower. And yes, a lot of beautiful fans did come to my defense, which I deeply appreciated. But of course, the negative comments seemed louder than the positive ones. Those bad comments were the ones I believed. I had to log off social media for a few days because I just couldn't handle it. That kind of intense scrutiny and meanness will break somebody. It broke me.

I love that, only four years later, we are living in an era when so many more different sizes and shapes of bodies are being accepted and celebrated. Of course I want everyone to love their bodies exactly as they are. But, for me, much of my embarrassment came from knowing that for many different reasons, I was behaving in a way that was not healthy for me—physically or emotionally. I wasn't taking care of myself. I wasn't eating healthy. I wasn't treating my body well. Unfortunately, feeling publicly shamed in the midst of all of the other personal turmoil I was experiencing did not empower me. I became even more self-destructive.

During the latter part of 2016, we were having all of these incredibly exciting moments. Jet-setting across the world, breaking records, and even beginning to headline our own arena shows, performing for thousands of screaming fans in Mexico and traveling across Europe. But I referred to my life behind the scenes as "the great sadness." I felt I had tried to make the best of challenging circumstances within the group. And even though we had achieved a great deal that I was really proud of, our day-to-day circumstances contained more stress than ever. Especially because we had to go out and project everything was great—better than ever—all of the time.

When we were back in LA, we stayed at a residential hotel in West Hollywood that I fell in love with. We stayed there for so long, and it became a home away from home for me. I loved it, and the staff there treated me like family.

But around this time, I was in a dark place because there were things going on behind the scenes that were unfair. It was one thing after another, and I was simply overwhelmed.

One night, I came into my hotel room, alone, and I was soon crying my eyes out. Although I've never turned to anything for comfort besides family and my faith, I was so miserable that I just wanted to escape.

I ordered a glass of wine from room service. I ordered a second and a third. For someone who's tiny and not much of a drinker, this was a lot of alcohol. I was so out of it I wasn't answering my phone. I didn't want to talk to anyone anyhow. Then, out of my drunken fog, I heard a noise and looked up. My door was swinging open, and our longtime tour manager, Will, was standing there, a concerned look on his face. Will had been looking after us when we were on tour for years, and I knew he always wanted what's best for me. Apparently, he'd been trying to call me for hours, and when I didn't pick up or even text him back, he'd become so worried that he'd rushed over and gotten a key from the front desk, who knew all of us by this point. As he told me later, he was shocked to see me so wrecked.

"Ally, what are you doing?" he asked. "Why?"

"Why is this happening to me? I said, choking out the words between sobs. "Why, God? Why?"

"Ally, I promise you, you're going to get through this," he said. "It's okay. I'm here for you. And you're not alone. God is with you."

And then I threw up. It was awful and embarrassing and scary. I slept on my bed in a pool of my tears.

The next morning when I woke up, of course, I felt terrible. But I also felt a little lighter. Maybe it was a relief to finally admit to myself—and a person close to me—that there was a limit to how much I could take. And to be reminded that, even in my darkest night, God was there with me. And I could feel His presence, if I just kept my heart open to Him. I definitely credit my faith as the thread that held me together during that darkest of times.

That's why I'm opening up about this now. Believe me, I know how hard it can get. But you can hold on. I did. Barely, but I did. And when I look at how far I've come in the four years since then, I am amazed by how powerful we all can be even when we don't think we can. So I know what I'm talking about when I say that no matter how awful it might feel right now, it will get better. It might take a year or two or four. But you can overcome even your most gut-wrenchingly difficult moments. And learn from them, and yes, even grow stronger.

It took a lot of strength to go through all this at the time and not to say anything to the fans, to the public, to the media. There were a few moments when I almost gave up. But I didn't. I prayed every day. It was only God who gave me the strength I needed. And also, I knew I had my personal angels, like my Grandpa Paul, with me all of the time, protecting me.

Toward the end of that year, we underwent a change. We became four: Normani, Lauren, Dinah Jane, and me. We still believed we had so much more to accomplish as a unit.

That Christmas, I headed to San Antonio to spend the holidays with my family as usual. I was definitely ready for Texas when I went home. I loved the instant reminder that I was still the same girl who'd grown up there. I wasn't only a performer or a star, or a member of Fifth Harmony in San Antonio, even though my hometown was proud of me. I was just Ally. I couldn't wait to get into my sweats, go without makeup, and watch Christmas movies with my beloved cat, Bobbi, especially after a long, crazy, hectic year.

But when I arrived home, my mom gave me some terrible news. I had known that Bobbi, my best friend for the past eight years, had experienced a few health problems that fall and that my parents were taking her to the vet once a month. But I had assumed the vet could help her, and I was not at all prepared for how sick she was.

"Mama, she's been struggling—she's been different," Mom said, trying to prepare me before I saw how skinny Bobbi had become.

There was no preparation for this most devastating of realities. I'd come home excited to receive that strong boost of perfect love from my sweet kitty, only to discover that Bobbi was much sicker than I'd known.

When I walked in, Bobbi ran up to me. My mom was shocked.

"She hasn't run in weeks," she said.

In that moment, I saw the proof of how special and extraordinary our bond was. It went beyond words. Even though she could barely walk by this point, she ran to me on her last night. Although I didn't know then that this would be my last night with her, I started crying.

I was stunned at how weak she was, how she could barely move. I tried everything to comfort her. Nothing else mattered. Bobbi became my only concern; everything else fell away. In a lot of ways, pets bring us a loyalty and affection that humans can't provide. They give this sweet, innocent love that requires so little in return. I couldn't imagine losing her.

She always curled up in my bed with me at night, but because she could only get her frail body on the couch, I slept with her there. She didn't leave my side for one moment, and we had our last night together. In the morning, we went to the vet. I still thought we were going to save her.

"I'm so sorry, there's nothing else we can do for her," the vet said. "This is a quality-of-life situation, where she's going to live in pain for the rest of her life."

I was completely shocked. I wasn't ready at all.

I pleaded with the vet, and even she had tears in her eyes.

Finally, when I understood that there really was nothing more they could do for her, my heart just broke into million pieces. Now I was saying goodbye to my best friend and my baby, all in one. I wasn't prepared. I had these Christmas tree earrings with me, and in that moment, I gave one to her as goodbye gift. I still have the other one tucked away in a special safe place at home.

As I gave her the earring, I told her how much she meant to me and how much I loved her. I held her for the last time.

I felt a pain like I'd never felt before. And then, just a few days before Christmas, on December 22, I had to say goodbye to Bobbi. I lost a part of me when I lost her.

While this experience was very different from losing Grandpa Paul, I was completely heartbroken. It was an enormous loss. I'd already been through so much in the past few months, and now I'd lost my best friend, whom I'd been looking forward to reuniting with because I missed her every second I was away.

We're all going to have hardships in life. We're all going to experience loss and moments of pain. But at the time, I wasn't prepared for this type of heartbreak. I tried to enjoy being with my family, telling myself I couldn't take anything for granted and I'd been blessed with many years with my precious cat. She'd brought me an unconditional love unlike any I've never known—it's just different with pets. I chose to be thankful for her life, but still, the holidays were full of grieving for Bobbi. Even at this point it's hard for me to talk about her, and I tear up just thinking about her. I will always miss her. She will forever be safe in my heart.

After spending a few weeks with our families, we regrouped as Fifth Harmony. We were determined to forge ahead. I believed in Fifth Harmony, and that we still had more songs to sing and more heights to reach. We weren't finished yet. I hoped the rest of the world would soon know that, too.

As we planned our next move with our label and new management, who we'd had since *7/27,* we ran through numerous ideas. There was talk of a worldwide search and a reality show that centered on our search for a new fifth member. There were also ideas on numerous well-known young artists and celebrities who might join us, and we talked over how that might work. But we strongly felt it would be weird to add a new member. And we believed our fans were the fifth member, so we stayed as four. There was some uncertainty about what we should do, but I felt like God was working through all of this. I wasn't afraid, but excited. It felt like a powerful moment of rebirth for us, and I was ready to give it my all.

We rallied together, and I knew deep down that we could show the world that we were amazing. And we were. We blasted into early 2017 with our first appearance as a four-member group, a high-profile performance at the 43rd People's Choice Awards in mid-January.

The stakes were high, with people anxious to see what we would do next. It was a pivotal moment. We had to go out there and kill it. There was no other option, and I have to admit, even with all of our experience, we were nervous. It felt like make-or-break.

We arrived at the venue with a huge entourage—everyone from our new management team and our choreographer to our hair and makeup artists and stylists and our parents. It was fast-paced and hectic but inspiring to be surrounded by such a large group of people who believed in us. I remember the girls and I worked so hard. We had fun in the rehearsals and dreamed together about our new future. When it was time, we gathered together backstage. We were so nervous that we were jumping up and down, trying to get out the jitters. It was my honor to lead our group prayer that night. "Dear

God, please give us favor, please give us peace. Please let nothing go wrong. Please let our show translate positively, and please let everybody love and accept us. Please let us enjoy our performance and take it all in as it's happening."

After we'd said amen, we all chanted together: "Good luck! Let's go!"

Our family members and team were encouraging us, yelling, "You're going to kill it!"

And then we walked out onto that stage. For the first time as a group of four. We'd put a great deal of planning into relaunching ourselves, including a revamped look that felt sexy and polished and powerful. As we danced and sang our way though "Work from Home," the crowd went wild. They loved us and gave us a standing ovation! It got better: we accepted the award for Favorite Group from DJ Khaled. As we did, we were sure to express our love for our fans.

Afterward, we returned to our dressing room, and our whole gang cheered wildly. We were moving forward, and everyone from the media to our fans was going ballistic. We'd done it—we'd survived, and even triumphed. We felt strong and empowered.

And then while we were backstage, The Rock (Dwayne Johnson) came up to congratulate us.

"You guys were fantastic!" he said.

What? We couldn't believe it. We were so hyped up; we even did a video with him, kicking off 2017 with lots of energy and laughs, and we posted it online. That's one of my personal favorite memories, because The Rock was one of my biggest inspirations as someone who has worked hard to get where he is. And of course he is one of the biggest movie stars in the world, and here he was, saying how amazing we were. He even met my dad. I was blown away. I thought then, and still think today, God bless that man.

What a beautiful night. This felt like another rebirth. I was very hopeful for our future.

We were feeling pretty good about our chances. We knew what we were capable of. We knew we had the talent, passion, and drive—not to mention the loyal fans—to create something special. Our management believed in us wholeheartedly, too, and fought to get us recognition and new opportunities at our label and internationally. We were not going to let anything stop us. Finally, after negotiating for months with our label, we were told we were going to record another album.

During this whole process, we were introduced to Chris Anokute, our new A&R executive. He had been behind the scenes of our *7/27* album. Chris was the one who first heard "Work from Home" and suggested that song go to us. Clearly, he had a good ear. But we'd had another A&R person at the time. After we became four, he was our designated A&R person.

Chris had tons of energy and excitement and gave us this amazing speech about how he believed in us. He made it crystal clear that he would fight tooth and nail to give us the best songs, writers, and treatment he could. We were more grateful than we knew how to express.

We were in the studio every single day, working our tails off to find the right songs. This time, though, Chris gave us an opportunity we had been wanting for a very long time—to write our own lyrics. We were so happy that someone was finally empowering us to express ourselves. We dove deeply into our songwriting, working on many songs. I enjoyed waking up that creative side of me again, and I was excited to have more input into all aspects of our group.

After weeks of recording, the time came to head back on the road to complete some shows. Then, in March, I was on a plane for our *7/27* tour in Asia. The fans were so kind and respectful. Some of my favorite memories in the group are of exploring Tokyo, visiting the martial arts temples, wandering the streets, going shopping, eating ramen and ice cream, and having other adventures. I first had Wagyu, the best steak of my life, there. I would also venture off to get sushi, which was incredible and so fresh. And I went to a cat café, of course, because I love cats the most!

Then I got to travel to my all-time favorite destination—my hometown. On February 20, we were invited to perform at our legendary

San Antonio Stock Show & Rodeo at the AT&T Center, which is a huge event in Texas, with about two million visitors each year. Everyone from Tim McGraw to John Legend to Rascal Flatts to Brad Paisley had performed there. I had grown up going to the AT&T Center to attend concerts and Spurs games, and I'd always wanted to be a part of the rodeo, which I'd also attended when I was young. Now it was actually happening.

Longtime friends and my entire family came out to watch, and the feeling of being together as the four on that massive stage in front of my hometown crowd was like nothing else. Afterward, my family gave me a ton of love, and we went to eat Mexican food, of course. We ate at one of my favorite spots, Mi Tierra. If you get the chance to visit San Antonio, go to this restaurant, which is a staple of my city. The interior is spectacular, with brightly colored decorations and so much cultural pride. And the food is delicious!

We started to become booked and busy all over again. After performing all over the place, we came back and finished recording for our album. We would write together every day for weeks, sometimes with two or three rooms going at the same time, and everyone switching writing partners. We were looking again for that one single—the song that would show the world who we were as a quartet. After months of recording, with the help of Chris, our management, and one another, the four of us announced our new single in May of 2017, "Down," featuring Gucci Mane. It was also a highlight working with Gucci. He was a ride or die.

We premiered the song on *Good Morning America*, and it immediately exploded worldwide—the reception was amazing. Even on the first day of its release, our song was already topping the iTunes chart. In that moment, I teared up, knowing that we'd actually done it. We had accomplished something personal and striking. After overcoming a lot, we were stronger than ever. Following our live TV performance, we were all beaming, and gave each other a huge hug.

By June of 2017, we'd hit our stride as a four-piece. I was feeling better on a personal level, too. It was wonderful to know that my mom was doing so much better since her surgery—better than she had been in as long as I could remember. I was feeling more empowered to speak up about what I wanted—in the studio and with the group. I felt like I was in a better place now. Overall, it was a moment with a great deal of energy and optimism, and I felt like it radiated out of all of us.

Early in the month, we were performing our song "Down" at an iHeartRadio event in Miami, Florida. This was a big outdoor event that was being televised live. All through hair and makeup, which I'd gone through a thousand times by now, everything was normal. Then, about twenty minutes before showtime, I felt a sharp pain in my stomach. I just didn't feel right.

We decided I should lie down while the other girls lined up to get their mic packs on. They were prepared, just in case I couldn't perform, but I was still hoping I'd be able to.

About that time, our tour manager, Will, came up and said that Mark Burnett was there with his wife, Roma Downey. They wanted to pray with us. This was stunning news. Of course I knew of Mark Burnett as the respected and successful TV producer who had helped to create some of the most popular reality-based TV shows of all time, which I had watched for years, including *Survivor, The Apprentice, The Voice,* and *Shark Tank.* He had been responsible for shaping culture as we know it. I would be honored to meet him. I was equally excited to meet both him and his wife, Roma Downey, who's not only a well-known actress and producer, but also that rare person in Hollywood who is very open about her Christian faith. I'd grown up loving her in shows like *Touched by an Angel.* I really looked up to them for not only playing an active role in the world of entertainment but also for being lights shining genuine faith in the industry. I'd wanted to meet them both for many years.

I still am not sure why Mark and Roma were at that event that day. Perhaps Mark's company was producing the online broadcast of the show, or they were there for a meeting. But it was such a generous gesture for them to ask to pray for us before we went onstage to perform. As I later learned, when Mark and Roma approached the girls, our manager immediately let them know about the circumstances we were facing up against just then. "Hey, Mark, before you pray, one of our girls actually is in horrible pain," our manager said.

"Let's go pray with her," Mark said without hesitation.

Meanwhile, I was back in the cabana waiting area right by the stage, unaware that any of this was happening. It was bizarre how horrible I felt. I rarely got sick.

Suddenly the door swung open and a crowd of people flooded into the greenroom. Before I really understood what any of this meant, I saw this couple surrounding me, and in a corner of my consciousness, I felt like I knew their faces somehow.

"Hello, Ally, if you don't mind, we are going to pray for you, okay?" Roma said in that calming voice, with her lovely Irish accent.

I nodded my agreement. They immediately lay their hands on me and started praying in the name of Jesus. At that exact moment of prayer, I felt the Holy Spirit come over me. This amazing peace and strength filled me as they kept praying. When I opened my eyes as the prayer ended, I was stunned. My pain was gone. After seeing how bad I'd felt, everyone stared at me as they witnessed this miraculous change. It was such a surreal moment, especially since Roma had played a TV angel, and there she was, praying for me like a real one.

"Let's get you all out there," someone said.

Suddenly I felt fine, and not just fine, really good. I ended up having tons of energy for the show, as if nothing had ever been wrong.

Since that day, both Roma and Mark have become such important people in my life. They are a beautiful, God-fearing couple who really just took me in. Roma has been such a dear special friend, almost like a mom away from home. She has a wonderful heart and has been a true mentor to me—both in the industry and as a spiritual example. Their friendship has led to numerous blessed experiences and time spent praying and talking about the Lord.

As if the day hadn't already been great enough, when I went back to my hotel room after the show that night, I found myself celebrating yet another exciting first in my career. Earlier in the day, a feature I'd done for the DJ duo Lost Kings called "Look at Us Now," which also featured rapper A$AP Ferg, had gone out into the world. To mark how special the occasion was, I did a live stream with my fans, and it was so exciting to see how proud and supportive they were. Having them love me for myself and for my personal musical expression, in addition to what I was doing with Fifth Harmony, was the best feeling in the world.

Even though all of us girls were starting to release features, we still had plenty of Fifth Harmony accomplishments to keep us busy. That summer "Down" was the most-tweeted-about song (according to *Time* magazine). We followed up with a live performance on *The Tonight Show Starring Jimmy Fallon,* and announced the release date of our self-titled album, *Fifth Harmony.* I'd been a fan of Jimmy Fallon's for years, hoping to someday be on his show. I thanked Jimmy for having us and told him how much I looked up to him. He was just as great as he seemed on TV, and this became another highlight for me of all the years in the group.

We'd been in the studio endlessly that year, trying to find the right songs, the right sound, the right lyrics. We were tirelessly writing songs, day and night. And it was incredible to experience the culmination of all of that hard work when our new album was released in August and debuted at No. 4 on the Billboard 200. It was a beautiful thing for us to share. We were all so proud. Have you ever been so happy you couldn't come up with words? That's exactly how I felt. The whirlwind continued; and everywhere we went, fans gathered around and supported us. We won several incredible awards, everything from People's Choice Awards to Teen Choice Awards.

We performed two songs on MTV's *TRL (Total Request Live).*

Then, much to my delight, we recorded another Christmas song, this one called "Can You See?" for an animated movie, *The Star*. Our first original Christmas song, it was a magical song about the Star of Bethlehem and the significance of the birth of Jesus. "Por Favor," our collaboration with Pitbull, was a catchy, vivacious Latin pop record in Spanglish. It was especially fun when we were able to perform it with him on *Dancing with the Stars*.

In November, our manager came up to us and said, "Guess what, girls?! You've been invited to sing at Disney World!" To say I was overjoyed is an understatement. I called my parents, and they were equally ecstatic. It immediately became a family trip. Here were all of my favorite things in the universe—getting to sing a Christmas song, at Disney World, on a trip with my family and cousins, during Christmastime! I couldn't imagine anything more magical, and that's exactly what it was. My parents were there, along with my brother and his girlfriend, and my cousin BJ and his wife and their three girls. It was my little cousins' first time at Disney World, and being able to give them that gift was priceless.

We ended up spending not one, but two and a half days in the park with VIP access, which meant we could go to the front of the line. We had the best time. Nothing, and I mean nothing, in my career, which has had some insane highlights, has ever compared to that Disney trip. Watching my little cousins' faces when they saw the Castle for the first time and got to meet their favorite princesses, Anna and Elsa, and also Mickey, that was something I'll always cherish. I could do nothing but thank God for these moments, especially because He had helped me to weather such difficult trials in the previous years. The beautiful part was that we all felt the same way—like we were in Heaven on earth. I will remember every laugh, every smile, every bit of pure magic that was felt on that trip for the rest of my life.

For Fifth Harmony's performance, everything was decorated to look like we were living inside a Christmas snow globe. We sang "Sleigh Ride" during the day, and then at night, we sang "Can You

See" and "The Christmas Song." We worked hard to perfect our renditions with our very talented vocal coach, and our voices were in fine form.

Singing in front of the Disney Castle made me feel like I was in a real-life fairy tale. I looked at the other girls as we performed and knew that with commitment and hard work we had survived a year of the biggest changes imaginable. It felt absolutely wonderful.

We did a few more shows before heading home for another holiday season with our families. I couldn't help but wonder what the New Year might hold. I never guessed that an even bigger change was right around the corner, whether I felt ready for it or not.

FOURTEEN

Changing Harmonies

I made a wish on the night of January 1, 2018, that the year would be filled with hope, joy, and beautiful opportunities. January was a great month for me. I found myself in San Antonio, back where it all began, thanks to the support of a local talent agent, Annette, I've known since I was little. She'd believed in me as a singer and performer, when I was young and unknown, and she'd always booked me around town whenever she could. She was so proud of how far I'd come. Having her in my life was such a blessing. It was so special to have family friends around me, who were there for me before and after my success in Fifth Harmony.

It meant a lot to me when I heard that she'd arranged for me to perform as part of the city's Tricentennial celebration. I'd be singing with the world-renowned opera singer Plácido Domingo—known for his role alongside Luciano Pavarotti and José Carreras in the classical music supergroup the Three Tenors—plus a 64-piece orchestra. My family and I couldn't believe all of this was happening in my hometown, making it all the sweeter. It felt like my journey had come full circle once again.

Now I had to prepare, and fast. There wasn't much time before the show. And I was in Mexico City with the group on a promo tour. Mr. Domingo had asked me to be ready to sing "Bésame Mucho" with him, and although I knew this classic song, I didn't have it memorized. So first I listened to it on repeat until I had it down. The night before I flew to San Antonio, I did a fitting with our stylist, who helped me to find just the right dress. I tried on several options, and then I slid on a beautiful white gown with a long train and sparkles sewn into the fabric. It was immediately clear this was the perfect one.

I wasn't able to leave the group for long, so I flew into San Antonio the day before my duet with Mr. Domingo. I was always happy for any time with my parents, and my dad took me out to eat at one of my favorite spots before driving me to rehearsal at one of the most beautiful churches in the city. I was so nervous. I had sung a bit of opera around town when I was younger. I loved the music from *The Phantom of the Opera,* as well as Luciano Pavarotti and Andrea Bocelli. It was an honor to be singing with Mr. Domingo.

After practicing with Mr. Domingo, I rehearsed the second song I would sing, just with the orchestra. It had always been a dream of mine to sing backed by classical musicians, but I'd never had the chance before this point. I loved how it felt different from my normal experience of singing—the sound was so grand and beautiful. I could see my dad tearing up from where he was watching, and when we finished, the conductor was so gracious. "Thank you so much," he said. "That was incredible. We're honored to have you as a guest. We'll see you tomorrow."

When Dad drove me home, he made sure to let me know that he was proud of me and that I'd sounded amazing. He couldn't wait for Mom to hear me. Neither of us could.

The next day when I arrived at the gorgeous Lila Cockrell Theatre, I was excited and filled with butterflies at the same time. I was anticipating a beautiful evening.

I had my local hair and makeup team do my glam—I love my San Antonio girls. Then I rehearsed one more time on the actual stage.

And suddenly I wasn't quite so nervous anymore. As I walked back to my dressing room, I was just taking it all in and enjoying myself. I slid into my sparkly white dress, which made me feel like a princess, and I got one last hug from my parents and my brother backstage. Finally I said a simple but heartfelt prayer for God to bless my performance that evening.

And then it was showtime. I stood behind the curtain, listening to the rustling of the crowd outside, so different from the animated screams that greeted the start of a Fifth Harmony concert. As I took my place in front of the orchestra and started to sing, joy washed over me. Now that I had more power to shape my musical output, I had returned to one of my first great musical loves, Selena. It was with tremendous pride that I sang one of my favorite songs by her, "No Me Queda Más," before I went on to sing "Bésame Mucho" with Mr. Domingo. I even wore my hair in an updo, also a special homage to Selena.

After we sang the final note, the crowd roared, and I was actually able to see my grandma standing up in the audience. That was so sweet of her. As I caught her expression of love and pride, I beamed, because my grandma is my heart. Next to her, my dad and brother wore suits, and my mom looked like a movie star in her gorgeous gown. Afterward, there was a reception, and it was so wonderful to be able to celebrate this special night with my parents. Of course, there were many opera fans there, and they were so lovely to me—commending me for being a young pop star who was also willing to sing classical music and telling me how impressed they'd been with my talent and versatility. What a wonderful way to start the new year. Switching up my element was a breath of fresh air. I loved the elegance, class, and beauty of the opera. Most important, I was enamored by the music and raw singing. Whenever I could I enjoyed showcasing the different sides of my passions, and I was glad to do so on this night.

Equally exciting, I was getting ready to release my second feature in just two days. My song, "Perfect," was a collaboration with a European

DJ/producer named Topic. I was really proud of it. The lyrics contained a message of self-love, which was exactly what I wanted to send to all of the boys and girls out there in that moment. I loved having music with positive, uplifting messages for my fans. Having weathered so many blows to my self-esteem in the past few years and having fought my way back to a place where I was finally starting to feel better about myself, I had a lot to say on the subject. My favorite way to express myself was always in song. We can all feel vulnerable or not good enough, but it's important to realize our worth and pick ourselves back up. We are all amazing in our own ways.

The response from the media and fans was immediate and so beautiful. It confirmed that when we allow ourselves to be vulnerable and honest, we can connect with each other. We should not be isolated in loneliness, pain, and our insecurities. I used to have a hard time being vulnerable, for fear of appearing weak. I was always the "sunshine" of the group, the positive big sister type, so I didn't want to let anyone down. But I realized being open is one of the greatest signs of strength. Vulnerability is a power. And now I was being honest, sharing my heart through these lyrics, and by doing so, I was helping others. We can stand together in the struggle and celebrate our strength as one.

I received some heartfelt direct messages from fans, who said they connected immediately to the lyrics. The thing is, I know how they felt. I'd connected to the song that way, too. I've had days when I was crying in my bed, thinking I wasn't pretty enough or I'd never be this or that. But being able to reach inside myself and find strength and security, to be able to give myself the love I need, knowing that I am enough in God's eyes, is a powerful thing. Also powerful was having found the courage to be honest and to have listeners connect with it.

One message I received from a fan summed up exactly what I've struggled with and all I've ever wanted to achieve. This is the real reason I sing: *It's a hard battle to love yourself. And sometimes nothing around you helps. But you cannot give up no matter how difficult it is. I thank you for being my strength. And for teaching me to love "me" with each passing day. Thank you for being so positive.*

I love being able to connect with my fans online, but meeting them in person is the best. Topic and I did a casual pop-up performance the day the song came out. It was super last-minute, at a club in Los Angeles called Bootsy Bellows. We sent out an invite over social media two days before the event. I worried that maybe that wasn't enough advance notice, and we might not have a very good turnout. But when I arrived at the club, a little before showtime, I was inspired to see that the space was packed—it could hold about two hundred people, and there were definitely that many eager fans squeezed into every inch of the place.

I had achieved so much with Fifth Harmony, but this was a different, special kind of moment, of which I was equally proud. It was personal, because this was from my heart and it was being launched into the world with so much goodwill. Some of the fans I recognized from Fifth Harmony shows over the years, but many new listeners showed up, too. Even though the song had just come out at midnight, the fans actually sang every word with us. They had already memorized the lyrics! It was amazing to hear them singing along with me, their voices singing together with mine as Topic played piano.

After our live set, we did a Q&A session and a meet-and-greet. Again and again I heard how much the record's message meant to people, and their love for it made me so happy. Some people drove a crazy number of hours just to attend. One girl said she had been trying to meet me for six years! I couldn't believe it. They were all there for me.

The club was open to the public for a regular dance night after our show. So the bouncers eventually had to kick us all out to make room for their usual Friday-night crowd, but no one wanted to go home just yet. Everyone met outside and we spent more time together, literally on the curb next to the club. We were taking pictures and laughing and joking and telling stories. I stayed until I'd personally met every single fan. We had so much fun. It was the best.

We were on fire, taking over the world. And we still had plans in the works for Fifth Harmony in 2018. We were supposed to do a summer tour, and then a European tour. So it seemed like we were booked into the fall. But then plans began changing. Soon I found us having conversations about the future of Fifth Harmony. All of the signals that we were getting from our team were that our label would not support another album. After several tough conversations, it was decided that it was time to move on from Fifth Harmony and go solo. Truthfully, I was disappointed and the last on board. I didn't want this, and it took a long time for me to process. However, I had to respect the overall group decision.

When I prayed, as always, I felt clarity and peace come over me. I knew I needed to trust what God was doing. By this moment in my life I had been through a long list of experiences in which God had showed me His unending faithfulness. I remembered how I didn't want to audition for *The X Factor,* and my mom pushed me to do it. I'd submitted my application only to make her happy. I'd prayed before doing so, even telling God that I didn't want to, but I'd trust Him whatever happened. That had led to the past six years with Fifth Harmony. During that time, God had helped me to grow stronger and more confident in who I was and to find my voice to speak and sing out. He knew what was best for me much more than I did. The past six years with Fifth Harmony had been unreal. I'd met friends along the way I'd have for a lifetime. I discovered my inner strength and womanhood. I shared memories with the beautiful girls that would last forever. I was a part of something greater than myself. We dominated the music world, even with so many odds against us. We built a success story from the ground up. We broke records. We impacted millions of lives. We brought fans together. It was incredible, all that we accomplished.

The official announcement was made on our Fifth Harmony Twitter account on March 19, 2018.

Reflecting on the past six years since we started on X-Factor, we've realized just how far we've come and we appreciate everything so much, more now than ever. We've really had one hell of a memorable journey together and can't begin to express our gratitude to y'all for coming along with us on this wild ride!

After six years going hard, non-stop, we also realized that in order to stay authentic to ourselves and to you, we do need to take some time for now to go on a hiatus from Fifth Harmony in order to pursue solo endeavors.

We are all very excited and grateful to be able to take this time to learn and grow creatively and really find our footing as individuals. In doing this we are allowing ourselves to gain new experiences, strengths and perspectives that we can bring back to our Fifth Harmony family.

To our Harmonizers, thank you for everything we have been able to build as Fifth Harmony. With your love and encouragement we will continue to build on ourselves, support one another in everything we do, and keep making you proud, each other proud and ourselves proud.

We do have some upcoming shows through the end of the year which will still happen as planned, and we can't wait!

All our love, from the bottom of our hearts,
Dinah Jane, Lauren, Normani and Ally xoxoxo.

Yes, we still did a few more shows and commitments, and a music video shoot for our song "Don't Say You Love Me." It was our final music video as a group. We cried at the wrap of our video shoot. It was strange and hard, preparing for the end of what had been a massive part of our lives. We were saying farewell to Fifth Harmony.

Our Fifth Harmony finale was that May in Hollywood, Florida, at Hard Rock Live. The first show was public for our fans; the second one, at a Disney property, was private. Since the group had originally been formed on July 27, 2012, in Miami, Florida, it somehow felt fitting to close out this chapter back in Florida, as if we'd come full circle.

The four of us came together. We prayed about our futures and for our last show. This collaboration was ending for all of us, and we each faced new things ahead. During these last weeks with Fifth Harmony, I was actually in talks for my own reality TV show, and I was filming a pilot. But I ended up deciding this was not the best fit for me at the time. Somewhere out there, however, is footage of our last show and last moments together as a group.

We stood there under the lights, in front of our fans and friends who had become like family, and said our goodbyes. It was a great show. I remember thinking during each song, *This is the last time we will sing this song together.* It was such a strange feeling. But overall, I felt really proud. Even with all of the insecurities and frustrations I had experienced in the group, I had always shown up on time, hit my marks, gone for my high notes, sang from my heart, gave it my all. I stayed true to who I was, and I didn't lose my integrity. I tried to be as selfless as possible. I tried to help when I could—just as my parents had taught me and reminded me to keep doing, even in my darkest times. I always advocated for the group. I didn't lose my faith. Even with the crazy schedule we kept up, I had only one or two sick days out of six and a half years. Now I was finishing strong, having honored my commitment to the group. I broke my back for Fifth Harmony. I gave it my all. It was an honor being a part of the group.

I'll always be thankful for Fifth Harmony, because it got me to where I am. It's been an incredible platform for helping to change people's lives—sometimes even to save people's lives. I always carried that big-sister role in my mind until the very end. We'd shared some wonderful moments over the years, and we'd grown up together in many ways.

After we'd finished our last number of our last show together, we walked off the stage single file for the final time. We changed out of our stage clothes in the dressing room and gave the outfits back to our stylist. And then we went our separate ways. There were some difficult times in Fifth Harmony, but I chose to focus on the positive. And one thing is true: I will always have love for them. And who knows, maybe one day, we will be at a major worldwide event together as a group again.

After the performance, I realized that the life I'd had for the past six years was ending. But a new day was dawning. I was ready to make my own music. It was time for a new chapter, and I was going to pursue the dream that I had been working on my entire life. Finally I would be a solo artist who would have the freedom to create something personal, something that was all mine. I sat down on my bed and took it all in: *My life is about to begin.*

FIFTEEN

Finding My Harmony

The next few months were spent gathering my thoughts, processing everything, and strengthening my faith in God. I was actually able to breathe and be myself again. I devoted myself to reconnecting and deepening my relationships with friends. It was a beautiful time. I was able to begin to rediscover who I was, and I couldn't wait to see what God had next for me.

As much as I needed a beat to regroup, there was an urgency for me to get my solo career underway. I wasn't the only one who thought so. Even while we'd still been together, our group manager, who also managed the solo careers for several of us girls, had said it would be a good idea for all of us to start looking for our own homes. I was all for that. Several of the girls had already signed their own recording deals. And because there were a limited number of labels we could work with, and there were four of us looking for our own labels, the pressure was on to get out there and secure a deal. It would have been nice to have had all of the possible label options to choose from, but that wasn't the reality. So I tried to stay optimistic about what I could make happen at this point.

One of the first and best positives during this moment of change was that I was able to focus on myself and my overall well-being for the first time in years. I'd always been very active, going running around the neighborhood with my dad as a little girl. And before *The X Factor,* I'd done a boot camp workout every day, and I'd been in the best shape of my life.

And then, during Fifth Harmony, there was so much happening that I'd lost sight of my health as a top priority. And then, of course, there had been my weight gain and online shaming that came with it, which led only to more self-destructive behavior and added to the problem.

After the group ended, I actually had ample time to work on myself and my well-being. It felt incredible to prioritize myself in this way after so long. I'll always love to eat—and I don't deprive myself of my favorite foods, like tacos and pizza—but finally I was able to find more of a balance.

Since I transitioned to being a solo artist, I've lost a total of twenty pounds. But it's not really about what I see when I step on the scale—it's about how I feel. When I work out, I feel strong, and I also feel this rush of energy that makes me feel powerful and unstoppable. It does wonders for my mind and spirit. I feel good about myself, and I feel healthy. I love a challenge, and I love working hard, so cardio is my jam. Plus, all of those endorphins feel amazing. More than anything, I could feel myself moving away from some self-destructive patterns I'd fallen into and treating my body with the love and respect it deserved. As a result, I could feel myself coming back to my true self, with even more self-respect than in the past, and that was so healing and positive.

I also began to take stock of where I was at personally, and I realized how much I'd grown in the past few years. I knew myself much better than ever before.

Many times, we all feel the way I did—out of our element, alone, self-conscious, and uncomfortable in our own skin. We can feel left out. We can not stand up for ourselves because we don't want to face conflict or rejection. I'm hoping that as I share my journey toward finding my identity and self-confidence, it will influence you to find out who you are and celebrate that person—without apology or excuses. Every one of us is unique and valuable, and if we know ourselves, we can be our best versions and thrive while realizing our dreams.

My main focus professionally was signing with a label. I also reunited with my 1500 or Nothin' fam and worked on a few songs with them. They were so proud of me, and so happy that I was finally on my own. It was beautiful to work with them again, and we still collaborate and record to this day.

My manager at the time was confident that I would get signed. He thought this part of the process would be easy and that I would be in a position to choose which label felt like the best fit for me and my music.

On a Friday that spring, I had my first label meeting as a solo artist. I'd talked to my parents the night before, and they were praying for me. Mom texted me: "We will pray. It is definitely going to be something God tells you. Ask him for a sign."

I woke up that morning feeling so excited. I looked all through my closet, searching for the perfect outfit and the perfect shoes. I tried on a few different choices, and then I pulled out one of my favorites, a pink chiffon minidress. When I put it on, I knew this was it. I carefully did my hair and makeup. I wanted to look just right for this potentially life-changing meeting.

During all of this, it helped that I was assembling a top-notch team. Will Bracey had been the tour manager for Fifth Harmony for several years. As I've already mentioned, he was the one who came and found me and took care of me on my lowest night at the end of Fifth Harmony. I knew he always had my best interests at heart and I could trust him, not only with my vision and artistry, but with my well-being and happiness. During the spring of 2018, I felt fortunate to have him transition into a full-time member at the core of my solo team.

As the three of us—my manager, Will, and I—signed in at the front desk, got our name tags, and took the elevator upstairs, I was nervous. Although I'd achieved quite a bit during the years I'd been pursuing my solo career in LA before *The X Factor,* I'd never met with a record label as a solo artist before. This was a full-circle moment for me, as I thought about all of the years my parents had helped me to pursue a label deal when I was younger, and then everything I'd done in Fifth Harmony. And now I was having my very first record label meeting on my own. But my manager was optimistic that everyone was going to want me. He told me: "You're part of the biggest girl group in the world. It's gonna be great!" So based on his optimism, I was hopeful about my first meeting.

My manager had brought along his computer to play the songs I'd been working on over the past few weeks, to demonstrate my vision as a solo artist. I hadn't had enough time to find my true direction yet, but I was proud of the songs and they definitely were strong enough to show my potential. So I figured it was a good showcase of the direction I was moving in. I was ready.

The office was so impressive. I was craning my neck to take it all in as we were ushered into a room. My team and I sat on one long couch. Three A&R reps sat across from us. My nerves kicked into high gear. I knew I needed to sell myself, but I wasn't sure how upbeat I should be or what exactly I should say, especially because this was my first label meeting.

They all introduced themselves to me, and my manager broke the ice with small talk and a few jokes. Everyone knew him through his many years in the music industry, and they were all really nice to us. But almost immediately, they went into business mode.

The three of them began to pepper me with rapid-fire questions:

"So what's your music about?"

"Who are you working with?"

"How are making yourself different than you were in Fifth Harmony?"

"What's your vision for yourself?"

"Do you write?"

Now I was really anxious. It felt like a job interview. I felt intimidated, but I tried to answer as best as I could, with the goal of finding the right words to show them who I was really was, impress them, and maybe even to make them laugh. But, honestly, the energy was all business—everyone was still being nice, but it wasn't as informal and fun as I'd hoped it would be. I felt like I had to sell myself and convince them why they needed to sign me.

When we played my music for them, it was so nerve-racking. I hoped they'd love it. I hoped they'd want to sign me right then and there. I hoped they'd get who I was as an artist. But it was hard to tell their thoughts from their expressions. Plus, I didn't know what to do with myself: *Should I get up and dance? Should I sing? Should I sit here and act cool? Should I bob my head?* In the end, I bobbed my head and sang along to a few of the lyrics. Even though I was nervous, I was always confident about my artistry and my vision.

They were very nice, but the meeting was over in thirty minutes. Before I knew it, they were standing to shake our hands.

"So nice to meet you, Ally. You have great energy and a great voice. We'll get back to you," one of the A&R people said.

My manager thought it had been great. Even though it was a quick and more serious meeting, I thought it had gone well, and I wanted to be as optimistic and positive as possible. And I figured if he was happy with how it went, then it must have been a good meeting. Maybe that was the standard for all meetings, and I had nothing to worry about.

I couldn't stop thinking about the label, and what we would hear from them, all weekend. On Monday, we got the devastating news that they had passed on me. Even though I'd had my thoughts about the meeting, my manager had assured me it was a sure thing. I had really hoped he was right and they'd make me an offer. I was crushed. I'd had big expectations, based on what my manager had said going into the meeting. But I also had to accept that things don't always go as planned.

"Do you know why?" I asked.

"No, they don't ever really tell you why," he said. "But don't worry. That's just one label. Who knows what's going on in their system? Maybe they already have a ton of artists. But I wouldn't worry at all."

A few weeks later, I had my next meeting. I could not have been more excited for this one. As we parked and made our way into the meeting, I felt this great positive energy. My mom had given me an idea during a recent phone call.

"Hey, Mama, go in there and have fun, be different," she said. "Even put one of your flower hairpins in your hair. Why not?"

So I'd put a flower pin in my hair, as a cute little touch, and I tapped it lightly to make sure it was still in place. I had a good feeling about this meeting.

It was a big meeting with one of the higher-ups at the label, who I was pleased to find out was a woman. She was friendly, telling me that she'd been looking forward to meeting me and was glad I'd come into their label. So right from the start, that made me happy, and I immediately felt comfortable with her. We enjoyed some pleasant small talk and I felt very satisfied with the feeling in the room. Then another male A&R person came into the office and took over. I felt the energy shift. He was more businesslike. I tried to make small talk with him and be friendly, but he wasn't very receptive. He just went straight to the point and got right down to it.

"What makes you different from the other girls in Fifth Harmony? Because you are going to be competing with each other, and you have to make yourself stand out. You can't stutter when you answer this question, either."

Whoa! In my mind, this was kind of an intense way to start off. I'd expected a little more small talk to warm up the conversation. He'd immediately gone for the biggest question of all. I was thrown off guard by his somewhat serious attitude.

I took a deep breath and went for it. I knew exactly what I wanted to say, about my Latin heritage and my vision for myself as an artist, but I was so nervous that I stuttered a little with nerves. I tried to calm myself down and get my point across.

"Well, you're going to be compared to each of the girls, so you'd better have an answer when people ask you that," he said.

Again, I was a little surprised by his tone. By now I was so nervous I lost my focus a bit, even though I knew no one else could see it. I took a deep breath and leaned into my positivity.

"Okay, well, how is your sound different than all of the other artists out there? And what is your sound like? And what is your album going to be about? Tell me about your stage show. What does your stage show encompass—dancers, music, a band?"

I answered confidently about my vision of having a high energy show with dancers and a band.

Finally I got through the question portion and queued up my music. I had been hoping that the music would be my saving grace, but I was quickly disappointed. When I played the music, the room was stiff, and no one really reacted. To me, when there's no reaction, that's a reaction in and of itself—and not a good one. I could feel my face getting warm, and I did not feel great—a mixture of awkwardness and disappointment.

I rushed to tell them what the song was about, and then I quickly hit play. As they listened, they nodded their heads just the tiniest bit.

In total, I played three or four songs. I knew I was still perfecting my direction, which I was hoping to get input on from my new label. But I was proud of them. Right at the end of the meeting, another member of their team came in, and he could not have been sweeter. But overall, I didn't feel good. I didn't feel like my answers were as strong as they could have been.

"Well, thank you so much for coming by," the woman said. "We loved meeting you."

As they walked me back toward the elevator, I had a gut feeling that it had not gone well. And after my first no from the other label, the thought that they might turn me down, too, was starting to make me feel a little frantic. By the time I got home and took the flower out of my hair, I was feeling defeated. But my manager again thought it had gone really well, so I hoped I was overreacting.

Next up was my third label meeting. Two higher-ups came out to meet me, and they were both incredibly welcoming and warm. They excitedly told me about all of the great artists they were working with. We had a fun conversation, full of laughter, and I felt like we were connecting. As I played my music for them, I felt hopeful that maybe I was actually landing this meeting.

This time I was prepared, when they began asking me all the same questions:

"What's your vision for yourself?"

"What's your sound like?"

"What's your show like?"

"Who are your inspirations?"

Not only was I ready with my answers, but I also felt much more relaxed, as if I was able to be myself, which was a huge relief. When we walked out of that meeting, both Will and my main manager felt there was no question it had gone well and I'd made a great impression. I even felt like, *Wow, that was a success. I had two of the label heads in my meeting, and it was so lively and fun, and they seemed so impressed with me. I finally got my vision of my artistry across just as I had wanted to.* We felt pretty sure we were going to get an offer from them, because it could not have gone any better.

Even though I was struggling a bit to find my footing as a solo artist, I had already been in the business for more than a decade— for six and a half years of which, I'd been part of one of the biggest girl groups in pop music history. I made a lot of connections over the years, from being in Fifth Harmony, from songwriters to producers. Just take DJ Flict, a producer we had worked with in Fifth Harmony, who had been a part of our early journey and albums. He was this hilarious, upbeat Filipino American guy, a total prankster. I loved his personality and thought he was great as a person and a producer.

Well, that summer he contacted Will, saying he'd heard I was working on music. And he'd love to work with me. I agreed we should do it. A date was set for us to go over to the Hollywood Hills studio he shared with a few other producers. I almost didn't go, because I had a different appointment that day. But I chose to meet with him—little did I know, that would change everything. It was all white and super homey, and it felt nice being in there with him.

At first we just talked, and it turned out that he'd actually shared many of my feelings about the group, and he'd always loved my voice and felt like I'd been undervalued. He thought I could be *the* next Latin pop artist, and he really wanted to work with me, even just to help me get down some music and lyrics and try to figure out my sound.

Through a little more conversation and lots of laughter, we just clicked. He has this big personality and the best laugh, and we were immediately joking around and having the best time. It also helped when he queued up the first song, one he thought would be perfect for me.

"I've been waiting for the right female to come in and sing this. I wasn't going to give it to just anybody, but someone who can make this believable and who can relate," he said. "I hope you like it."

As the song, "Vamos," started playing, Will and I looked at each other. We both loved it. I loved it. It was so fun. Flict knew of my love for Selena, and this track definitely brought her to mind. It was this upbeat pop-Latin hybrid, with mariachi horns that reminded me of San Antonio. I immediately loved the vibe. And so we recorded it.

It was amazing to have creative freedom on my songs. Recording solo, all by myself. I could sing the song, exactly how I wanted to. I could play around with whatever I wanted. I was in control of the lyrics and what I wanted to say. It was an indescribable feeling. Working with someone who understood me, and believed in me, and who I had so much fun with, meant everything to me.

After we'd worked on the song for a few days, we were really loving how it was coming together, but there was an empty spot for a feature. We kept kicking around the possibilities.

"Man, we've got to dream big here," Flict said. "We've got to come up with the right feature, and it has to be someone Latin."

We tossed around all kinds of possibilities. As a producer, Flict was well connected, so he started reaching out to people, seeking a good fit. Literally the next day, Will was listening to a Spotify playlist while at the gym, and he heard this song, "Bien de To'." He couldn't get enough. It was by this Latin rapper, Messiah, who had an unreal tone. He sounded like nobody else; his flow and his lyrics were amazing. We checked out more of his music. He was the real deal.

"This guy on 'Vamos' would be insane," Will said.

The next day we had a meeting with Flict. Will was still pumped about Messiah.

"We need to get him before he explodes," Will said. "Because there's no doubt this guy's going to explode."

Of course, in a crazy coincidence, Flict happened to know Messiah's A&R rep, Nick Ferrer. He called him right up. Within a few hours, Nick came over to the studio, met me, and heard the song. He was really into the idea of having Messiah do it, and soon Messiah agreed. Although Messiah is based in New York, amazingly enough, he happened to be coming to LA in a few days. We set up a session together.

A few days later, it was time for us to meet. I was excited to work with such a great talent. It was also exciting for me to have my first real collaboration as a solo artist, post–Fifth Harmony. I was eager for what we could create together. When Messiah walked into the studio, he had such a great energy and vibe to him. He pulled up with his entourage, including a guy named Charles Chavez. Charles signed Messiah to his JV label, Latium, under Atlantic Records. Charles has had a long and illustrious career in the music industry. He was responsible for the record-breaking success of Pitbull and had been his manager for a decade. When Fifth Harmony performed at Pitbull's New Year's Eve special, going into 2014, Will knew of Charles, and had the chance to meet him backstage. I had met him only once, very briefly. But I definitely knew who he was.

We all hit it off right away and were instantly at ease, just talking and catching up.

"How's everything going, Ally?" Charles asked. "It's funny, I submitted a feature for you to Fifth Harmony's management. Did you ever hear about it?"

"Hm, I don't remember them ever bringing it to me," I said.

"Wow," he said, taking that in. "It ended up going to this other artist. But . . . you mean . . . they never even told you about it?"

"I don't think so," I said.

"That's very unfortunate," he said. "It's not right."

"That's crazy," I said. "We could have known each other sooner. And I'm sorry, too, because I definitely would've listened and probably loved the record."

He was kind of shaking his head. But neither of us was surprised. Stuff like that happens in the music industry all the time, unfortunately. Then Charles started asking questions about my new journey: "How's the solo transition going? Are you signed?"

"No, sir, she's not signed yet," Will said. "She's meeting with people, but we could use all the help we can get. We're taking meetings right now."

The whole afternoon was a good time. We had a lot of fun in the studio. I loved being around Messiah and his team. They felt like a piece of home. I am an energy person, and I definitely loved the energy in the room. Having my first collaboration experience was the positivity I needed. And I fell in love with Messiah's verse. He killed it.

And then soon after that, Will had a side conversation with Charles about me and my career. He was very open with him.

"You know, sir, we're a big fan of you and your work," he said. "You're someone who breaks artists worldwide. We're looking for someone who knows both the Latin and mainstream pop market. Would you be willing to meet with Ally?"

"Sure, just bring her into my office, and we'll talk."

This was a huge relief. We really needed to meet with everyone we could. Charles was a powerful force in both the Latin and mainstream pop music worlds. And we needed all of the connections we could get. A few days later, Will and I went to Charles's studio for our meeting with him. We had already been talking about making a shift in my management team, so we were very interested to see what Charles would have to say and where this would all lead.

Charles made me feel at ease right away. We bonded over the fact that he was a fellow Texan, was Mexican American, and he had been a radio DJ at a station in San Antonio at the beginning of his career. He was clearly someone who understood my culture and values, and how they were mixed with American values. It was amazing to feel so seen. It was as if we had known each other for a long time. It didn't seem like just another business meeting, even though he asked me some of the same questions I was used to hearing by now. It seemed like he actually cared about my answers.

"Tell me about your artistry, your vision, your songs," Charles said.

I quickly felt comfortable with him, and I put it all out there.

"Listen, I have a dream of being an artist who can do both—I want to sing not only in Spanish but also in English. And to have global records and pop records, and I also want to dance and entertain people. That's who I am."

"Wow, I do see that," Charles said.

When I was in Fifth Harmony, we'd done a lip synch battle, and I'd chosen to perform a Selena/Jennifer Lopez medley. I showed it to him, with a disclaimer. "Obviously, this is playful and for fun, but if you look at the Jennifer Lopez part, that's kind of how I see myself onstage. Very high energy, fun, commanding the stage."

He watched closely, and it was clear he was impressed.

"Wow," he said. "I know that's for fun, but I can see your potential and what you could be. And that's what separates you from other artists. There hasn't been an artist like you who really can sing but can also have that performance value that can make people be entertained. And in Fifth Harmony, I feel like they didn't highlight you the way you should have been."

We kept talking and talking and talking, and it felt like he understood me and my vision.

He asked me to play him some of my music, and I did.

"Listen, these songs are really good," he said. "I know it's just the starting mark. You're recording with whoever you can right now. But I think it needs to be a little bit more cohesive and kind of tell a bit more of a story. I love being able to work and collaborate with artists."

I appreciated his honesty. It meant that even if my music wasn't quite right yet, he cared enough to want me to get it right, eventually, and maybe even help me to get there.

"Even without the music, I love what you represent, what you strive for," he said. "I haven't been a manager in a while. I'm more on the label side, but I really think you're amazing."

We talked some more, and it was obvious he was weighing everything in his mind. "Let me really think about all of this and then contact you guys," he said.

Of course, I would have rather gotten a yes right away, but I respected that he was taking my career seriously enough to make sure, if we decided to work together, it would be a good fit for all of us. A few days later, he called Will with some news.

"I think I'm willing to take Ally to Atlantic," he said. "Let's set up a meeting."

SIXTEEN

Going Solo

As I went into my fourth label meeting, my whole team was Will. I trusted Will completely because we'd already been through so much together, but we both felt we needed a big power player on our team. Finding the right team can be a challenge, but it's essential to a successful career. My family will always be part of my decision-making process, but it's also important to find the right fit when it comes to management. Searching for a manager is kind of like dating someone new or investing in a new relationship. You get to know someone and allow yourself to be vulnerable, and then if it's not working out, you have to end the relationship. The thought of starting all over can be overwhelming. But from the beginning with Charles, I could tell we saw things the same way, and we were both excited to see what he could make happen.

One of the heads of the label, chairman and CEO Craig Kall-man, who had the power to sign new artists, was in town for a few days from New York City. We were supposed to meet with him at the Atlantic building in LA, but he was very pressed for time, so he asked Charles if we wouldn't mind if we met with him at his hotel in Beverly Hills. We were so excited for this meeting, but from the moment we got there, everything that could have possibly gone wrong went wrong. We struggled to connect to the Wi-Fi so we could play the songs we'd brought. When we finally managed to get online, the computer speakers wouldn't work. Craig had clearly had a long day, and this meeting was just one big mishap.

"So tell me about yourself," Craig said, quickly asking questions.

"What's your sound?"

"What's your vision?"

"Who are you working with?"

I tried my best to be funny and charming, but all of the technical problems had rattled me. I was starting to feel nervous. I played my songs for him. By this point, I wasn't feeling very confident. The whole meeting lasted only ten minutes.

"Thank you so much for having me," I said with a big smile, trying to stay upbeat.

I knew he was incredibly busy, and I'd been fortunate to meet with him, but we all walked out of there knowing it could have gone better. And with all of the other difficult meetings I'd already had, I was feeling pretty insecure and defeated. *Dang, this is a lot harder than I thought it would be.*

A few days after I met with Atlantic, I had a private show in Bentonville, Arkansas, for Walmart and Coca-Cola. It was my first paid solo performance. Will was traveling with me in his role as my day-to-day manager. I could tell that something was off with him, but I couldn't figure out what it might be. He looked like he'd had the life sucked out of him, but I couldn't think of why.

"Hey, Will, are you all right?" I kept asking him.

"Yeah, I'm fine," he said, but he wasn't very convincing. He had sad eyes, and he was definitely keeping to himself more than he normally would have when we traveled. He was quiet the whole flight. By the time we landed, I was really starting to worry.

"Will, seriously, what's wrong? Are you sure you're all right?"

"Yeah, I'm just really tired," he said.

"Okay," I said, trying to give him a little space.

Making matters worse, we had touched down on a dark and stormy evening. The sky was overcast, and it looked as if it was about to start raining any second. If there's one thing I'm terrified of, it's thunder. It's because of my sensitive hearing from being a preemie baby, but when it thunders, my ears can't take it—the sound is so loud it is very painful. I always end up hiding somewhere, crying. Seeing those clouds, I was already feeling queasy with nerves.

"Excuse me, does it thunder here?" I asked an airport employee.

"Yes, and it might rain tonight," he said.

I had to sing in the morning, and it was just going to be me with a piano player, so I had to make sure my voice was in great shape. And for that, I needed sleep. I'm always up all night during thunderstorms, and so now I was worried that I'd be awake because of the weather and be a mess the next day. When we reached our hotel, I immediately went up to my room to practice my songs for the next day.

This was one of my first solo performances, post–Fifth Harmony, and I'd had to come up with a thirty-to-forty-five-minute set list of songs I could do with just a piano player. It took me a few days, and what I settled on was a bit random, I'll admit—everything from Whitney Houston to Bruno Mars to Selena. One of those songs was "Jesus, Take the Wheel," which had always resonated with me in a similar way as "On My Knees." I'd been a huge Carrie Underwood fan since I rooted for her on *American Idol*. I loved her music, her voice, and what she stood for—I saw her as a light in the entertainment industry. I'd loved this particular song of hers forever, but I'd never performed it before. For someone reason, I was led to put on my set list for this show. Little did I know how much I would end up needing it.

Will was there, attending to his normal duties, but he still seemed off. Finally I couldn't let it go anymore. "Will, I can tell something is wrong with you," I said. "And I need to know."

"Okay."

He let out a long exhale. I could tell he didn't even want to look me in the eye.

"Ally, it's going to be okay," he started off.

I knew right then what was going to happen next. The bottom was already dropping out.

"I'm so sorry, but all of the labels passed."

When those words came out of his mouth, I was silent with shock, but my reaction had been immediate and gut-wrenching. Then I shouted out: "No. No! NO!"

"There's no way," I continued. "Someone got the information wrong."

"It's not true," I said. "It's just a mistake. They're going to come back."

And then, I just fell on the floor.

I started bawling my eyes out, like I'd never bawled my eyes out before. There were no other options. I could have tried to be an independent artist without a major label, but that's a really hard road for a pop artist. You need the support of a major to help finance everything that goes into funding a career—everything including the cost of songwriters, producers, engineers, recording studios, promotion, travel, hair and makeup, wardrobe. Every single detail of a career that needs to be funded, including music videos and stage shows. There are a seeming infinite number of costs.

I felt this piercing doom, this sinking thought: *Will I ever be able to make music again? I may not, based on everything that's happening. There are only so many labels to choose from, and once the other girls got signed, that already eliminated those choices for me. And now basically all of the doors have been shut.*

I really felt like this was possibly the end of a dream that went all the way back to me being a little child, and all of that hard work and patience, and sacrifice by my parents. Would that ever be rewarded? Would that dream ever come true?

I'd had such high hopes. I'd had it all planned out in my mind. I'd worked so hard, putting energy and effort into my new music and into meeting after meeting, no matter how discouraged I felt in the room. All of the doors had closed in my face. I was shattered.

Not even one label out of four wanted me. This is a nightmare. Someone wake me up.

It had already come out that the other girls had all found labels, and the question from the public remained: "Where was Ally?" Of course I was happy for them, but it also upped my anxiety, reminding me how far behind I was, and that there were not an infinite number of labels to choose from.

Our fans were super supportive of me, even when things were slow for me. They didn't doubt that I'd get signed. Their mindset was: "Oh, Ally must have been signed, and she's just keeping it on the down low for now." When I saw their encouraging comments or excited questions about what was next, I tried to quiet my jitters and assure myself that I'd soon have the kind of news to warrant their excitement—a fantastic label, a partnership with the best in the biz. But I was in panic mode. Around this time, I also realized how many lingering scars I had from the group—all of those negative online comments that had picked apart my body, my dancing, my talent, had been an emotional beating. And the sympathy had been its own difficult pill to swallow. The last thing I wanted now was to fail at securing a label and have people say, "Oh, poor girl, she can't do this, either."

Will was right there by my side to encourage me. He admitted he didn't understand why God was allowing this to happen. He was devastated, too, seeing everything I'd been through to this point. But he also reminded me that God was in control and that He would take care of us. That it wasn't over. I tried to see the truth in his words, but for that moment, I couldn't. I couldn't figure out why I always had to fight for every small step of progress I made. And then I had a worse thought: *Oh my God, I have to tell my parents that I got rejected by all the labels. There's nowhere to go.*

I couldn't do it. I couldn't disappoint them like that.

Having all of this hit me at once was gut-wrenching. I was devastated. I was angry. I stayed down and kept crying.

Why, God? Why are you putting me through this? Why? I've been so patient. I've held onto my faith. I've tried to follow You always. This whole journey to my dream has been so hard. God, I thought you were going to take care of me. Why is this happening?

Just then it got worse. The sky started cackling with loud thunder. I hid in the bathroom, terrified. Every part of this moment was my worst nightmare come to life. I put on my headphones and, on repeat, I played "Jesus, Take the Wheel," the only solace I could find. *Please, God, take the wheel of my life. I can't do it on my own.* I gave it all up to Him. It was hard, because I was upset and questioning God, but I mustered a seed of faith. I curled up there on a pile of towels, awash in tears, until I'd cried myself to sleep.

I do not know how I got up and sang the next day, except that it was with God's help. I was a zombie. I was so heartbroken and sad. I felt like a body with no spirit inside of me. But I had to perform. Then I got to the moment in the set list when I sang, "Jesus, Take the Wheel." Just then, those lyrics hit me harder than ever. I sang it with all that I had left. I was a brokenhearted girl, who desperately needed Jesus to take the wheel of her life. Little did the fans and audience know how much that song meant to me in the moment and why I was singing it. It took all the strength I had not to break down. I belted out those words to God and surrendered myself to him.

After the show, I did my best to carry on, but I was really low. Looking back, I can see how significant that moment was. What I didn't know at the time was that this crossroads in my life, which felt so dire, marked not the end, but a new beginning. I would spend the next few weeks praying and waiting, but the answer was on its way, and I just needed to stay strong.

Charles reached out. He believed in me, in spite of the noes we'd received. "Let's try this again," he said. "We've got to prove ourselves. Let's swing the bat and hope that we get a home run."

At least this time we had some information to go on. One of the pieces of feedback Charles had gotten from Craig was "the music's a little all over the place." Craig had also said: "She needs more direction. However, she does have superstar potential."

So Charles had a plan. "I really do think if we work together on finding a cohesive sound and go in with a clear plan, there's a great shot that they could say yes and sign you," he said. "I'm willing to do a two-week period, where we record as much as we can, and we pick the best records, and we go to New York and meet with Atlantic again."

"Wow, that means the entire world to me," I said. "The fact that you did not give up on me, you see what I see in myself, you have the same visions for me, and you want to try this again. Thank you so much. This means so much to me."

"Listen, there are no guarantees," he said. "I don't know what's going to happen, but at least we can try."

Charles had thought the reason I hadn't gotten signed was because I hadn't been able to provide a clear enough picture of what I had to offer as an artist and entertainer. He suggested that when we went into the studio, we dig deep and make some crucial decisions about my sound and vision—who I was and what I had to say on my own. It was a risky proposition. As Charles had pointed out, they could still say no. But I was immediately game.

Oh, and as if I wasn't already juggling enough, I became a mom that summer—to two of the cutest kittens I'd ever seen. As a way to honor sweet Bobbi's memory, I'd decided to become an ambassador for the ASPCA and to help rescue other cats, because she'd rescued me. Even though it had been almost two years since she had passed, I was still grieving her loss in my life, and I definitely did not feel ready to adopt again. I didn't know if my heart would *ever* feel ready to adopt again. And then there was my travel schedule. But when staff members from the ASPCA emailed me in June and asked if I could foster two cats, my heart immediately told me that I had to help these poor homeless kitties, in Bobbi's honor.

The email read, in part: "These kitties are looking for a home . . . One of them was born with a deformed tail, but don't worry, she's still healthy and as cute as ever." As soon as I saw those words, I immediately started crying. Bobbi had a deformed tail, too, and I just knew that Bobbi had sent them to me and it wasn't a coincidence. It was a sign that I was meant to say yes.

Oh, my baby, I thought. I know that's my baby.

I believe it was God who orchestrated all of that, so I knew right then and there that I had made such a beautiful decision.

"Yes, I'll do it," I said before I'd even fully thought through the logistics.

It dawned on me that I'd never raised a kitten before, let alone two, and I didn't know how much work it would be. And that when I'd had my other pets, I'd still been living with my family, so we all helped to take care of them together. Plus, my parents were there to step in when I was away, traveling the world. My life was very different now that I had my own apartment in Los Angeles, and I really had no idea what the next few months of my life would look like, as I hopefully secured a record deal and launched my solo career. When I started to worry myself that it might be too much and that I might let the kittens down, I reassured myself that I was just fostering them for four days.

But then when the kittens were brought to my home in the ASPCA vehicle and I saw them crouched together in this single crate, these precious little angels—they were only four weeks old—I immediately started to cry. I knew these were *my* babies, and I was going to take care of them. To be honest, I had no idea what I had gotten myself into. It was going to be a lot more challenging and emotional than I'd ever expected or felt ready for, but it changed my heart in that very moment. It was something from God, even though the timing made no sense at all. They were gifts from Heaven. And there was no question that I was never giving them back. I knew they were mine. We were chosen for each other. I ended up adopting them, and it was one of the best decisions I'd ever made. They opened up my heart again, and I couldn't imagine loving anything as much as I loved them.

Being able to give back through the charitable organizations I work with means so much to me. In recent years I've also become an ambassador for the wonderful nonprofit March of Dimes. It's so special, because I was born a premature baby, and now I can help babies like me, which is such a beautiful thing. I'm so thankful that, through my dreams, I'm now able to have a platform to help the organization that once helped my family and others like us.

It's tough when you're in the middle of a transition, but during this season of seeking a label, I worked on releasing worry and trusting that I was just where I was supposed to be.

Will always tried to reassure me. "I don't know what's happening or why God's allowing this to happen," he said. "But I promise you, he's got a plan."

One of the hardest parts was that I could not bring myself to tell my parents about my bad news. I was so scared of breaking their hearts. Of course they'd be disappointed for me and upset that I'd had to go through this. But even more than that, I felt like I'd let them down, like I'd let down our entire family. After everything they'd put into my career, we were in this together, and my defeat was something that had happened to all of us. I just couldn't devastate them like that. As fragile as I was, I knew it would break me. I normally told my parents everything, and this was the worst possible secret to keep. I felt so alone during this time.

I still talked to or texted with my parents every day. During a few calls, my dad brought up the labels and asked me if I'd heard anything back from any of them yet.

"Oh yeah, it was a great meeting," I always said. "They said they're going to call us back and let us know. But I feel great about it."

I wasn't lying on purpose. I was hoping that by buying myself some time, I could put another record deal together. So that by the time I told them about my label saga, I'd already have a wonderful big yes in place. And then I could just casually drop in the noes.

But my dad soon got real with me during one of our talks.

"Mama, are you hiding something from me?" he asked.

"No," I said.

There was silence on the line for a long beat.

"Dad, I have to tell you something," I said, my voice timid. I took a deep breath and prepared to tell him the news. "Dad, they all said no."

I had tears in my eyes.

"I'm sorry," I continued. "I don't want to disappoint you guys. We've all worked so hard on this. And this is testing my faith, and I just didn't want you to worry."

"Oh, Mama, I am so sorry," he said. "Don't worry, God's going to take care of you, and even though I can't believe it myself, this is happening for a reason. And God has a plan for you in all of this. It's going to be okay, Mama. I'm so sorry. And, Mama, you don't ever have to hide anything or feel alone. I'm always here, through the ups and downs. That's what family is for. I don't want you to ever to battle anything alone. And as hard as it is, we have to trust God and know that He is going to take care of you."

Just hearing him say that and having the weight of my secret lifted, I felt better.

"Can we just hold this information for a little bit, just you and me?" I asked.

"Of course, Mama," he said.

For the next two weeks, Charles and Will and I went into the studio every day. Sometimes they would sit in for a bit, and if I needed them for anything, they were always available to me. Charles had paired me with several different songwriters, and day after day, in different sessions, we just wrote. Sometimes we recorded two songs in a single day. First Charles helped me to verbalize what my sound was. He was open to letting me try anything, which was incredibly freeing—songs in Spanish, songs in English, songs in Spanglish. What I wanted for myself were high-energy songs, definitely with a mix of English and Spanish lyrics and a positive message. Really, I wanted to be free to do it all.

We listened to hours of music, picking out my favorite songs by my favorite artists. I would share what I loved about each song, how I was inspired by it. Now that we knew where we were going, we went in that direction, hard.

Charles worked with and had signed incredible songwriters, and so he set up sessions for me to record with them. Mostly they would play me a complete song, and I'd love it right away and decide to record it with my own particular spin. Or they'd play me an instrumental track that had already been written. If it caught my imagination, I'd say, "Ooh, I love that. Let's write to that!" We'd start working on lyrics to go with the music. A few times we'd have nothing more than a beat or we'd even start from scratch, creating a track from the bottom up.

The whole process was so comforting after what I'd just been through. Because Charles had a studio and all of these relationships with successful people in the industry, I felt so supported. I didn't have to worry about the cost of studio time or scrambling to set up meetings. I could focus on my creativity and listening to that true voice deep inside of myself that had grown silent during the years when I'd been unable to tune in to it with any regularity. I was coming back to life as an artist. It was amazing.

At first I was just nervous to write with other songwriters. But Charles and Will were always supportive and encouraging. As always, I talked to my parents every day, and they were always my number one fans.

"I know you're nervous sometimes to write," my mom would say. "Go in there, show them your talent. Don't be shy. Mama, you got this."

I don't care how old I am. I'll always need advice from my mom, and I'll always cherish it. She's helped me to believe further in my voice, my talent, and what I'm capable of. No matter what age you are, you always need that.

After meeting with a few of Charles's writers, who were all talented, with great personalities, and who created a no-pressure, stress-free zone, I gained more confidence. It took a few sessions for me to be fully comfortable. But I soon saw I was free to say what I wanted, what I didn't like, what I wanted to sing about and what I didn't.

One of the absolute best parts was working with Charles. He is known for being honest. It means a lot that he respects me enough to tell me the truth, even when it's to say something isn't working. I love rich feedback. Let me tell you, in this industry, that kind of truth is hard to find. It can make all of the difference in creating a vibrant, long-lasting career. But he's always funny and upbeat, even when he's delivering bad news or he's shaking his head at some wild thing that's happened.

"Who does that?" he always says when he doesn't understand something or when someone does something crazy.

When we were working in the studio together, he'd give me the best notes.

"I think you're trying to sound like the demo singer here," he said several times. "And I would suggest, have your own flavor, have your own flair. Be yourself."

I realized he was right. Because I'd always been working hard and hoping for good parts in Fifth Harmony, I'd often tried to sound just like the demo singer the songwriter had chosen, thinking that might make me more likely to receive a bigger part. But of course my path forward now was to sound more and more like myself. Charles gave me helpful notes about that, too: "I think on this record, you can just kind of more be relaxed in the way your tone is."

Now that I was free to think for myself and tap into my own creativity, I would take a beat to consider what he'd said and check to see if it seemed true to me and to what I was going for in my music. When I listened back later, he was always right.

Before I knew it, we had several songs I was really happy with.

We finished a rough cut of a new song, "Lonely," that we all really loved. It was based on the Rob Thomas song "Lonely No More," which I'd always thought was great. We'd put my own take on the theme and sound and come up with an interpolation, where we took the melody from the chorus, "You don't have to be lonely no more," and from there created an original. It sounded fresh and was a great showcase for my voice. We needed only three or four songs to take back to the label. We'd managed to put together a group of songs I was really proud of, and which felt representative of my potential new sound. I was so thankful Charles had been willing to go through this again. Honestly, out of all the labels, I truly loved Atlantic. It was my ultimate dream label. I had grown up being a huge fan of Bruno Mars, and my dad was also a fan. I was always proud of the fact that Bruno was also a Hernandez, just like me. He was one of my biggest inspirations, and I dreamed of being on the same label with him. That would be the ultimate for me. Plus, the label had the greatest of the greats, Aretha Franklin. And the most powerful, relevant, successful artists, everyone from Cardi B to Ed Sheeran. So my parents and I were just praying, "Please, God, Atlantic."

But if I'd been nervous before, the stakes were even higher now. There was *literally* nowhere to go from here. Everything was riding on this one meeting. It was time to put it all on the line and see what we could make happen. I was still feeling the pressure to catch up to the rest of the girls, as far as making announcements about where I was going to land, getting music out, starting a solo career.

Charles set up a meeting at the Atlantic offices in New York City for June 20, 2018. We booked our tickets and flew into town. The day before, I had put on "Amazing Grace," sung by Chris Tomlin, and listened to it all day. That night I set it as the song for my alarm the next morning, because it was the song I really needed to hear. I just needed that reminder of God's grace and love—how God can transform anything—and of His power and his plan for me. The lyrics were so comforting, at a time that I was truly scared. This was my last possible label meeting. And I had to wake up not with fear, but with the peace of the Lord. And that's what that song gave me. Listening to it while I got ready reassured me.

Are you seeing a pattern here? I am. So many times, God has used other artists and their songs to encourage and strengthen me. That's the true power of music.

Because of Charles's role within Atlantic, he knew the label in and out and was right at home in the building. But Will and I were nervous. We started the day with a prayer, and it was running through my mind all day: "Please, God, please bless this meeting. Let it be the one."

When we arrived at the office, we prepared to put Charles's plan into play, which was to meet with his friend Inigo, who was the label's Latin/International head, play him the songs, and hope that he loved them. And then if he did, he would go to his boss, Craig, with an enthusiastic assessment of me and my music. Hopefully, Craig would also love them and sign me. We went into the conference room with Inigo, and I felt so at home with him right away. He's such a kind man, and because he had a good relationship with Charles, he was excited to hear what Charles had been working on most recently.

"Ally, how are you?" Inigo asked. "It's so wonderful to meet you."

His voice was so warm. It also helped that he took a few minutes to introduce himself, his history, and his role at the label. I wasn't put on the spot right away.

And then it was time for me to show him what I could do. Charles hit play.

"Wow," Inigo said after the first song. "Your voice is beautiful. And that song is amazing, and it has such a vibrant feeling."

I was beaming when we played him the next track, and then the next.

"This music is really good," he said. "We don't have that true Latin pop artist here. And you are amazing, and so personable and lovely and loving. And I love your music."

It was shaping up to be a beautiful meeting. As nervous as I was, Inigo was such a kind soul that I felt comfortable and able to be myself, relaxing enough to smile and laugh. Not because I was trying to make a certain impression, but because I was happy, and that's what I felt like doing. When it was time for me to tell him about myself, I found that the words came easily. I spoke from my heart about where I'd come from, how hard I'd worked, what my dreams and goals were, and how much it meant to me that he was taking the time to meet me and listen.

Again, as we were winding down, he summed up his feelings in a most encouraging way: "We're missing your market, and your artistry," he said.

While we were still in the building, Inigo went off to meet with Craig. A few minutes later, Craig came into the room. He was so inviting, and he gave me the biggest smile. "Welcome to Atlantic Records," he said. "We are so excited to have you as part of our family."

I was having trouble absorbing what he was saying.

Wait, was that a yes? Did I hear that right? Did he just . . .

I looked around me and Charles and Will were bursting with joy. It had finally really truly happened for me. Tears formed in my eyes, but I held them back.

Wait, I have to get confirmation that he just said that. Please, God, let me have heard right.

"Thank you so much, sir, this means a lot to me," I said.

"We're so excited," Craig said.

"Thank you so much," I said, elated. Although I was a little in disbelief, I had the biggest smile on my face. "I'm more excited."

The meeting ended on such an up note. I was still trying to take it all in, but little by little, I was starting to let myself trust that this was really happening. Next, they introduced me to Julie Greenwald, the head of Atlantic Records. I'd long heard about Julie, and what a strong, ferocious woman she was. It was amazing to me that she was the woman who ran one of the biggest record labels. She was the type of boss that you hoped to have. I was very excited to meet her, but also a little intimidated, because she has this very powerful presence.

"Oh, we're so happy to have you, congratulations," she said. "You ready?"

"Yes, I am ready!" I said.

"Better bring it, girl," she said. "You'd better bring that home run record, because we can't just have a great good record. We need that home run, especially coming out of Fifth Harmony. You have got to break out on your own."

"Yes, ma'am, I will do that. I'm going to hit a home run for you."

"All right, go get 'em."

While we rode in the elevator down to the street, I almost lost it, but I knew I had to keep it together in front of these people. I was looking around me in a dazed way, wondering if I'd dreamed it all, hoping I hadn't.

"Did that just happen?" I asked.

"They loved you," Charles said.

"What does this mean? Do you think they're going to sign me?"

"Yeah, they're going to sign you," Charles said. "They're going to make an offer."

"Are you serious? Are you sure? This isn't just a case of you *think* they're going to make an offer, is it?"

"I just talked to them," he said, laughing. "Yes!"

I was practically skipping across the street to the sushi restaurant where we were going to have lunch. Right before we sat down, Charles got a phone call and excused himself. When he came back, he was glowing. "I just got a phone call from Atlantic Records, and they are officially going to offer you a record deal."

Immediately I started crying. I squeezed Charles and Will so tight. *We did it! After all we'd been through.*

I needed to call my dad right away. I ran outside to the sidewalk, where there were people walking all over the place. Some of them were looking at me because I was crying and carrying on, but I didn't care, because I had the biggest news to tell my dad.

"Dad," I said, so excited to tell him the good news that I was tripping over the words. I stood there on the sidewalk, yelling into my phone, crying. People were staring at me. But I did not care. I had done it. We had done it. That was one of the happiest moments of my entire life, made all the sweeter by how low I had been brought a few weeks earlier.

Of course Dad was unbelievably proud and overjoyed for me. Next I called my mom. She was also ecstatic and soon crying. She later sent me a text that summed it all up:

Pinch yourself, Mama, because this is all happening. Enjoy the beginnings of a long successful career. The ride is about to begin. God will take you to great places. He has blessed you and found favor in you. All this is happening because of God's grace and mercy. I love you so much. I'm so happy for you.

Later that day, my parents went to our local H-E-B grocery store, and what do you know? My parents shopped there pretty much every day, and on this particular day, they happened to see a vinyl record by Bruno Mars on one of the shelves—when they'd never seen the store carry records before. Our favorite Atlantic artist as a family. If that's not a sign directly from Heaven, then I don't know what is. We all agreed that it seemed like the best sign.

Finally, all of my hard work—my blood, sweat, and tears—had paid off. I will forever be grateful for how that meeting changed my life. The lesson I learned is to never give up. As often happens, it's a lesson that I've had to learn more than once. You see, sometimes a no just means you have to approach something again in a new way. A no is not permission to give up. A no is a sign that it's time to make some changes and try again.

My advice to you, if you have dreams of your own, is to go for them. Don't be afraid. Life is too short. If you want to put yourself out there, do it. Not everyone will believe in you, but that's okay. If you want to write songs, write songs. If you want to put a cover out on YouTube, put it out there. If you secretly dream of starting your own business, do it. Try new things and don't be afraid to fail, because it will always lead to a new path. It might even lead you to a place you couldn't have dreamed of.

My record deal with Atlantic was really happening, and so many of the pieces of my new solo career were falling into place. I was happier than I'd ever been. My lifelong dream to get signed had actually happened. Now the real work began, and I couldn't wait to dig in.

SEVENTEEN

——

That Right Song

A few months had passed since I'd signed my deal with Atlantic, and I was in and out of the studio almost every day. My team and I were focused on building momentum for me as a solo artist, and that meant finding me an amazing debut single.

In August 2018, in the midst of my initial recording sessions as a signed solo artist, I hit the red carpet for the Teen Choice Awards. It was one of my first public appearances since our final group show, and where I announced my new label. I felt amazing, with a brand-new confidence, being on my own. And people immediately noticed the difference. This just reinforced my desire to keep working on myself and to stay healthy. Around this same time, I was approached by the producers of *Dancing with the Stars* about being a contestant on the next season of their show. They made it clear—they really wanted me. I'd watched with my mom since I was a little girl, and I was a huge fan. I'd experienced the joy of performing on the show several times with Fifth Harmony, and those were some of my favorite memories in the group.

It was very flattering to be asked, especially when the producers went so far as to personally call me several times to try to convince me. But the timing wasn't right. My solo music career was still in its infancy. I'd just signed with Atlantic, and I didn't have any new music out. I was still trying to find my first single. Because of all of those factors, I felt it just wasn't the right decision for me at that moment.

Plus, agreeing to do the show was a huge commitment, depending on how long I lasted as a contestant. It would have taken all of my available time, when I could have been working on new music or traveling to make appearances. Because the future was so unknown for me, I really needed to keep my schedule open, just in case. So I had an easy excuse for saying no.

I did need time to regroup. But the deeper truth was that I was really nervous about my dancing, especially on a show that was *all* about the dancing. I didn't want to embarrass myself. I'd already been made fun of, mercilessly, for my dancing when I was in Fifth Harmony. Online trolls would make videos highlighting what they saw as my bad dancing, and those videos would go viral, but not in a good way. Everybody made fun of me and it seemed that a lot of our fans thought I was the weakest dancer. That was a big wound I was still trying to heal and move past.

Charles and Will both felt the show would be a great thing for me to do that fall—to be introduced to a new audience on such a big and beloved platform, which would allow me to show the world the real me. Plus, I'd have a chance to work on my dancing and to get in even better shape. They both encouraged me to say yes. They had good points, but this was one of those instances when I felt this very confident *no* rise up within me. I trusted in my answer, no matter what anyone else said. The producers reached out a few more times to try to convince me, but I was quite sure about my decision.

In the late summer of 2018, I flew to London for my first solo performance in the UK. It was my first festival performance as a solo artist, since the group had ended. The country's main radio station was putting on the Fusion Festival in Liverpool, and I had been invited to take part. I was ecstatic to be traveling to London for this incredible moment in my new solo adventure. Everything about the trip was exciting—even packing my bags and being on the plane for hours. I was looking forward to what came next with so much anticipation and joy.

In the months leading up to the performance, we'd thought we had everything dialed in. I had booked the show in the spring, after I knew that Fifth Harmony would have finished up all of our commitments by that time. And my team and I had thought, no question, we'd have new music out in the world by September 2, the date of the Liverpool festival. But time had flown by, and before we knew it, and much to our surprise, we were getting ready for London, and I had not even one single to perform at the show.

However, we were excited about a feature that I'd recorded with these producers Kris Kross Amsterdam, who were from the Netherlands. It was called "Vámonos." Now, in a crazy turn of events, Messiah was on the song as well, after he'd already guested on my earlier song, "Vamos." Although the names of the songs sounded similar, they were not at all the same. When Charles first sent me "Vámonos," he acknowledged the similarities to the song I'd already recorded, but he decided to go in this direction because it had more of a high energy, reggaeton vibe. I truly loved both, but at the time, we decided to release "Vámonos." It was so upbeat, vivacious, and had this amazing island feel to it. It was also entirely in Spanish and had female empowerment lyrics. I loved all of these elements of this song.

Because Messiah was signed to Charles's label, Charles was easily able to bring him onboard. When we were done, I absolutely loved the record. And so I was excited that at least I had this song to debut live. But four days before the festival, Kris Kross Amsterdam's team informed us that we couldn't perform it after all. An earlier song of theirs was doing very well, and they didn't want to drop another new track yet. So they had decided to push the release date back. This was so disappointing. I'd been excited to meet them, because I hadn't been able to yet. And it was extremely important to perform new music in Liverpool, and with this little notice, I didn't have anything besides my old features and covers. I started to panic.

I was also worried about money. When they pulled out, it put me in a tight spot. The team for Kris Kross Amsterdam had planned to share some of the expenses, and now paying for the trip and the performance would fall completely on me. It was stressful. But once again I prayed hard, and I just gave it over to God.

Well, as God does so many times, He worked out all the details. Right before we were set to leave for London, the team for Kris Kross Amsterdam called and said that we could premiere the song there after all. They still weren't going to officially release it yet, but the guys agreed to perform it with me. I was so relieved! Just in time, I'd received a saving grace.

Will called the production team in London to let them know about the last-minute change to the set list, so the dancers could learn the specific choreography for the song. They already had so little time to prepare, we wanted to give them every possible minute to rehearse that we could. I was excited to have dancers and a whole production behind me for such a meaningful performance.

When I flew to London, it felt surreal to be there on my own merit and to be launching this new adventure. Will was with me as my day-to-day manager, and when we landed, we looked at each other and smiled. Will knew how much this moment meant. He had been with me when I was in London the first time with Fifth Harmony years ago, and now, after everything that had come to pass, I was there on my own as a solo artist. He has been with me through it all, and I'm eternally grateful I had someone special to share the impact of that moment with me.

My love for London had been immediate, as soon as I first landed there with Fifth Harmony. I love the culture. I love the people and their accent. They always seemed to me to be the coolest—so on-trend.

I love the restaurants. Most of all, I love being able to wake up and have a proper English breakfast, with scones, and a proper English breakfast tea (my favorite). I just love the whole vibe of London. I had always longed to return. It was a surreal feeling to be back, because I had so many memories from being there in the group, and now it was wild to be there on my own. Not only was I doing a solo performance, but I was doing it in a whole different country, on a whole different continent. I was ecstatic.

I arrived in London on a Friday, and I was set to perform in Liverpool on Sunday. I had two days to rehearse. It was nonstop. It was madness. I went to the hotel to quickly drop off my luggage and freshen up—I had ten minutes before I went straight into rehearsals. Drained by lack of sleep and jet lag, I was running on adrenaline, determined to give it my all, no matter how tired I was. I met with the choreographers, the creative team, and the dancers. Everyone was incredible. They showed me the routines they had created to go with my music, and seeing them, I teared up. I had flashbacks of my life before *The X Factor,* when I was struggling to get anyone to listen to my songs, performing at schools, singing my heart out to anyone who would listen. And then I thought about the *X Factor* audition and everything I had since done, digging deep to overcome such a rough start. Memories flooded me. I realized how, at each step along the way, I had grown professionally and personally, and I had learned so much. I was filled with gratitude for all that had brought me to this day.

I could see how hard this group of dancers and choreographers had worked to make me happy. My set list was my two features, "Perfect" and "Look at Us Now." Plus a cover I'd remade into a new song, "Cupid," and last was "Vámonos." They showed me the entire set, with all of the songs back-to-back. I was thrilled. But I had a lot to learn, quickly. And we had only a short time to make it all work. Somehow we did it. They were truly a dream team. If I could have told my twelve-year-old self that this time was coming for me someday, I would never have believed it.

It felt as if I had been preparing for that moment onstage in Liverpool my whole life, because of everything I'd been through to get me there. Listen, I know it may seem as though it's just one performance of many in my career, but it meant so much to me. I couldn't help but think of all of the struggles and all of the trials I'd gone through when I'd been trying to grow into who I am as an artist. And it was incredible to feel it all come together, just in time for my first solo performance, right there at that festival. I felt a powerful emotion that seemed to take on a life of its own. This was the beginning of a new life and a new career for me. The weight of it hit me all at once during our prep days in London, and it was truly beautiful.

We rehearsed hard. I didn't care how tired I was or how hard I had to work—I wanted the performance to be perfect. I wanted to do my best. For those two days, I rehearsed long hours with the entire production team to make it seamless.

The night before the show, I called my parents. It was nighttime in London, but daytime in San Antonio, because of the time difference. We had the best talk. I thanked my mom and dad for everything they had done for me. They had wanted to be there, but they couldn't because my mom had experienced some medical issues that prevented her from traveling. My dad had to be with her. I completely understood and wanted my mom to get better, and I wanted my dad to be with her.

"Mom and Dad, I'm going to go out there and show the world who I am as an artist," I said. "You always have seen me for who I am, even when I was a little girl. You sacrificed everything and you believed in me. I'm so grateful to you both."

They told me that they would always believe in me, and that they still saw everything that was special in me. My parents reminded me that I had worked hard for this, but God also had blessed me with my talent and with this opportunity, and He was blessing me with this moment. They told me they were proud of me and reminded me that all I had to do was go out there with my confidence in Him.

It was a wonderful, heartfelt conversation, and I went to bed feeling good. As I drifted off to sleep, I practiced the routine in my head, and I even dreamed about it during the night.

The next morning I was nervous, of course, but my excitement was stronger. I had to have my English breakfast and my English breakfast tea. I enjoyed every sip while taking the time to reflect, pray, and prepare for the long, important day ahead. We all piled into a big van together—Will, the local hair and makeup team I'd hired, and people from my label—to make the four-hour drive to Liverpool.

When we arrived at the venue, my team scattered to get ready for my performance, and I walked over and looked at the stage. It was big, and a great crowd was starting to build. Although I was used to doing a sound check before live performances, I didn't get one on this day, which was a little nerve-racking. But I knew I was as prepared as possible. As I went into hair and makeup, the time was winding down, and I was getting more and more nervous.

Finally, I was called to perform. It was showtime. By this point, I was super nervous. There was a lot riding on this set. I hoped I would do a great job. I hoped I wouldn't forget anything, especially because I'd had so little time to prepare. I hoped the audience would like me. I couldn't wait to see the reactions online from my fans because I would be showcasing a new Ally, and I hoped they would love the new me, too. I was excited, especially as I pulled my dancers and my team into a huddle so we could say a prayer together. This felt familiar and safe—I knew how to do this!

The intro music started playing, and it was time to go. When I was announced, a heavy scream rose out of the crowd. My heart was pounding in my chest. I said one final quick prayer to myself, and before I walked out, I took a deep breath. Only in the last few days had it really sunk in that I was stepping into my own identity as an artist. It was my time, and it felt liberating and really just phenomenal. The stage was outdoors, and as I took my place, I surveyed the beautiful scene.

I had twenty minutes to win the crowd over. I was still nervous, but I could feel the excitement of the crowd. As I began to talk to them and then to sing, they responded with cheers and applause— some of them were even singing back to me.

When it came time to premiere "Vámonos," I was ready. How would people react? Oh yeah, and one other crazy curve ball was that "Vámonos" had just leaked online. It wasn't due to be released yet, but somehow it got out. So that was another delightful wrench thrown at us during a hectic time. It actually ended up getting the fans very excited, so in a way, it turned out to be a good thing.

Neither the audience or my fans knew that I was performing "Vámonos" at the festival, but I brought Kris Kross Amsterdam out, and they made the introduction. It's a very fiery, sassy female empowerment song, all in Spanish. And then the crowd was getting to see a whole new Ally perform it. I think they were kind of shocked. I basically came at it like it was the performance of my life. I gave everything I had in that moment, and I also remembered to have fun. It was a blast, and I could feel that the audience was loving it. The energy onstage was electric. The crowd ended up being so kind and enthusiastic. I couldn't have been happier.

People had come from Scotland and Ireland and all over the UK to see me perform, and it meant so much. After the set, interviewers from several radio stations and even some artists came up to me and said things like:

"Whoa, that was amazing. I can't wait to see what the future holds for you."

"We can't wait until your music is released."

"We can really see an all-new Ally. You were fantastic up there."

Then we had a meet-and-greet, and I got to spend time with some fans, some of whom had even been waiting to meet me for years, and that was so much fun. One girl gave me a book that she had put together, including messages about why she loved me, messages from other fans, and photos of me. Her thoughtfulness meant so much to me.

The social media response was what I'd hoped for and more. One fan said: "Ally is here and did not come to play."

Yet another comment was: "Who is that girl? Wow, Ally set the stage on fire."

At that time, such positive feedback meant the world to me, because I had worked so hard to get there. I had been an underdog, and I always felt it. I had to fight for everything I got. Some people doubted me. Didn't believe in me. Thought that I couldn't dance, that I wouldn't have great music. But now look! I had sacrificed and powered through obstacles, and apparently it had paid off. It was incredibly rewarding. I was filled with hope and joy, and it made me want to keep going and to work even harder. I realized that I had held myself back when I was in Fifth Harmony. But I'd learned from that experience. Now I felt confident. A whole new Ally was inside of me, and I felt a promising feeling.

I ended up trending on Twitter, No. 2 in the world for that song and performance, and many media outlets were loving it as well. I was a happy girl. This was so much bigger than me.

Little did I know, I was about to hit some even bigger performance milestones. But first I desperately needed to find my debut single. Time was of the essence.

As soon as I got back to LA from the UK, Charles and Will and I met to discuss what we were going to do about finding me the perfect song. As much as I loved "Vámonos" and was proud of my part in it, it was just a feature. I needed to start defining my own sound with my own music. As great as I felt about how things were going, I did notice that whenever I did interviews I'd be asked: "Ally, all the other girls have their singles out. Where's yours?" And I couldn't help but see the articles in the media that said the same thing. I knew they weren't being mean—they were just curious. It was the same with the fans. In a way I did feel that I was behind.

"Oh, it's coming," I kept saying.

But really I had no idea when, because I hadn't found the song yet. So that was hard.

For months, I was in the studio every day—sometimes recording three songs a day. Charles worked hard to bring me together with so many different talented writers, from some of the biggest songwriters in the world—like Max Martin's team, Rihanna's team, and Cardi B's team—to some less prominent but still amazing songwriters. I worked with everybody.

Day after day, I would go in, love a song, and become so excited. But then I would listen to it and work on it more, and I'd have to admit that it wasn't my next single. Since this song was going to be the calling card to launch my solo career, it had to be perfect.

Then, in August of 2018, Charles introduced me to an outside A&R person from APG, a record label and publishing company under Atlantic, so we could meet and talk songs. He played several records, one of which was called "Lips Don't Lie." Within a few seconds of hearing it, I was hooked.

"Oh my gosh, I need this song," I said. "That's my song."

"Yeah, that's a really, really amazing track," the A&R guy said. "I'll set up a date and we'll record it."

When I played the song for Charles, he loved it just as much as I did. I couldn't wait to get into the studio and put my stamp on it, making it my own. But there kept being delays that prevented us from recording it. Finally the magic day came, and Will and I headed over to the APG recording studio for the session. The whole drive over, I was so excited.

"I love 'Lips Don't Lie' so much," I said. "I want it to be my first single. I can't believe I finally found my first single, after so many weeks and months of searching."

When the A&R guy approached our car, I rolled down the window and tried to look cheerful as I said, "Hi."

But I could tell something was wrong, just from looking at his face.

"Oh no, what happened?" I asked.

"Listen, I'm so sorry, but the songwriters and the producers won't let us record the song yet because it may go to another pop artist," he said. "I'm so sorry. We can't record it today."

There had already been so much waiting to find the right song, and then more waiting to find the right time to record it. And now guess what? Oh, it might go to another artist. You can imagine how frustrated and disappointed I was. I held it together until I got home, and then I just started to cry. I felt so defeated. *This is so challenging. Everything I do is so challenging. I'm already super behind in releasing something, and now this is happening. Why?*

I had no choice but to move on. For the next few months, I kept recording songs, because I had to find *the* record. But I knew in my heart that none of them were *the* song. Finally I couldn't pretend anymore. I was so down that I took refuge in my bed, and I cried into a pillow. I decided to called Charles and just be real with him. When he picked up, I was still crying.

"Charles, listen, to be honest, I'm getting so frustrated and discouraged," I said. "All I want to do is to be out there, performing. I want to have my music out. I want to show people who I am as an artist. I want people to know what my sound is like, what I have to offer. I just want to put something out into the world, finally."

"Hey, Ally," he said. "Listen, I know this is very frustrating. And I hear you. I know you're working day in, day out. I know you always have a positive attitude, you never complain. You always work, no matter what. And no matter with who, whether it's the best or the newest writers or producers, you're there with a smile. I get how frustrating it is, for the media and people out there, to be pressuring you. I know it's a lot. Trust me, I want the same thing for you, too, because I see your potential and what you can bring to this music world. But hey, take a breath. When the song is right, you'll know it, and we'll all know it. It's all about timing. It doesn't matter when it is—when you have that right song, everything will fall into place."

"Okay," I said, already feeling better. This was just the pep talk I'd needed.

"You've just got to be patient and trust the process. Know that I'm here and I only want the best for you," he continued. "I don't want you to put out any old song—a song that's not right. I truly value you as an artist. I believe that you are too good to just put out any song as your first single. You only get to make a first impression once. Trust me, it's all going to work out. We're going to find that song soon. I just know it. Keep your head up high."

That was just the dose of perspective I'd needed. Even though I was feeling pressure, I couldn't let that outside noise affect me as an artist or influence my path forward. Charles had reminded me to value myself enough not to rush this process for anybody, but to wait until I found the best song that I truly thought was my first single, even if that took weeks or months. Right then and there my inner restlessness and anxiety started to go away. From that moment, I gained a brand-new peaceful, optimistic spirit.

With all of the recording that I'd been doing, I'd amassed an amazing body of work. In fact, there was one song, "If You Want to Be Mine," that came very close to being my single. Yes, we all loved it. I trusted my team and my label, and they thought it was the one. They kept moving forward with the process, and it was set to come out in October or November 2018. At the same time, we couldn't quite nail it—we kept recording and recording, until we'd done literally ten versions. We were all frustrated by this point—Charles and Will wanted a song out almost as badly as I did—but Charles has amazing musical instincts, and he kept making us hit pause.

And then, because it was an interpolation, which meant we'd sampled a melody from an existing song as the basis for a new song, we couldn't get clearance from the original artist. That meant we couldn't release the song. Now I was really upset to hear that there was going to be yet another delay in getting out my first single. At the same time, I tried to focus on the words Charles had spoken to me.

Not long after that, I was filming for a press day for a company when Charles popped up out of nowhere. Sometimes he comes to my events, but not always, because he's very busy with meetings and managing so much. But he was so excited by whatever he wanted to talk to me about that it couldn't wait. He actually pulled me out of the shoot.

"Hey, so, I have something I want to play for you," he said.

This felt different, special, and I was already getting excited.

"It's called 'Low Key,' and I love it," he said. "A lot of big, heavy-hitting songwriters and producers are a part of it. I think the song is amazing. I want it to be your first single. That's how much I love it. I hope you love it as much. So I want to play it for you. Are you ready?"

"Yes," I said, my heart fluttering with anticipation.

We climbed into his car and he cued up the music for me. "I'm nervous," he said, laughing. "I hope you like it."

After I pressed play, immediately, within the first ten seconds, I fell in love. It was different from any song I'd heard, and it gave me a different feeling from any record I'd been sent. It had this Latin flair that reminded me of home and the music I'd grown up on. But it also had this cool, urban sound as well. When the chorus came, I felt it: *This is a big record, and not only that, it feels like me.* Also, the lyrics, "Low key, low key, you should really get to know me," could not have been more perfect, since it was my first solo single, and that's exactly what I wanted my fans and new listeners to do. I loved how it had the perfect double meaning.

"Wow, that is my first single," I said. "I love it, Charles. I'm so excited about it. Let's get it locked in, please."

Finally, after months and months of working so hard, and being in the studio every single day, and recording forty or fifty songs, I'd finally found my single. But as with everything else, challenges awaited me. When Charles tried to secure the song for me, the producers said they loved me, but they wanted to see how I sounded before they agreed to release it. The song had originally been written with a male artist in mind. They thought it was a big record, and it almost did go to a male artist.

So I prayed: "Lord, help me to secure this song and sound amazing. I pray that it's mine." There was so much at stake. I was determined to kill the song and make it my own, so that everyone who heard it knew: *This is Ally.* Throughout the whole recording process, we were nervous that we wouldn't be able to secure the song. And because it had been written to be sung by a male artist, I had to raise it by two keys. But when the producers heard my version, they ended up loving it, and so we secured it. I'd earned it—that was the best feeling.

But we still had to get the label's approval before we could move forward. Charles was convinced the song could go to the top of the charts. So he flew to New York to meet with the Atlantic heads, Craig Kallman and Julie Greenwald, hoping for the green light to make it my first single and secure a budget for marketing, promotion, and the music video. For the next week, my family and I prayed every single day for the outcome of that meeting to go my way.

When Charles called me, I could barely stand the suspense. Well, not only did they love it, but they believed in it as much as we did. Julie's exact words were: "'I wanted you to get a home run. And that is a home-run record that we're looking for. Let's go."

Finally, after everything that I'd been through to get here, and all the obstacles and roadblocks, we had my first single. Now we were going to make it even better. Craig from Atlantic is a genius when it comes to music. He'd worked on Cardi B's "I Like It Like That" record, which was the biggest song in the world that year and happened to be my favorite. And now he wanted to help me on "Low Key."

Craig flew to LA to go into the studio with me. He wanted to help me improve a few elements of "Low Key" that he thought could be even better. He was a big deal. But I knew that to be working with him meant that I was definitely doing something right. He pushed me, but he was also so gracious and encouraging, every step of the way. In the end, he brought the best out of me and got the record to exactly where it needed to be. It was a *long* process, but I didn't give up; neither did Charles or Will or Craig. We kept finessing that song until it was as perfect as could be.

I was so excited, I wanted the whole world to hear my new song *immediately*. But of course the music is only the first step—there's a whole process to launching a single. My label got to work laying the groundwork. In the meantime, it felt like I was conquering smaller challenges nearly every week. In early November, I was asked to perform "Vámonos" at the ALMA Awards, my first solo performance on a TV awards show. It was also a huge honor to be part of a ceremony honoring other Latin artists, including actors, actresses, and entertainers in our community.

Only, I had just two days to rehearse. And I was already nervous going into rehearsals. We'd been looking for the perfect choreographer, and Charles had a relationship with Aníbal Marrero, who had worked with Pitbull and also Shakira, doing the choreography for "Hips Don't Lie." So obviously I was very excited to be working with him. Of course, I hoped that he would be impressed by me and think that I could dance, especially because I was still healing from the old wounds caused by the comments I'd received about my dancing in Fifth Harmony.

But as soon as we met, both he and his assistant choreographer, Susie, were so warm and vivacious that I immediately felt at ease, and he actually went on to become my creative director and main choreographer to this day. He immediately felt like family and understood me as an artist. He saw something special in me and believed in my talent. We got straight to work. It was so much fun. I ended up picking up the dance moves really quickly, and I really did impress everybody. The whole vibe of the room was amazing and fun, and it was really awesome to have the six dancers and team with me, and to be preparing for my first awards show.

The next day, we did camera blocking, and I had to work with a new unconventional stage. Plus, I had to remember all of the choreography and to sing, so it definitely put me to work, but I was excited. Charles was there to watch.

"How was that?" I asked him.

"Honestly, I'd give you a seven out of a ten," he said, with a smile.

I took that to heart, and as hard as I'd already worked, I was determined to do even better. I really did appreciate his feedback, which pushed me to go further. That night, I rehearsed more, alone in my apartment. When I showed up to the show the next day for the final camera blocking, I dug in and had this deep focus. After rehearsals, I started to get ready. What made me even more nervous was the fact that my wardrobe didn't come together until the absolute last minute—it's crazy what we artists go through. But I wouldn't have it any other way, because it makes the business and the payoff that much more exciting. Finally, as always, it came together last minute, and I was ready. The show's host, actor Wilmer Valderrama from *That '70s Show*, had been so wonderful and sweet and encouraging about my solo career when we'd met in rehearsal, and he gave me a beautiful intro: "I love this girl. I'm so excited for your next chapter, Ally. Ally Brooke! Let's go 'Vámonos.'" Then I went out there and released the fire.

After we got offstage, we all gathered together for a big hug—the dancers, Aníbal, Susie, Charles, Will, and me—and we were all filled up by this electrifying energy. We all felt that we had really given it our all, and it was such a spectacular feeling. This remains one of my favorite performances I've ever done. You can see me embracing who I am, coming into my own for my first solo TV performance. I have this confidence that roars. You can see it in my face—just how much fun I was having. It was the beginning of me finally showing the world what I could do.

When I saw Charles afterward, he was beaming at me. "Ten out of ten!" he said, giving me a huge hug. "That was amazing. I'm so proud of you. Wow, I don't even know what to say because I'm that proud and that blown away."

After the show, Wilmer also tweeted the most positive message, which meant so much to me: "Couldn't be more proud to see you win, you deserve it all Ally . . . ilysm twice! Blessed to have met you then, and thrilled to see you be your dream! Un abrazo!"

All of this positivity was fueling me and giving me more confidence for my first solo single, which was still my biggest dream of all. I also had the honor of performing the Christmas song I'd recently recorded—a cover of Wham!'s "Last Christmas"—at the historic Macy's Thanksgiving Day parade! Fifth Harmony had performed in the parade during our first year, back in 2013. Ever since then, it had been a bucket list item to do it solo. When I received the invite to grace the 2018 parade, I was giddy like a little kid. Fun fact: When I was on my float, I literally almost froze. It was biting cold, and I had worn this gorgeous, custom, white snow-princess dress, with an elegant white faux fur coat and matching earmuffs. But I hadn't layered enough. Every moment I was on that float, I soaked it all up, with wide eyes and infinite joy. When I was done performing, though, my body was shaking uncontrollably from being so cold. But I posted a funny video online about how "frozen" I was, which ended up going viral. Cardi B commented on my Instagram, saying: "I saw your performance at the jet airport, and I said I know she cold as hell. You did amazing tho." My near-freezing experience was totally worth it! Plus, soon enough, I finally returned to normal and celebrated with Dad. It was magical.

EIGHTEEN

Dada

It was December 2018, and I was gearing up to prepare for the release of my first single, "Low Key." Things had finally started coming together. Then I got a call that changed my life.

"Mama," my mom said. "I need to tell you something. Your other grandpa, my dad, is very sick. I know you are working so hard out there. I am so sorry to have to tell you this."

I was heartbroken. My mom had not been close to him, for reasons she doesn't like to talk about. But the times I saw him at family gatherings, I always felt respect and love for him. He had a strong masculine presence, always had a smile for everyone, and always shared with me how much he loved my voice.

I couldn't believe that these could be his final days, and I was shattered that I wasn't there at home. Immediately I wanted nothing more than to be with my family, but I had to be in LA to prepare for everything we were setting up for "Low Key." My mom and aunts reassured me that they wanted me to stay in LA and finish up all that I was working on.

"We are all at the hospital, visiting him, and he wants to talk to you," my mom said.

I took that in, and by the time he came to the phone, I had tears in my eyes.

"Mija, oh, mija, I love you so much," he said, crying like I've never heard before. "You are my granddaughter. I have always loved you."

I kneeled beside my bed and broke down. "I love you too with all of my heart, Grandpa," I said. "My Dada. I wish I could be there to hug you." Dada is what our family called him.

My mom then told me that the doctors had to come in and check on him. In that very moment, we reconciled with Dada. It was a day that changed who I was. To hear my mom be with her dad, to have his love surround her and her love surround him, it was beautiful.

That night, I thanked God for answering a lifelong prayer I'd had that my mom would reconcile with her dad. Then I fell asleep, crying my eyes out, so agonized that I could not be there. I prayed for God to please give him strength to survive until I got home for Christmas.

It was excruciating, balancing my grief with the joys of "Low Key." The day after I'd talked to my grandpa on the phone was the morning I met with Craig in the studio to work on my single. I'd tried to be professional and focused, but of course I was struggling internally and dealing with a great weight. By the almighty strength of God, I was able to savor the studio time with Craig, as well as the preparation for the filming of the "Low Key" video.

We'd decided to push hard and try to do the shoot before the holidays. We met with my amazing director, Mike Ho, a few weeks before our shoot to start planning. We wanted something that was striking, to introduce me to the world as a solo artist. First, we had to settle on one of our five possible concepts, called treatments. We wanted one that really told a story. I'd always been inspired by film, and therefore, I wanted my video be like a mini-film. I was inspired by a dance sequence from *A Chorus Line*, as well as an old Hollywood dance between a woman and a man. Once we had our story, we only had five days to prepare. Every aspect came down to the wire—from the treatment we finally chose, which we kept revising until the day of shooting, to the dancer I was filming with, who had to be replaced at the last minute, to the dance break, which I had two days to learn and rehearse. In the end, we were able to cram in five different dance sequences in just forty-eight hours. I decided to take a risk with the wardrobe I was going to wear, which I was still deciding on until the night before the shoot, going through the racks of wardrobe we had at the ready. The lyrics to "Low Key" say "really get to know me," so I wanted to show who I was as an artist through bold, killer outfits. No more second-guessing myself or my body. No more hiding. I was finally proud of who I was, and I was going to show that to the world. I was shedding the old me and transforming into the artist I'd always wanted to become. Yes, this was my chance for people to really get to know me.

In the final days before we were set to shoot the music video, we were still brainstorming who the perfect feature for the song might be. I was on a group text with Charles and Will when Charles wrote: "Hey, Craig thinks he can get Tyga." Immediately I knew that would be incredible. He's amazing, and I especially loved his song, "Taste," which I'd been listening to a lot those past few months. I was so excited.

I sent a giant YES and prayed that it would come to pass. The next day, Charles sent me Tyga's verse for "Low Key," and I was hooked. I listened to it over and over again, about twenty times, in my kitchen. I couldn't believe it. He was huge. And he'd killed it. His verse was perfect. Then once Tyga was confirmed, we asked if he could be in my music video. We figured it was a long shot, because the shoot was in less than a week, but amazingly enough, he ended up being able to do it. All of the stars were aligning perfectly.

We'd actually done a song with Tyga, "Like Mariah," when I was in Fifth Harmony, and it had been great. That song was a fan favorite. But now it was a different story, having him on my own song. In 2018, he basically became the biggest rapper of that year, with hit songs out on the radio and all over the world. To have him feature on my first single was incredible. I could hardly believe it.

On December 19 it was time to shoot my very first music video since I'd signed to a major label. It was a sweet victory to see this day, after so many years of my parents and I chasing my music dreams. I was sure to take it all in. My dad flew in to be there for my special day.

"Wow, Mama, I can't tell you how happy I am to see this day," Dad said, tears in his eyes. "You're finally recording your very first music video on your own. I'm so proud of you, Mama."

The set was at the Los Angeles theater where Mariah Carey had filmed her music video "Heartbreaker." It was also used as a location for many films. The theater was majestic, with glamour dating back to the 1930s, including a glass-ceilinged ballroom, grand central staircase, crystal fountain, and multiple stunning chandeliers.

We were hurrying to film everything in a matter of hours. I was anxious because this would be my first time, dancing on my own in a video, and I was still healing my scars from the teasing I'd previously received. I'd worked tirelessly with my choreographer, but I hadn't had a lot of rehearsal time overall. I worried that I might not be able to remember all of the sequences. And now there was no one but me. It was my time to bring it. This would mean the difference between confirming that the fans had been right that I couldn't dance. Or this could finally destroy every preconceived notion and show them all I could do. I actually messed up a few times in the first takes, because I was getting a little bit in my head. But then it was like a light switch flicking. I felt this energy pour out of me that you can see in the video. Everyone on that set was blown away. I was so proud.

My outfit for my main dance sequence was originally supposed to be a black bodysuit with high-waisted black shorts and black thigh-high boots that I had fallen in love with. However, that was getting lost against the background. My stylist and I had less than seven minutes to tear through all of the possibilities and come up with the outfit I ended up wearing, which was a sparkling nude and crystallized bodysuit with high-waisted leather shorts and crystallized, bedazzled boots. Another onset wardrobe change was that the gold bodysuit I wore was actually supposed to be a green bedazzled crop top and skirt that we'd made into a dress. But since I was lying on the floor in that shot, it wasn't going to work. Again, we had five minutes to change the look and came up with the bodysuit, which I ended up loving. It looked incredible onscreen.

After doing multiple hairstyle and wardrobe changes in no time flat, I had less than ten minutes to shoot the final scene. We'd added it on the fly, as the director had done with several shots added the morning of the shoot, such as the floor shot and the final shot. As quickly as possible, I had to select my dress, change, and redo my hair. I couldn't make it all the way back to my greenroom, because we had no time, so I ran into a nearby room. The light wasn't working, so I had to change with my stylist, by the light of a cell phone flashlight. Then my regular hair stylist Preston quickly did my hair. He's been with me since my solo career started, and he's so close to me, he feels like family. He is the most hilarious person ever and has the biggest personality. I adore him. In the end, we pulled it off. I credit this to my amazing team that day, everyone from the director and choreographer, to the dancers and stylists. Everyone brought it. The energy on that set was euphoric— pure bliss. I'd gotten to record the music video of my dreams, and I was very proud.

Still, family and my grandpa were always in my thoughts. Each passing day I prayed with all of my might. On December 21, I flew to my beloved hometown. After I landed, I waited for my dad to pick me up. When I saw him, I gave him a big hug. Nothing meant more to me than family, especially at this time. As soon as I got in the car, I called my mom. She was distraught.

"Mom, mom! What's wrong?"

"Your aunt just called and told me he might not make it until you get there!"

I started sobbing. "Dad, we have to hurry, please!"

We raced to pick up my mom, and then to drive over to my aunt's house. I prayed every second of that drive, crying out, pleading with

God to please let me have one moment with my grandpa before he passed. That time would be invaluable; it would mean the world to me.

"Ally, we just need to prepare you," my dad said softly. "Your grandpa is really bad, and he's pretty unrecognizable. He's just not the same."

"What do you mean?" My heart was pounding.

"We just want to warn you so you aren't shocked when we get there."

I spoke to my aunt for some comfort over the phone, and she told me the same thing.

"Oh, Mama, but don't you worry, you still talk to him like normal and tell him everything you want to tell him from your heart," she said. "All he wants is to see you, and to have one last Christmas with his family."

None of us could hold back our tears.

Dad pulled up to my aunt's house, and we jumped out and hurried to the door. I had prepared myself for the worst, but as we walked in, we couldn't believe what we saw. Grandpa wasn't in his bed. He was standing, and not just standing—he was walking with the help of a walker. We were shocked by this amazing turn of events.

"Grandpa!" I shouted, going straight to him.

"Mija," he said. He reached out to squeeze me.

I couldn't believe what my eyes were seeing. It was a miracle. My grandpa was walking, and he didn't look anything like what I'd been warned to prepare myself for.

My aunt explained that he'd suddenly improved and had wanted to get out of bed. Her face showed just how miraculous this was. I'd been so worried that I wouldn't make it to his bedside in time, and here my grandpa seemed to have rallied and might be getting better.

We had an amazing day with him as a family. I felt God so strongly there with us. I watched as my mom talked with her father. It was evident there was peace between them after so many years. Grandpa told her how much he loved her. We were all tearful. That right there was one of the most beautiful moments we've had as a family. I just know there were angels in that room. There was God in that room. It was a miracle.

Seeing this moment of deep forgiveness and love changed my perspective on life and on God. It truly expanded my sense of what is possible through Jesus. That Dada had rallied when everyone thought he was about to die. But even more so, getting to see him telling my mom things that were so meaningful to her—I don't know if I can find the words to fully describe it. Words from God came to Grandpa's lips, words of affirmation, words that were so healing to my mom and to all of us. I've never seen so much love radiating from someone, as it did from Grandpa on that day. He had this childlike wonder in his eyes.

Before we left, my mom and grandpa embraced, and she kissed his cheek. Knowing how many decades of emotion were dissolving, I felt sure that I was witnessing the true meaning of Christmas right before my eyes—new life through Jesus, grace, mercy, love, wonder, and miracles.

In the car, we all tried to absorb what had just happened.

"Ally, he was not like this a few days ago," Mom said. "He was bedridden. He couldn't talk very much, couldn't move. He couldn't open his eyes. Now he's walking and talking. This is such a miracle! Thank You, Jesus."

The next day, we went back to my aunt's house. Grandpa announced that he was going to fight to live. He also had a special request. "I want some of Jerry's pies for Christmas," he said.

We all laughed. It was true that my dad, Jerry, makes amazing pies, and it just touched our hearts that this was what Grandpa wanted for Christmas.

I was enjoying getting to know my grandpa in this beautiful way. It was like his real self was able to come out. I could see that even though he was sick, he was also a very strong man full of overflowing love. He now had joy in his heart, and he had discovered an immense love for Jesus, even more than he'd had before.

"God loves you," he said. "God loves you so much. You don't even know."

It was a remarkable turn of events, and we thanked God so much for this extra time with Grandpa. I suddenly felt hopeful that he could beat his infection and return to full health. I imagined getting to spend more time with him, seeing my mom and her dad create new memories together.

Our plan was to return to my aunt's house on Christmas Day, when my mom's side of the family would all be together. We wanted to be with Grandpa, to celebrate a wonderful Christmas with him and create a beautiful memory for all of us.

On Christmas Eve, I was at our house with my brother, and he had just proposed to his girlfriend! It was a truly special night. As usual, my dad had gone all out, decorating the outside of our house, and my mom had filled the inside with Christmas magic. But we couldn't fully enjoy the season, as our thoughts kept going to Grandpa and his health. At the same time, we were grateful for what God was bringing to pass in our family—reconciliation, healing, and peace. During this time, our extended family on my mom's side had become much closer. My parents, brother, and I have always been close, but this reminded us further that family does come first.

I had been watching *It's a Wonderful Life* and wrapping Christmas presents, when all of a sudden, my dad received a call from my aunt. Grandpa wasn't doing well at all. My mom asked if we should make the trip over right away, but my aunt said to wait until the next day, as we'd planned.

That night, we stayed up until midnight, helping my dad bake those pies for my dear grandpa, accepting that this might be our last Christmas with him. We had a beautiful Christmas morning together at my parents' house. Then we drove back to my aunt's house with the pies. All the family was there, just like Grandpa had wished. He wasn't up and in his walker this time, though. My aunt had unfortunately been right. He wasn't doing well. He'd been given a lot of medicine, so he mainly just slept. But even though he was very weak, he knew we were all there, surrounding him with so much love.

The whole family tried to make the holiday special. Grandpa had his family together on Christmas, just as he'd hoped. But at the same time, we were heartbroken that he had taken such a quick turn for the worse. During this night, his favorite movie, *The Godfather,* was playing in the background. I saw a scene of a baby being baptized, and as I turned to my grandpa, I saw that his life would soon be drawing to an end. That signified so much.

I sat on the edge of his bed and sang to him one last time as sweetly as I could.

> *"Silent night. Holy night.*
> *All is calm, all is bright,*
> *Round yon virgin mother and child.*
> *Holy infant so tender and mild,*
> *Sleep in heavenly peace.*
> *Sleep in heavenly peace."*

"I love you, Grandpa," I said, with tears streaming down my face. I felt him squeeze my hand. I leaned down to give him a kiss and prayed over him. We were all crying by this time.

Grandpa wasn't really eating or drinking at this point, but later that night, we were able to feed him a small taste of my dad's pie. Our family gathered around his bed. We all cried over him as a family, we prayed, and we played him his favorite songs. Everything from the theme song from *Rocky* to "My Way" by Elvis Presley. We shared so much with him as a family that Christmas.

Two days later, on December 27, my grandpa went to be with Jesus. Christmas Day was the last day that I saw him alive. From my mom's first phone call about his decline to his passing was only two weeks. It had all happened so fast. It felt overwhelming to go from not having him in my life, to having a change in my heart and all of our hearts as a family, to experiencing that reconciliation of peace, to losing him immediately.

My mom was devastated. She wanted that time with her father that she'd never had. At the same time, we were so thankful for what God had brought to pass in Grandpa's heart, and in all of our hearts and lives. Christmas will never be the same again. I know now the true meaning of Christmas, which I will carry with me forever. I will never ever forget that day, as long as I shall live. I will always be grateful that we had that precious time with him.

His funeral was in the first week of January. We had such sorrow in our hearts. It was such a hard process, welcoming a new year, which my parents and I did quietly, and being excited and hopeful about all that was on the horizon for me, while also grieving. Thankfully, we were able to feel peace that Grandpa was free of pain and was in the arms of Jesus now. That's the most beautiful thought in the world. And one day, we will be together again. *I will always love you and keep you in my heart, Dada.*

Of course, as always happens when you're grieving, it took me several weeks to get back to myself. I had to be back in LA the day after Grandpa's funeral. I was still processing what had happened. It was so painful, all I wanted to do was be home. I wished with all my heart that I'd had more time with him. But I was grateful for the time I did have. This was a deeply personal experience, not just for me, but also for my mom and her father, that forever changed us all.

I decided to share it with all of you, to hopefully encourage you to believe more deeply in God's grace, his reconciliation, and his miracles. I have seen them with my own eyes. I can't describe it; it goes beyond words. But it's strengthened my faith even more. It has changed my heart, and I hope somehow this story can change yours, too.

NINETEEN

"Low Key"

As I looked ahead to the new year, I paused to reflect on how far I'd come. Standing in my apartment in Hollywood, I took a deep breath and stared up at the moon, wishing, dreaming, and wondering what was on the horizon for me. It had been a difficult holiday, and I was still grieving, but I was also still ready to look forward, with hope and joy, to all of the amazing music I would make on my own. At this point in my career, this was the biggest moment in my life: the release of my debut single, "Low Key," which we'd pushed from earlier in the month to January 31, 2019.

I knew my grandpa would have wanted me to not only live my life, but also to continue to chase my dreams. He would smile when he talked to me about my music. He asked me how I felt having so many fans all over the world. He was indescribably proud of me. And so that was fuel to make me work even harder and give even more than I ever had before. It's my life's mission to live in his honor.

Although I still had grief in my heart, it felt like things were finally turning around for me. I was invited to perform at the international sales meeting for Warner Music (which Atlantic is under the umbrella of). It was amazing to be flown first-class to Stockholm,

Sweden, where the label showcase was. I quickly put together a team of dancers and rehearsed for this incredible chance to show the label's offices around the world, from Brazil and Mexico to Australia and Japan, just what I could do. I was a little nervous that one of my songs might leak, especially "Low Key," which we planned to drop with a big roll-out, but the show couldn't have gone better. The room was very high-energy and everyone was super excited about my performance and how well I'd done up there on my own. It felt incredible to hear that, literally, the whole world was behind my release and ready to help me succeed. There was genuine enthusiasm about my artistry; it was amazing to feel that support, within my label, all around the globe. I couldn't believe it. I was flying high and incredibly excited about the future. Of course, there is never any guarantee that new music will hit. But getting all of that positive feedback at that crucial moment—and with genuine enthusiasm from industry insiders who'd seen so many artists come and go—was just the boost of confidence I needed right then.

It had felt like it had taken forever, but suddenly, it was January 30—the night before my big release. I recorded a special message for my fans, telling them how excited I was to have new music for them, and how much it meant to me to have my baby coming out finally, after they'd loyally been waiting for more than half a year. I knew they had high hopes for my first single, just as I did, and I was so grateful for their continued support.

That night I looked out the window of the hotel where I was staying in New York City. It was cold and quiet and peaceful, and I prayed: "Please, God, let people see me, finally, through my first single. And let them love it. Please. And especially the music video. Please let people receive it in the way it's meant to be received. Let people see my journey, my evolution, how far I've come. Let them see a new Ally." And then, I gave it to God.

The next morning, just before eight A.M., when my single and video would actually be released online, the energy in my hotel room was way up. Everyone was there—my dad, Will, and my whole team, including my publicist and my hair and makeup artists. It had been a long time since I'd seen my dad that nervous, but I also saw him more excited than ever. We gathered together, prayed, and with the biggest butterflies in my stomach, we watched the YouTube premiere countdown begin. It was all actually happening!

10, 9, 8, 7, 6, 5, 4, 3, 2, 1!

"Low Key" met the world. All of the hard work had paid off, and now it was time to see what everyone thought. But truly, just the act of releasing something I was so proud of was already a sweet success.

It was amazing to release something I was so proud of. My dad and I had both read the online comments and we were both in awe of the unbelievably positive responses. My dad teared up when he read a comment from a fan that basically said: Wow, this was the Ally that was made fun of. This is the Ally that people doubted. And now look at her, she just proved everyone wrong. The press response was equally glowing. I did interviews with everyone from *Harper's Bazaar* to *People,* where I was quoted as saying, "For so long I was in this box and now I'm out of it. I'm able to be who I want to be." I was so proud when I read praise like, "Brooke's vocal chops were never in question, but with 'Low Key' she's making a statement . . . 'You should really get to know me,' she sings on repeat and, well, that seems like a fair request for a star carving out new space for herself as she pursues her solo career," from *Time,* and "With a catchy chorus, an eye-catching video, and Tyga's added star power, Brooke has everything she needs for 'Low Key' to be a hit," from MTV.

It was so exciting to run all over New York City, filming the whole thing and doing press everywhere, from MTV to *Entertainment Tonight.* My video was played on one of those giant screens in Times Square, where there was also a huge digital Spotify billboard, spreading the word about "Low Key." Of course I was overcome with emotion, just seeing that major proof of my accomplishment. And then that night we had a party for my fans. The head of my label, Julie Greenwald, even stopped by to support me. The best part was that, as soon as they saw the video, my fans' enthusiasm went through the roof. They were, screaming, crying, joyously welcoming a whole new Ally, and they were praising every aspect of the video, including my dancing, which meant so much to me. It felt so incredible to celebrate this moment with as many fans as possible at my meet-and-greet at my party, which even had a photo booth. Their response was beyond anything that I could have hoped and prayed for.

And it was all so much more special because my dad was with me, and I felt my grandpa with me, too. I could only think what this moment would have been like if my grandpa had been there, but I saw signs of him that day and felt him around me. And I knew that he was so infinitely proud, watching from above.

Right there, my solo career was launched! "Low Key" ended up reaching the Top 20 of the Pop Radio Billboard Chart. Almost everywhere I went, I heard my song on the radio. I was excited that I'd be doing my first solo promo radio tour all across the United States, including my hometown of San Antonio, where I said thank you with a free concert for my local fans. I was scheduled to go to Corpus Christi, Texas, during my promo run. It has a special place in my heart because that is where Selena lived. I'd also grown up with my parents taking us to the beach there, so it basically felt like a second home.

One day, I got a call from my record label rep, who was going to be taking me around Texas to promote my record, from Dallas to San Antonio to Austin to Houston.

"Ally, oh my goodness, are you ready to hear this? Are you sitting down?"

"Yes!" I said, holding my breath. I was super curious.

"Suzette Quintanilla heard that you were coming into town and wants to meet you."

I screamed. I could not believe it. I didn't even know that she knew of me, and learning that she did was one of the most amazing feelings. She, of course, had had such a tremendous impact on my entire life. If it weren't for her family—for her sister, Selena, and for her—and all of them chasing their dreams, I wouldn't have been inspired to chase mine. I was in awe.

Of course I told my parents right away. They were amazed. They remembered so clearly how I watched her movie so many times, and how I would sing and dance to her music. "Mama, I can't believe that she wants to meet you," my mom said. "What an honor. Wow."

I couldn't stop thinking about my trip to Corpus Christi. I would finally meet Suzette. It really did feel like my whole life had led up to this moment.

The plan was to drive to Corpus from San Antonio. So I got my hair and makeup done by my local San Antonio makeup artist and my regular hair stylist Preston.

"Preston, I have to do a Selena-inspired hairstyle!" I said.

He did a beautiful job with my hair. It was exactly what I had envisioned. Then I had my makeup done. I had already picked out the perfect outfit. I wanted to look perfect for them.

Suzette wanted to take me on a tour of the Selena Museum, which I had never been to before. I'd always wanted to go to the Selena museum, but I'd never gotten a chance to visit. There was no better way to see it than being given the tour by Selena's own sister.

I rode to Corpus with my dad, Will, Preston, and my Atlantic radio rep. During the car ride, I was listening to every single Selena song and watching almost every single interview she'd done, plus as many music videos and live performances by her as I could find on YouTube. For as long as I could remember, I'd watched Selena videos almost every single day. I'm not exaggerating. I just love Selena with all of my heart, and I always have. It had been a lifelong dream for me to meet her family, and now it was happening. It really felt like it wasn't real, like it was an out-of-body experience.

Finally we pulled up to the Selena Museum. I said a prayer, along with my dad, and we walked up. I met Suzette in her office inside the museum. She was more beautiful in person than she'd even been on the interview of her I'd watched earlier that day. And she was so down-to-earth, fun, inviting, and welcoming.

"Well, I know how much you love my sister," she said. "And I want to thank you for always trying to honor her whenever you can. It really means the world to me. Congratulations on all your success. Girl, we're rooting for you. We see everything, and we're so proud of you."

I was blown away that she said that. What an unbelievable honor.

As promised, Suzette took us on the tour of the museum. While we were walking around, Mr. Quintanilla walked in, and I literally got goose bumps because that was Selena's father. He was wearing his signature glasses and hairdo, just like in the movie about Selena. He looked unbelievably young, and exactly like I'd imagined he would. My dad actually started tearing up, as soon as he saw him walking toward us with his cane, because my dad couldn't believe that we were meeting someone who meant so much to us, to our family. We were meeting a legend, a great man who had changed many, many lives.

It was just a beautiful moment. We ended up staying there for hours, talking about almost everything—my journey as an artist, and of course, how much Selena meant to me. I was able to ask them questions about some of their favorite memories, and they told me the stories behind some of the different outfits she'd worn and the songs she'd sung. They showed me never-before-seen videos. The experience was incredibly meaningful to me because so many strands of my life journey just intertwined in that moment, especially since my dad was there with me.

They showed me the studio where Selena actually recorded "Dreaming of You" and some of her final songs. As soon as I walked into that recording studio, I got goose bumps all over my body. To be in the same room where Selena recorded her last songs was overwhelming. I took a moment to savor the weight of what this meant. I had tears in my eyes. It was so special and unforgettable.

The beauty of meeting them was that they're so down-to-earth. They made everyone in our group feel welcome, like part of their family.

Soon Mr. Quintanilla had to go back to recording, because he was working on music. He never stops, and it was just so inspiring and moving. Soon it was time for me to go because I had other commitments that day. I didn't want to leave. I would have stayed there the whole day if I could have, but I had to get back on the road. Before we left, Suzette had a final message of encouragement for me.

"We're here, rooting for you," she said. "We're behind you, Ally, and anything you need, you please let me know. We love you."

That was one of the most amazing days of my life. Although we had never met it felt like I'd known them my whole life. They made us feel so comfortable. And I am forever grateful that my dad was there to experience it with me. A few months later, I performed for a radio station in Corpus, and Suzette came to see me sing. I was honored that she would take time out of her day to see me perform.

I'd always honored Selena when I could in Fifth Harmony, and since being solo, I've made sure to include a special tribute to her in my set. I had a Selena medley prepared and realized that Suzette would see it. *Oh my gosh, I'm going to perform Selena in front of her sister, Suzette,* I thought. *That's crazy. I pray that I can do her justice and make her proud.*

After the show, Suzette gave me a compliment that was literally priceless. "Ally, I don't ever say this, but you reminded me of my sister up there," she said.

"Suzette, oh my gosh, that is an honor," I said. "I don't know what to say. That is just—wow. Thank you. You don't know what that means to me."

"You know, Ally, you're so bubbly and cute and fun in person," she said. "But on that stage, you become a different person, just like my sister."

That comment will never leave me. Even now, I don't know how to even put into words how much her words meant to me.

Nothing could possibly top that experience, but everything felt like it was finally coming together. My next single, after the battle to secure it, was "Lips Don't Lie," which now included a feature by A Boogie wit da Hoodie, and dropped in late May. That also got a lot of radio play and went to No. 38 for Pop Radio on Billboard.

Of course, even when things were in full swing, I was learning that the entertainment industry requires a lot of flexibility. In this case, we'd recorded a simple video that was supposed to be the lyric video. At the last minute, the label decided to make it my official video for my single, as they didn't want to delay its release in order to take the time to shoot the more elaborate concept I'd had planned. My vision for my second video didn't come to life, but as I was learning, it was best to roll with whatever came my way.

However, at a time when I was busier than ever, my family was still trying to find its footing after the sudden loss of my Dada. And then that spring, while I was preparing for my first solo European promo tour, with dates scheduled in London, Paris, Milan, Berlin, and Brussels, my family was struck by another blow, while we were still grieving Dada. My dad was visiting me in LA without my mom, who couldn't come. My dad is usually so upbeat and full of joy, he's basically a big kid. Everybody loves my dad, because of his big heart. But he wasn't acting like Dad. And he tried to hide it, but I could tell that something was bothering him. We were walking out of a restaurant when I brought it up.

"Dad, is there something you need to tell me?" I asked.

"No, Mama, we're fine," he said. "We're fine."

"Dad, I know something's wrong with you, and you're my dad," I said. "And listen, I know that you want to protect me, you and Mom. You have the biggest hearts in the world, and I know you just want to protect your daughter, especially while I try to pursue my dreams. You don't want anything to take my focus away from that, but family is first, and family is everything. And now I'm an adult and I have to be able to handle life, the good and bad. I have to be strong for you guys. I don't want you all to ever go through anything alone. I know something's wrong, please tell me."

Finally, with tears in his eyes, my dad told me that my uncle Rene had cancer. Uncle Rene is married to my mom's sister, Diane, whom we all called Aunta Nana. We were very close. They'd never had children of their own, but they had a way of taking care of and being there for all of the kids in the family. She was the kind of big-hearted person who you wanted to protect from ever having anything bad happen to her. And now this. *Cancer? How could this be?* I had never faced a cancer diagnosis within the family before, and I was in disbelief, and I felt so cold, angry, helpless, afraid, and incredibly sad. It hit me with the force of a speeding train.

The next few months were a trying time for our family. We had to pray that he would beat this awful disease, but the doctors were not too sure that he would, which made it incredibly discouraging. Our faith was tested. I woke up crying and went to bed crying, and the whole time, I just kept praying for God to heal my uncle and to be there with my aunt to comfort her and bring her peace. The cancer had spread from my uncle's throat to his lymph nodes, which was bad. He would have a hard road ahead of him. I hated being so far away from my family. Again and again, I said I wanted to go home. But my aunt and my parents begged me to stay where I was and to continue pursuing my dreams. They told me how happy and proud it made them, knowing how amazing my career had become. And what a good distraction it was, hearing that I was doing so well. All they needed was my prayers. So I got down on my knees every day, and I prayed. I was in the middle of another promo tour and juggling a busy schedule, but with this kind of tragedy at home, it was hard to be present and think about anything else. It was very difficult to manage my emotions that whole summer.

My uncle was doing chemo and radiation treatments. He also had to have a major surgery to increase his chances of weakening the cancer. We prayed that it would help, but the doctor said that, unfortunately, there were no guarantees. In addition, he would have a long road to recovery from the surgery. These next few months were painful for us all. When I did go home in the middle of his treatment, he didn't look like himself, and it was so hard to see. I prayed harder than ever. Finally in mid-October we got word from my aunt. Her text said, "We're having the doctor's appointment tomorrow. Please pray that it is gone in Jesus's name."

And we just prayed and prayed, like we never prayed before. Just telling the story now, it still gives me the chills.

The next day, my uncle called me. "Mama," he said.

"Uncle, oh my gosh, how are you?" I said. "Are you okay?"

"Guess what?" he said.

"What?"

"I'm cancer-free."

When I heard these words, I lost it, right there on my kitchen floor. I was so thankful to Jesus.

"Uncle, oh my gosh" I said. "God bless you. Praise the Lord. Praise the Lord."

Then I spoke to my aunt, and she was crying. And I spoke to my uncle again, and I heard the smile in his voice, something I hadn't heard in months. That was a miracle from God. And having witnessed it firsthand, my faith was deepened once again.

This is what I want people who read my book to understand, if they take away anything from these pages, it's that faith, and God, can move mountains. God can change people's hearts. God can change destiny. God can change the doctors' reports. God is a God of miracles. I've seen them with my own eyes. These are the things that cannot be explained, which make my whole soul believe in God. Because of His will, things that are impossible have become possible.

To this day, I am proud to say that my uncle remains cancer-free.

Our family could not be more grateful for each day. We are forever a family of faith. We have been through everything. Cancer, death, rejection, pain, loss, but through all of it, God has always showed up. God is always there, in the midst of the worst trial and the deepest sorrow. He has saved us from so much, and he's brought us unspeakable joy and miracles. That's why I will always serve in honor of my God and Jesus. That's why I believe in God and I believe in miracles. Believe, believe, believe. I wear a ring every day that my mom gave to me. It reads, "Believe." As I've said before, that is my word, the one I hold closest to my heart.

In the midst of these miracles, there were also plenty of ups in my music career. To promote "Low Key," I went on my very first solo international promo tour to Europe, an incredibly exciting opportunity. I had stops in Milan, London, Paris, Berlin, and Brussels, and it was an exhilarating experience, full of tender bliss. I am enamored by Europe and traveling abroad is one of my favorite things to do. Paris had been a bucket list destination for me. I was able to travel there in Fifth Harmony, during our European tours. Now I was able to embrace that extraordinary city again, this time on my very own merit. Being able to travel to Europe in my first year of being a solo artist was sensational.

I also went to beautiful Brazil during this time. The fans are unbelievably passionate, full of pure heart and love. They treated me the same way as they'd treated Fifth Harmony, mobbing me (in the best way possible!) at the airport. Hundreds of fans stayed outside my hotel and came to my first solo show there, at a theater. It was last-minute, but they packed every square inch to double capacity. The room shook with their beautiful, high-pitched screams. The love and rush I felt was phenomenal.

That spring I was driving from Los Angeles to San Diego to promote "Lips Don't Lie," with Will and one of my label radio reps, Mo.

The promo for the second single had been going really well. But I had my sights set on Wango Tango, one of the biggest, most coveted radio show lineups of the year. Only the top artists took part, and Fifth Harmony had performed at it three years in a row. When you were on Wango Tango, that meant you'd made it. To land a spot on it during my first year as a solo artist would be an incredible sign that I was getting real traction. The head of radio for Atlantic, Andrea, called Mo while we were in the car. She started screaming. "Okay, wait, Let me put you on speaker!" Mo shouted. "Okay, Andrea, tell her."

"Ally, guess what? You're going to be playing Wango Tango!"

I started screaming!

We were so shocked and overjoyed. Usually artists don't play Wango Tango until later in their careers, but I'd landed it my first year. That meant things were heating up for me even faster than we could have hoped. A funny detail is that I was eating an RXBAR when I received the news. And it was so exciting and so big for me that I actually kept the wrapper as a reminder of that moment.

That June, I performed at Wango Tango, kicking off a summer of many big radio festivals, which was a goal for me. Not only does it show that you've reached a certain level of mainstream success, but it also gives you the chance to reach new fans and to connect with other amazing, high-profile artists. But no show meant more to me than that day at Wango Tango. During the afternoon, I performed on one of the smaller stages. It was a beautiful day, the sun was shining, and the crowd was having so much fun. All day I ran on adrenaline, buzzing from here to there, doing press, glowing, and feeling so proud to be there. It was also amazing to run into my fellow artists backstage. Halsey was so sweet and excited to see me, giving me a quick hug when we ran into each other in the hallway. I also saw the Jonas Brothers and quickly caught up with them before an interview. I also ran into Zedd, and he was so happy for me and all that I had been doing. It felt amazing to be recognized by my peers.

That night I was due to perform on the main stage, along with the other major artists I've mentioned. It was a huge moment. I'd changed into a new wardrobe for my second show—a customized outfit with boots featuring lip kisses all over them, in honor of my new single "Lips Don't Lie." My dad was with me for my special day, which made it that much more meaningful. And as he walked me over, he was just grinning. My team and I loaded up into a golf cart, because this was how the staff transported the artists from the dressing room all the way to the main stage. The energy at Wango Tango is always electrifying.

"You deserve to be here, Mama," he said. "I'm so proud of you."

When I walked on that stage, for the first time in my career, I truly get overwhelmed for a moment—by the huge stage, the bright lights, and the sea of screaming fans, stretching out as far as the eye could see. *Whoa,* I thought. And then instantly I pulled it together. *It's go time!* I ended up feeling this incredible electricity on that stage for my twenty-minute set. It was the biggest stage I'd ever been on. I had this huge production, a crew of eight dancers with me, Tyga was cool enough to be my surprise pop-up guest, and during my final song, "Low Key," I had huge sparklers going off behind me. It was a sensational moment.

That month of summer radio shows was an incredible ride. I was soaring. I also performed at the AT&T Center in San Antonio. Thousands of people sang along with me, welcoming me home, and it was remarkable to share this spectacular moment with my family and hometown fans.

I was already riding a career high from all of these long-awaited triumphs when, that July, I was in the office with Charles and Will on a normal workday. I happened to glance at Will's phone in his hand, and I saw the subject line of an open email: DWTS.

Could it be possible? Were they actually going to ask me again?

"Ally, we have to talk to you," Will said.

TWENTY

Dancing with the Stars

M y eyes had not deceived me. Will had just received an email from the producers of *DWTS*, asking me to be a part of the show for the 2019 season. I was surprised they'd asked me again, and I thought it was nice that they'd considered me for yet another season. My life looked different now than when they'd first approached me. I was much more established now and had a real career going. And I was happy that I'd proved I could dance since I'd started my solo career, in my "Low Key" video and other performances. Even so, my dancing was still an area that could make me insecure. Plus, this was ballroom dancing, which I had never done before.

"Let's think about it," Will said.

"Okay, I'll think about it this time," I said.

And then Charles weighed in: "Hey, I really think you should do it this time. The timing is perfect now. It'd be great for you to let people get to know you even more. We haven't had that moment yet where people know Ally as a person. This could be the opportunity."

"Okay, I'll definitely think about it, but I'm still uncertain, and I still feel like my answer is no," I said.

I kept putting off my decision until three weeks had passed. And finally, *Dancing with the Stars* gave us a deadline for getting back to them. I was in Atlanta for my best friend's wedding. I was a bridesmaid for the first time, and it was such a beautiful weekend, I was just in bliss with her. But I had this nagging worry in the back of my head: *Dancing with the Stars, Dancing with the Stars,* you've got to give them an answer.

Charles and Will really wanted me to do it, but I really didn't want to because I was scared. True, Fifth Harmony had performed on the show a few times, and I'd always loved being on the set. There was such a wonderful feeling of being part of this close-knit family, and I knew I'd get even more of that goodness as a contestant. That was one of the main draws for Will, too.

"Ally, remember we would have such great memories on that lot?" he said. "That *Dancing with the Stars* family is something else. And we could get that every day."

I was conflicted. So of course I prayed about it, and I asked my parents for their advice. They are always amazing at sharing their wisdom with me, and as far as I was concerned, they were basically entertainment industry veterans by this time. So they really knew what they were talking about. The previous year, they had agreed with me that it was not the right moment for me to do the show. Now I called my mom to discuss the pros and cons all over again.

"I've been thinking about it a lot, back and forth," I said. "My team thinks I should because it's a wonderful opportunity for people to get to know me. It's perfect timing. There are so many possible benefits from doing it, but I'm nervous, Mom. I don't want to do it. Even though I love the show, I'm scared."

"For the first time, I feel like you should do it," she said. "I feel good about it, like it's going to be a challenge for you. You're going to have to push yourself, and you've got to be ready for that challenge, but I think it could be amazing. It could help you with your confidence. And, Mama, remember, we would watch the show together. I think it could be special."

I was not expecting that at all. My mom and dad were saying yes? I sought advice from a few close friends, including my close friend Tori Kelly, and they all said the same thing—don't let the haters or fear stop you; nothing but positives can come from the show. I prayed even harder: *I'm so nervous, but this could be great. Please, Lord, show me what to do.*

I was terrified by the thought of being on reality TV again after how much I'd been misrepresented on *The X Factor*. I didn't want to be judged or ridiculed again. I had a near breakdown before I made my decision. But in the end, I knew I had to surrender those feelings to God and trust him. Not to mention all of the good people I trusted, whom I'd have all around me. I knew I should go with that, so I picked up the phone and I called Charles.

"My answer is yes!"

He was so happy. This was the start of a whole new journey. It was real and final now, and I began to get excited.

Saying yes was just the first step. The producers sent me a questionnaire that would help them to choose my music for the show. The questions included: "What is your favorite song? What song reminds you of your childhood? What song has gotten you through a tough time? What's your favorite Disney song? What's your favorite Halloween song? Your favorite song to dance to? Your favorite song to cry to?" I filled it out carefully. I knew it would help everything if I had the chance to dance to the songs I loved the most.

Now I was really nervous and excited. It was hard to believe that I was really going to be a contestant on a show that I had watched and loved for years. I envisioned my family back in Texas being proud of my performances and voting for me. I pictured my friends from all over, seeing me dance. I imagined getting all of that love and support, and it was so exciting.

From the time I said yes, there was about a month before it was time to fly to New York City to reveal who that season's contestants would be. In the meantime, the show released teasers on social media to keep people guessing. Soon, there were all of these rumors flying around on social media about who the other contestants would be. I was right there with everyone at home, trying to guess. It seemed like one of the contestants might be country music superstar Lauren Alaina, whom I'd loved and voted for when she'd been on *American Idol*. I felt like that would be amazing, and maybe we'd even become friends. My mom had that same thought, too, and hoped she was on the show with me because she loved Lauren. There were rumors about everyone from Dwyane Wade to Jessica Simpson. Trying to guess the other contestants was a fun game and the perfect way to stir up my excitement.

During this time, the producers were in touch to let me know how thrilled they were that I was competing this season, especially after they'd waited so long for my yes. They couldn't tell me yet who I'd be dancing with, but they assured me that they had picked the best possible partner for me and I would love him. After years of watching the show, I was a fan of all of the dance pros. I ran through all of the possibilities in my mind—could it be Val, whom I'd become friends with when he was Normani's partner, the season she was on the show? Could it be Sasha, who was small but mighty, like me? I'd just have to wait and see.

Finally it was late August, and time for me to fly to New York City for the announcement, where I'd meet the rest of the cast. This year, to make it even more suspenseful, the producers were trying a new approach—none of us would know who the other contestants were until we met them in New York. So we'd be almost as surprised as the viewers at home. And instead of being announced along with our partners, as a pair, on *Good Morning America*, we wouldn't learn who our partner was until the first day of rehearsal.

When I landed in NYC I went straight to my label's office for meetings and a photo shoot for my next single, "Higher," which I'd done with the Norwegian DJ Matoma. It was due to drop in conjunction with my time on *Dancing with the Stars*, on the same day as the show's premiere. From there, I rushed over to the hotel the show was putting me up at, which was located in the heart of the city. It was literally across the street from the *Good Morning America* studios. They put us contestants there, so we could walk over together first thing in the morning. I met with my publicist, did a quick fitting for the next day, and got my hair and makeup done. As the clock ticked down to our first event that night, I was so unbelievably nervous.

Who are these other contestants going to be? Am I going to like them? Are they going to like me? Are we going to get along? Is it going to be awkward?

I rode the elevator downstairs to the ballroom floor, where there was a small area with a bar, tables with candles, and a very casual, kind of loungy vibe. When I walked in, the first person I saw was Sasha, one of the pros on the show, and his wife, Emma, also a pro. Now, the crazy thing was that Sasha and I'd had the same tour manager, and several years earlier, he'd told me that Sasha had said, "I want to be Ally's partner if she ever does the show." My response had been to tell him thank you. And then, the previous summer, I'd been at The Grove in LA with a friend, when two people ran up to me from behind, all excited.

"Ally!" a male and female voice yelled to me.

I turned around and instantly recognized Sasha and Emma, whom I knew and loved from the show, and I was so happy to see.

"Oh my gosh," Sasha said. "Okay, you have to do *Dancing with the Stars.*

He was so energetic, just like how he is on the show.

"You have to do it," he said again. "I would love to be your partner. Please."

"Aw, I'd love to be your partner! That would be awesome. We'll see what happens."

Well, what had happened was I had said no that year when I'd been asked. But now, fast-forward to a year later, I was going to be a part of *Dancing with the Stars,* and it was so awesome that the first person I saw at the party to launch the season would be Sasha.

"Oh my God, Ally, it's you!!" Sasha and Emma cheered together when they first saw me.

He lifted me off the ground and twirled me around, so over the moon to see me. We were so excited to be there together, and it was an amazing surprise for them, because the pro dancers did not know in advance who the contestants would be that season.

"Yeah, oh my God, you're doing the show," Emma said. "Finally!"

It was one of the most excited, high-energy greetings I'd ever received, a fantastic way to kick things off. I was still nervous, but I was already starting to feel at home. As we chatted, I was looking around to see who the other contestants would be. It had been rumored that the Bachelorette, Hannah Brown, would be on, and there she was.

I kept peering over toward the door, excited to see who might walk in next. There was Kel Mitchell! Internally I was freaking out because I was a massive fan of his. *All That* and *Kenan & Kel* were my brother's and my favorite shows on Nickelodeon. Kel was part of the network's glory days and my childhood hero. I had been able to perform on the reboot of his sketch comedy series *All That* a few months earlier. I'd been so happy that I was able to meet him there, but it was even more amazing to be able to spend more time with him on *Dancing with the Stars.* I loved that he was also a fellow believer and couldn't wait to become friends with him. I met about half the cast that night, including Lamar Odom, who was so nice. It was so exciting, having the other contestants finally revealed to us and getting to meet some of them. The rest of the cast included Karamo Brown from *Queer Eye,* actor James Van Der Beek, NFL legend Ray Lewis, *The Office*'s Kate Flannery, Mary Wilson from the Supremes, Sean Spicer, and Christie Brinkley. As soon as I could, I ran upstairs to call my parents, who were eagerly waiting to hear who my castmates were going to be. My parents were beyond excited. "This is one of the best casts they've had in years," they said. My mom even shouted: "I can't believe you're going to be with Christie Brinkley! What a dream!"

But how would my fans and the general public react when they heard I would be dancing? Luckily, I was too exhausted to worry about it that night, and I fell right asleep. The next morning, it was go time. I got up at two A.M., had a little bit of hair and makeup done, and went downstairs to meet the rest of the cast, so we could walk across the street and do a live announcement on *Good Morning America,* in my favorite city, other than San Antonio, of course.

I was stepping out of my comfort zone in a big way, and on top of that, I was subjecting myself to the terror of being a contestant on a reality show again. I was nervous as we walked over—and then outside the studio, I saw a few of my fans who had guessed I'd be on the show from the teasers, and had come out to support me. That meant so much to me. I was starting to feel excited to reveal to the world that I was taking on an all-new challenge. All of the contestants were there, except for Mary Wilson from the Supremes, who Skyped in for the interview. It felt really amazing to be up there with so many people that I had watched, and admired, in their different fields, and it was so fun to be doing all of this together, live, on *GMA.* To my excitement, Lauren Alaina ended up being one of the contestants after all. She flew in on a red-eye and I met her the morning of *GMA.* I gave her a big hug, and I told her that I'd voted for her on *American Idol.* I couldn't wait to be a part of this amazing cast.

I decided I was going to take another risk and be vulnerable with the public. During our initial cast interview on GMA, one of the anchors said "I understand you're doing this show for a number of reasons. You were a big fan growing up, but you also say you want to stop the haters." I bravely came right out and said: "I was in Fifth Harmony, and there was a lot of dancing, and I feel like sometimes some of the dance moves were a little harder, and some people would leave not-so-nice comments, and it wouldn't feel good. So this is an opportunity for me to prove not only to them but to myself that I can really tackle this. And I want to be able to help those people who've felt like I do, that too, like, anything that they might feel that they are insecure about or they feel uncomfortable with, that they can go, and they can do it."

Of course I was happy my fans were excited when they heard that I was going to be on the show, and they were immediately rooting for me. I received so many messages of support from friends who texted me directly, and also messages online, from people who couldn't believe that I'd been through such cruelty and who offered me encouragement now.

We had a crazy press day. It was super long. Plus we were filming some behind-the-scenes promo footage for the show. It was all happening!

I flew back to LA later in the day, after my press. The producers had told me that I would officially be meeting my partner in a few days. My parents and I had spent more than a month excitedly guessing who was going to be my partner. And then Charles had guessed. And Will had guessed. And my brother had guessed. And now, after all of that buildup, I couldn't believe that the moment for the big reveal was almost here. Finally I got word from the producers that it was time to begin rehearsals. We pulled up to this big, beautiful building that had five different rehearsal spaces. It was spacious and grand and very *Dancing with the Stars*–esque. And it all felt so real. I met my individual producer, who got me mic'd up and prepared me for what came next: right through those doors was my partner.

They started filming and asked me to tell the camera who I thought my partner would be.

"I'm so exited," I said. "I can't believe I'm here. This journey means a lot to me. I don't know who it could be, but I'm excited to find out."

I was so nervous, I put my hand over my mouth. And then, *bam,* who should walk through the doors? Sasha! I was beyond ecstatic that he was my partner. I let out this big scream. I told him my story about doing the show to try to overcome the pain of having been teased in the past, but also because I was a huge fan. And so it was for the little girl inside of me who didn't think she could do it. And for all of those little boys and girls out there who got bullied.

My mission on the show may have been serious, but we were immediately laughing. He gave me a quick mini-lesson before our first true rehearsal the next day, and I immediately felt so comfortable with him. Every moment was new and exciting.

At the start of the first week, Sasha told me that for our first dance, we'd be dancing the cha-cha, and all of us contestants would be paying homage to our roots. With a flourish, he revealed that our music would be none other than Fifth Harmony's "Work from Home"! Since I'd gone solo, I hadn't really performed any of our songs. I knew that this could be amazing, and if so, the fans would go ballistic. On the other hand, if I didn't do well, this could be really bad.

We had three weeks to prepare our first dance, and I practiced as much as I possibly could with Sasha. During that time, I also filmed the music video for "Higher." Just because I was on *DWTS,* I couldn't put my music career on pause, so for as long as I stayed on the show, I'd be juggling both. From the beginning, it was pretty nonstop. We also had to think of a team name for ourselves and we were stumped. Then Sasha got a brainstorm.

"Ally, this is your time to shine," he said. "So . . . we have to be called Team Time to Shine! Because not only is it your time to shine, but when it's our turn to go onstage, it's time to shine."

I loved that message and felt invigorated for all we had to do. Toward the end of the third week, we also started learning our dance for the next week's taping. It was a lot. Around this time, I also had my first wardrobe fitting. It was a dream to work with the show's wardrobe team, who were known for making the most gorgeous, stunning outfits. And of course I loved what they'd made for me. I got to wear so many dream outfits on the show, and I was so happy about my very first one. It was tailored to my body and exactly what I wanted. I felt incredible.

The night before the very first live show, I had memorized our cha-cha routine, but there were a few tricks that I still hadn't mastered. I kept trying and trying, but I just couldn't get them. I could feel the clock ticking down to the end of the day, and that was very stressful.

"Don't worry," Sasha reassured me. "We've done all we could. Let's just have fun tomorrow. And if we need to change it at the last minute, we will."

The next morning was officially the day—it was show day! When we pulled into the gates of CBS studios, I took a moment to take it all in. The journey was beginning. First up, we were going to do a full dress rehearsal of the entire show. And then that night, we'd tape the show live. Mondays were always long days, but the excitement buzzing around me always kept me going.

One of the most amazing things about being on the show was the cast. As soon as I started to get to know them, I immediately felt right at home. Although we all came from different backgrounds and had different personalities, the producers had chosen the perfect group of people to mix together—we had our share of jokesters, and everyone had so much heart. Sadly, Christie had broken her arm in rehearsal and was replaced by her daughter, Sailor, whom I quickly became close to.

After I got my hair and makeup done, my family and a few close friends came to my trailer to pray with me. "You've got this, Mama," my parents said. "Go out there and have fun."

As I'd hoped, Lauren and I had immediately become close friends ordering Cheesecake Factory and talking and laughing until 1 A.M. on our first friend "date," and we hugged and wished each other the best of luck. I was excited to watch her dance. It was actually so fun to watch each of the other contestants take their turns. But of course waiting in the wings just made me feel more nervous.

Once you were on the ballroom floor and those cameras were on you, it was live on the East Coast. So whatever happened on that floor—whether you messed up or tripped or fell—it was all live. You couldn't go back and do it again. Plus, it was my first time dancing on that ballroom floor, which was so different from the rehearsal studio. As I would soon learn, it could play tricks on your mind, as far as which direction you were going.

My nerves had built up and built up, but as soon as I set foot on the stage, a jolt went through me and something just clicked into place—there was nowhere else I would have rather been. I loved my costume, my hair, and my makeup. I felt amazing and powerful. It was a little strange to just be dancing to a Fifth Harmony song, when I was so used to singing the words, but it also felt wonderful to give a nod to where I'd come from.

During a high-precision moment, it's amazing how fast the human mind can spin and the number of thoughts it can cram in—a million details hitting you all at once: *Am I doing my steps right? How are my facials? Is my costume okay? How are my feet? How are my lines? I'm going to be judged on every single technical aspect of this. I'm killing it.*

And then, while we were dancing, I saw the face of one of the judges, Len, and his head was down, in his hand. That was *not* an enthusiastic response, and it threw me off.

Oh no.

I was so rattled that I messed up during the end of our routine. I recovered pretty smoothly, but it was still obvious that I had misstepped. When I went to stand before the judges, I had no idea what was about to be said, and I was just praying: *Please, dear God. Let the comments be good.*

All of the judges gave me constructive criticism that wasn't exactly positive, so that was a bummer. Then Len said something about how it was too much Beyoncé. People later took exception to that online, along the lines of: "Oh my gosh, you can never get enough Beyoncé." (Which, yes, I agree.) But the truth was that I didn't do the best job technically on our first night. I felt it, and so I wasn't surprised when the judges' comments reflected that. But it was still hard to hear. And we ended up getting a score of sixteen, which was not the lowest score that night, but it was one of the lowest. That was such a bummer for me. *Wow, I went out there. I did a Fifth Harmony song. I tried my best. But did I just embarrass myself on TV again? Did I not do well? Are people going to have even more ammunition to say I can't dance?*

The rest of the night, I was pretty low on myself. I was frustrated and disappointed, because I'd put in so much work. And I'd felt extra pressure, because I'd been dancing to a Fifth Harmony song. We'd had three weeks to learn this dance, which was way longer than we'd have for any of the next ones. And even though I had put in so much effort and really tried my best, still, the feedback hadn't been great. I'd seen it all go down so differently in my head, assuming the first night was supposed to be amazing for me, especially as I was doing a Fifth Harmony song. I was bummed through and through. As always, my parents were quick not just to cheer me up, but to put everything in perspective: "It's just night one. It's just dance one. That's okay."

I didn't have long to wallow in negative feelings, because the next morning we had to immediately get back to work on our next dance, which we had started to learn the previous week. Sasha picked right up where he'd left off, teaching me the steps. We wanted to give ourselves as much time to rehearse as possible. I'd already been struggling with the next dance, which was a waltz, and now I was worried about what my comments for week two would be.

But after a few weeks, at least my anxiety had happily vanished in another area. After my *X Factor* experience, I'd been worried about the way they'd edit my packages, especially because the same producer was now in charge of *DWTS*. When I first said yes to the show, I had voiced my concern, and they reassured me that they would make sure to not skew my edits, and to represent me in the most positive way. But I was pleasantly surprised, each week, to find myself fairly and accurately represented. Maybe my family and everyone on my team had been right, and this show would help more people get to know the real me. When I next had the chance, I made a point to pull the producer aside and give him the compliment I felt he deserved. "I've been seeing the packages, and I've really been happy," I said. "So I want to say thank you, I really appreciate it."

"Oh, my pleasure, darling," he said in his lovely British accent.

It was so healing to have a more positive reality TV experience after my past trauma. And no matter the challenges I would face on the show—and there were plenty of them—I was overjoyed to find that I was always treated fairly by the producers and never felt like my story line had been manipulated for drama. In fact, the day-to-day producers had a very collaborative approach that I really enjoyed. Each week they'd come to Sasha and me and talk to us about what they were thinking for that week's package. They were always suggesting angles that gave me an opportunity to be candid about something that mattered to me—how I'd gotten started as a performer, how I felt about dancing, how much I loved Selena and why. At the same time, Sasha and I were collaborating in our own way, trying to figure out how to tell our tale of working together. We considered several different angles, before realizing the real story was our actual relationship, in which he was like a real-life brother to me, sometimes silly, sometimes tough, but always putting in the extra effort to help us be our best team possible.

I loved my rehearsals with Sasha. His number one goal was for us to have fun, and while we did have fun, of course he wanted to make me the best dancer I could be. Some days were more frustrating than others, and he would be more serious and disciplined with me, but I was always happy to practice longer and harder. Most of the time, we were joking and laughing, and he was thinking up hilarious little pranks that kept the mood light, which was great, because even when it was going well, the hours were long.

During the second week's show, Sasha and I danced the Viennese waltz, an emotional moment that allowed me to dance out my feelings. Again, my performance was not as strong as I'd hoped it would be, when I'd been putting everything I had into our rehearsal. And my comments from the judges weren't great. Len Goodman said: "I would have liked to have seen a little bit more rotation in there, and your footwork, you didn't know what you were doing with your feet. You reversed turns. Listen, it was pretty, and I liked it, and I understand the audience going wow, what a lovely, lovely dance, and it was a lovely dance. Technically, it wasn't so good." The audience sweetly came to my defense, booing his negativity. And Bruno gave me an amazing compliment: "First of all, you can dance. Second, it was a very compelling, heartfelt performance, and there were some wonderful, wonderful moments." Carrie Ann got up to give me a hug and said, "You are a dancer." But I still knew I had my work cut out for me.

Going into the show's third episode, which had the theme of movie week, we got some exciting news. Our dance was the rumba, and to my excitement, I was going to have the chance to dance to a Selena song! And so I chose one of my all-time favorites, none other than the movie Selena. The producers had a say in the song, and to my excitement, they picked "Dreaming of You." Not only that, but in order to show people how much my hero had always meant to me and where I'd come from, they were flying Sasha and me to my home state of Texas, so we could film my package there.

I was so excited to be going home! Of course, the thought dawned on me that we'd have one less day to rehearse, because of the travel. It was totally worth it to me, though, because the trip meant getting to see my family and inviting viewers into our home so the whole world could meet the amazing people who had made me who I am today.

First up, we flew from LA into Corpus Christi. In the morning, the show filmed us going to the Selena Museum to meet Selena's sister. Sasha had rented a car, and we had a camera crew with us, filming everything. I was so excited to get to introduce Sasha to Suzette, Selena's sister, and to show him who Selena was. Suzette gave us a personal tour that allowed Sasha and viewers at home to learn about the incredible talent and reach of Selena, who had inspired not only me but millions of people worldwide.

It was such an honor to be at Selena's museum now, with a successful singing career of my own, helping to make sure that her voice and spirit are never forgotten. During the tour, Suzette took us into the studio where Selena had recorded much of her music, including "Dreaming of You." I felt the significance of knowing that my hero had stepped foot in this room, but it was also hard not to let thoughts of her loss weigh heavily on my heart.

Once we'd taken a moment to breathe in where we were, Sasha and I showed Suzette a bit of the rumba. Then I was deeply touched when Suzette showed me a Selena pin she'd just had made as part of a new line of merchandise. She handed it to me.

"I would be so honored if you would wear this," she said.

I started crying, holding on to the pin and vowing that I would wear it during my performance. As I had the first time we met, I told her how much Selena meant to me.

"Oh, you're going to make me cry," she said.

It was a beautiful experience through and through, and I felt so proud that my voice and my hard work had given me this opportunity. Although the footage of this special moment didn't make it onto the show, I'm so glad that we shared that moment, and it only deepened my appreciation of Selena and her family. I was really disappointed when I heard that it wouldn't be included, but the producers let me know that due to time constraints, they could show only the package of me with my family.

From there, we drove to my sweet hometown, San Antonio, to my cousin BJ's house. Before we went inside, I stopped short and tried to prepare Sasha for what was inside.

"All right, Sasha, are you ready?" I asked. "Because it's about to be crazy in there."

"I'm ready, Alz, bring it on."

So we went in, and *BOOM*, everybody was there. The entire down-stairs area was crammed with all of my family. This was the first time they'd seen me since the announcement of *Dancing with the Stars*, so they were welcoming me as their hometown hero. As soon as Sasha and I walked in, my whole family started cheering and my grandma came up and gave me a big hug. The room was hot and loud. With my family, it's always crazy, energetic, hilarious, and full of so much love—and food. Everyone talks at once, welcoming guests, hugging, laughing, making them feel at home.

"*Sasha!* Oh my gosh! Nice to meet you! Make yourself at home. Let me get you a chair. Here, sit down. We'll serve you food."

Everyone was talking at once and laughing and loading up enor-mous plates of food for our out-of-town guests to enjoy, including the camera crew. It was so beautiful for me to have Sasha, who was quickly becoming like my second brother, get to have family time with me. I've always felt that it's hard to really explain to someone who you are and why you are the way you are until they meet your loved ones who mean the most to you. And for me, of course, that's my family.

I was tired, but I knew we had only two hours before we had to fly back to Los Angeles. The show ran until November—and if all went well, I wouldn't be home again until after the final episode. So I made sure to enjoy every second and soak up all of the love and laughs. And to eat plenty of the amazing food, which had been donated by our dear family friend Jay, who manages one of our favorite San An-tonio restaurants, Palenque Grill. When I was little and first getting started, long before I became successful, I performed everywhere I could around San Antonio. I used to sing with Jay at local hospitals, and he'd been friends with my family ever since. So when he'd found out about the show taping, he'd reached out via my parents. "I would love to cater for you for free, Mama," he told me. "I want to do this because I love you and I believe in you." He piled long tables with my favorite foods—beans, tortillas, queso, tortilla chips, rice, steak, tacos, picadillo—all arranged in the most beautiful way.

In my family, we have one another and our vibrant community of friends, and we love each other hard, and that's all we need. Sasha was immediately welcomed in as one of the family. They treated him like a king. We piled his plate high with food. And Sasha danced with my mom and my aunt, which made everyone cheer. My parents told him embarrassing stories about me, and everyone laughed, even me. It was a whirlwind, but we had such an amazing time. It was a perfect day, even though it was over too soon. Before I knew it, we were headed back to LA.

I would need all of the love I could get because I had a long journey ahead, and it would be awhile before I came home for another visit. When we returned to LA, I pushed myself, and I worked harder than ever. Sasha was right there with me every step of the way, to push me and to help me grow. Together we had instantly formed a close-knit team, so we both really cared about the outcome. We tried not to get discouraged when we didn't do so well, and eventually my hard work began to pay off. Suddenly, there was an amazing turnaround in the competition for me. It started with "Dreaming of You." I got all eights that night. Things began to change.

Week after week, I kept advancing in the competition. And I was ecstatic to have made it to the coveted Disney week! I had prayed I would make it to this night. Of course this was one of my favorite moments on the show, because I was able to live out my Disney princess dreams, dressed up as Belle, my favorite Disney princess, while dancing to the theme song from my favorite movie, *Beauty and the Beast*. That night we were the first couple of that season to score all nines across the board. Finally, it seemed like we were gaining momentum. The next week, when we danced the quickstep to "Take on Me" by A-ha, our score of twenty-five wasn't even the lowest of the night, and yet we landed in the bottom two, based on the votes cast by viewers. If the judges hadn't voted to save us, we could have easily been eliminated.

Week by week, I knew I was getting better, but I didn't always feel like this was reflected in my position on the show. Week eight, I had the amazing opportunity to dance the paso doble to my very own song, "Higher." What made it even better was that I was able to sing the first few lyrics. That was such an electrifying experience—I really let out the beast in me on that one. I became a different powerful Ally, and soon it became one of my favorite moments from the show. I also got the first tens of the season! It was phenomenal. I was positively beaming with pride. And yet we were again in the bottom two. That was horrible, because I never saw it coming. I'd just had the huge high of singing and dancing to my own song and scoring all tens.

I felt like I was finally winning over the judges, and they could see my hard work, my growth, and most important, my heart. Having always been a big fan of the show, I highly respected Carrie Ann, Bruno, and Len, and I'm so grateful for their comments about how much I improved from week to week, and how I really COULD dance. The next week, we again earned tens across the board—this time for both of our dances. And so it hurt to be in the bottom two a second time. I vowed to work even harder and give even more.

The show gave me so many unbelievable moments. I loved going out to high-five/say hi to the live audience before they entered the building every Monday. One of my favorite dances was to "Wannabe" by the Spice Girls, where I got a special shout-out from Emma Bunton, aka Baby Spice. Another glorious moment was dancing jazz to "Step by Step" by New Kids on the Block. That was one of the most fun dances of my life. Afterward, Bruno compared me to Paula Abdul, which was such a tremendous honor. I loved her. I even got a shout-out from Paula, telling me how amazing I'd done. So many incredible moments. While we were rehearsing for this week, I was also excited to be invited back to be a part of the same magical Christmas special at Disney World that I had sung in years ago as part of Fifth Harmony.

Sasha and I traveled to Orlando, where I juggled rehearsals with him and filming the Christmas special, which amazingly was being hosted that year by Emma Bunton.

No matter what happened, I had to get up the next morning and try all over again to learn a new dance, to be better than I'd been before. And as my mom had predicted, it was good for my confidence. Sometimes doing something really hard is the best medicine, no matter how it turns out, because it helps us to believe in ourselves more. But nothing I'd been through yet prepared me for what happened going into the semifinals.

TWENTY-ONE

All Heart

By this point, I didn't know what to expect on the show from one week to the next. It had felt remarkable getting high scores along with incredible comments from the judges, week after week. Finally getting my redemption in dancing was so rewarding. I also felt I was becoming a fan favorite and that meant the world to me. I was soaring. But I was also scared of what the results would be every week. At the same time, I knew how hard I'd been working. I tried to reason with myself: *It's not possible to be in the bottom three a third time.*

During my months with the other contestants, I'd bonded with them over the amazing catering, and formed some special friendships with each of them. They were like family to me. One of my most cherished friendships was with actor James Van Der Beek. He became like a mentor to me. He is such an amazing soul—always so calm and poised in how he walked and spoke and everything he did. He had this amazing presence. He was a brilliant, beautiful dancer—one of the best on the show that season. From early on, I wasn't alone in assuming he'd definitely be going to the finals.

Part of his journey on the show had been to open up about the exciting news that he and his wife were expecting a baby, which was a huge blessing, after they'd gone through the devastating experience of several miscarriages. By the time of the show, she was far enough along in her pregnancy that they felt okay about sharing the news with the world. Everyone had fallen in love with him and his beautiful family and were rooting for them on every level.

And then, over the weekend before the Monday night taping, the week of the semifinals, the unthinkable happened, and his wife had a miscarriage. Sasha's wife, Emma, was James's partner on the show, so she was one of the first people to know. And then when Sasha saw me at rehearsal, he told me the awful news. When I heard, I started crying. I felt this awful pain for James and his wife and their other children. The other contestants and I had become a family during the course of the show, and we were in it together by this point.

Of course James didn't come to the studio on Sunday, when we did camera blocking for the next night's show. The rest of the cast was devastated for James and his family and in shock. We all felt this intense sadness, and there was not a dry eye among us, because we all adored James. He's just such a wonderful man, and our heart went out to him and his family. We didn't know if he'd dance on Monday.

When we arrived on the next day, James was there. We all rallied around him, hugging him and crying with him and telling him: "We are so sorry. We are here for you."

He had the unbelievable strength to talk on the show about their excruciating loss, and to explain how he had somehow gotten the strength to dance that night. I was incredibly moved by his honesty and his bravery. I so admired his strength.

When he danced, we were all cheering for him so hard. I could not believe it when I saw the judges' reaction. They were tough on him, and I thought they had underscored him.

Are you kidding me? I thought. *I mean, this situation aside, he was amazing. He just went through a miscarriage, but he cares so much about honoring his commitment, he's here.*

On that particular night, we each did two dances. And he redeemed himself on his second dance and got higher scores. That made me feel better, but the whole situation had left me with a weird feeling. Still, this was one of my last chances to dance on this stage, and so I dug in and really gave it my all. My first dance was a redo of the waltz, which I did not get good scores on the first time. And now I received much higher scores, which felt amazing. And then, on my last dance for the semifinals, we danced the Charleston, and I received all tens. So I was riding high. It was one of my best nights that whole season, and I was so excited, because I felt like I had a good chance of making it to the finals.

When it came time to announce who was advancing, we all crowded onto the stage as we had done so many times before, but now there were fewer of us, and the stakes were as high as they would get. My nerves jangled as I listened to them call the people who were making it to the finale, one by one. Finally, there were only three of us left: it was Kel, James, and me.

I immediately thought: *No, there's no way that I could be in the bottom three again, a third time, and especially not after how I danced tonight. On top of my results and the comments from the judges, and how the past few weeks I've been getting better and better, climbing and climbing. Oh my gosh, there's no way.*

At the same time, I felt gutted.

I had already been in the bottom two twice at this point. And now there were only three of us. I had fallen in love with the show in its entirety and with every aspect of my whole experience there—the cast, the producers, the judges, the crew. It truly was a family, a space full of love and positivity. I'd never felt anything like this on any show or in any environment before. I was fully invested. I'd been working so hard. Sasha had never won before, and I wanted that so badly for him. I knew it was just a mirror ball trophy, but it symbolized so much more than that. By this point, I was so freaked out, I felt like I was going to throw up.

There was nothing I could do but to wait for my fate. Then Tom made the announcement of which couple would be joining Hannah and Lauren on the finale: Kel and Witney.

In that moment it hit me—as shocking and horrible as it was, I was left in the bottom two. And not only for a third time, but also, now I was up against James to possibly be saved. It was the most horrible situation possible. That was it, then. It was over for me. I was crying, but I was also working toward acceptance, telling myself: *You know what? My time on this show may be done, but I'm proud of myself for making it to the semifinals. Even though I didn't go all the way to the finals, I'm going to walk out of here with my head held high.*

I was disappointed to not make it to the finale, but I was doing my best to process all of this, and in front of the cameras. At the same time, I was comforting Sasha—even though we didn't win, we were going to be fine, and it had been an amazing experience, and I loved him.

We still had to get through the part where judges could each save one of the bottom contestants from being eliminated. Of course the judges were going to save James, because he was so incredible, and especially after the night he'd had.

"The couple I want to save, and I'm so sorry, is Ally and Sasha," Carrie Ann said, obvious emotion in her voice. "I'm so sorry, James."

I was shocked.

The second judge, Bruno Tonioli, also voted to save Sasha and me.

"What?" I heard someone say in the studio audience.

"What?" I said, starting to tear up. "No, no."

Emma started crying. So then, of course, Sasha was upset that his wife was crying, even if we were maybe advancing. Now he was crying. And in the audience, James's daughter, Olivia, was crying. This was awful.

"Sasha, I cannot do this," I said. "This is not right. This is not fair. I cannot move on in the competition like this."

I felt so unworthy. I didn't deserve to be there. I was heartbroken. It was not at all what I'd been envisioning, and it sucked the joy out of going into the finals for me. I had to fix this, even though I didn't know if my action was allowed. I turned to our host, Tom Bergeron, and I think I startled him, which made me feel bad, too. "Can I give it to James, please?" I said, crying.

"No, but that's lovely of you to say that," Tom said.

Tom got back to finishing up the rest of the show, but he was still trying to comfort me. During the course of the show, he had always supported me and become like an uncle figure to me.

Then I turned to my castmate: "James, can I give it to you, please?"

James began trying to comfort me. Now I was really crying. I still wanted so badly to make it to the finale, and I had, but I didn't want it to be under these circumstances. I actually did feel tremendous love from *Dancing with the Stars* fans. But I'd been in the bottom two once again. I'd advanced by being saved, which I felt awful about. And the judges had chosen me over James, after what he'd gone through.

And now I feared that I'd be known as the girl who'd taken James Van Der Beek's spot. In the moment, I was starting to second-guess myself. I was devastated for James, and I was angry that I'd been put in this position. It didn't seem fair—I knew I deserved to be in the finals because of my hard work and how much my dancing had improved. I knew James deserved to be there, too, because he'd always been an incredible dancer and worked just as hard. And now this.

The show was done taping, and I went back to my trailer. I couldn't stop crying. My parents had been there for my big night, as well as Will, my pastor, my best friend, and some of her friends, and they all tried to comfort me. But I felt so embarrassed. I started to have flashbacks to past experiences when, no matter how positive my attitude was and how hard I'd tried, I just couldn't seem to prove I was good enough.

I was hysterical and shocked by what had happened.

Normally I did press after the show. But I was so emotional, I didn't feel well enough to do press.

Finally my mom and dad calmed me down and got through to me.

"Mama, listen, I know you're sad, but you deserve to be here, too," they said. "You deserve to be in the finals. Yes, James does, too, but it's not your fault. Please don't think for one second that you don't deserve to be here, because you do."

I pulled myself together enough that I was ready to hear from my friend, the ABC publicist, who was very sweet. She came in, with my personal publicist, and they both comforted me. They told me that they weren't there to persuade me to do press. But that they would love me to do it as a chance to tell my story. They also had strong feelings on the matter.

"Don't think for one second that you don't deserve to be here," they said.

I ended up doing a few interviews, and really, I wanted to take that moment to highlight James. And rather than burying my emotions, I wanted to express them, to be honest with the viewers about how bad I felt about everything.

At the end of the night, before I went home, I had one more thing to do. I knocked on James's trailer door, which happened to be right next to mine. He was sitting with his daughter, Olivia.

"I just wanted you to know how sorry I am," I said, soon in tears. "And how guilty I feel, because I'm going on and you aren't. Please, I'm begging you, I want to offer you my slot. Please, please, please. This is not just me trying to be nice. This is a real gesture. Please take it."

It was a very emotional moment.

"Ally, I will never let you do that," he said. "And it's crazy that you're over here even doing that. It just shows your heart. Ally, you go out there, and you be unapologetic."

He'd always encouraged me to feel empowered to be myself, with pride, and that's how he'd become like a mentor to me.

"You go up there and you shine," he continued. "No apologies. Please do that for me. Please, Ally."

It took a few more minutes of my crying and still offering him my spot. Finally I accepted that he had made up his mind, and the best thing I could do was to respect that.

"Okay, but I want you to know how sorry I am," I said. "If you do change your mind, please let me know."

He turned to his daughter, with a twinkle in his eye. "Hey, Olivia, who was your favorite, besides me?"

"Ally," she said shyly, with a big smile. I hugged her.

In that moment, I felt that love from her, how sweet she was. As little as she was, I needed to hear that vote of confidence. The fact that she did love me and I was her favorite besides her dad really meant a lot to me. It's amazing how kids can change our entire hearts and moods in a single moment. I now felt like it was okay for me to be there and to move on.

"Ally, you've got my support and my blessing, a hundred million percent," James said. "I love you. You go kick ass out there for me. Don't you cry anymore. I want to see you shine, okay?"

I nodded my head, wiping away the lingering tears on my face. And I vowed to make the most of this difficult life lesson I'd been given, in honor of him and his kindness and his family. But for the next day, I was really sad, and I couldn't shake it. Nothing could cheer me up. I didn't want to go to rehearsals.

But I had made a promise to James. And I couldn't let Sasha or my fans down. So I did my best to put one foot in front of the other. The first day was tough. And the second. But throughout this whole time, I was getting overwhelming messages of support from Sasha, my parents, the other dancers and contestants, and the producers, and they all said: "Ally, don't you dare think that you don't deserve to be here. You deserve to be here more than anyone."

Lauren, who had become my close friend, cheered me up in the way only she could.

"Ally, you deserve to be here," she said. "Don't let the show change you or change your belief in yourself. And if it's anybody who doesn't deserve to be here, it's me. I don't know what the hell I'm doing here."

We both laughed. Then, she gave me a big smile and an even bigger hug.

"You deserve to be here more than anyone," I said. "Thank you."

I was so glad that James could see my heart and that I did receive so much support. Because as I'd feared, for the first day after the show, I did receive some negativity on social media. Many were so mean to me online, treating me like it was my fault. Saying I didn't deserve to be there. Making and posting videos of the mistakes I'd made on my last dance. I tried to focus on how far I'd come, but I got into a little bit of a negative head spiral, where I was brought right back to that dark place I'd been in right after my *X Factor* audition aired and when Fifth Harmony fans had ridiculed me online.

Oh my God, people hate me. I'm not good enough, and I'll never be good enough no matter what I do.

But after that, the love started to pour in for me. Finally love triumphed against hate. I felt the support I was receiving more deeply than I felt the negativity. It was empowering. I came back stronger than ever. It finally sunk in: *I do deserve to be here.*

What I learned from all of this was that even though I hadn't been given a choice in what had happened to me, I'd still had the power to choose what kind of person I wanted to be, what kind of values I wanted to live by.

It was amazing to have that support behind me, and slowly it began to energize me.

I began to get excited. This was the culmination of all Sasha and I had worked toward, our last time to shine together. I had really cherished my time on *Dancing with the Stars,* and I felt like I'd been a part of the most wonderful family, just like Will had predicted I would. I had felt like a fan favorite. And now this beautiful escapade was coming to an end. The last few days of rehearsal were bittersweet. Most of all, it had been a safe place for me to grow. From my dance in week one to my dance in the finale, it felt like I'd gone from being a tender little cub to this fierce lioness. It gave me the confidence I'd needed to move on from the scars of Fifth Harmony, not just as a performer but in my life. When I looked ahead now, I was so excited for the next chapter, and I couldn't wait to take all I'd learned and implement it in my music, my live shows, and every aspect of my career.

But first I had one more dance to do. When Sasha had approached me with the music, before he'd even pushed play, he'd been excited. "You're going to love it," he said.

And then he played "Conga," by Gloria Estefan, which I had told the producers in my original questionnaire was one of my favorite songs of all time. I'd always loved Gloria and Emilio Estefan and looked up to them for breaking down barriers for Latin artists everywhere, being among the first to really go mainstream. Now I was going to have the opportunity to honor them and their inspirational story, which I'd admired since I was little, on national TV. We started working on the choreography right away. During the finals, we also had to repeat an earlier dance that had been a highlight for us, and we'd decided to do "Proud Mary" again.

Every day we were taking it all in. We had a big hill to climb. Thankfully, Sasha was in a much better headspace than me, and he began cheering me up from our first day back at rehearsals. Obviously, he was heartbroken for his wife and for James, but he had seen our evolution as a team. He was so proud of us. He didn't want anything to take this moment away.

It took me two or three days to snap out of the sadness, but then after receiving so much love from fans of the show, and a very loving pep talk by phone from my aunt, I started to feel better. By the third day I had completely transformed my mind to think: *This is my last week on the show. I have to cherish it and take it in and absorb it and enjoy every single second, because it's going to go by so quickly.*

I was so unbelievably overjoyed for "Conga." Sasha kept building out the choreography as we rehearsed. By the time we finished the whole dance, I was amazed by his talent and vision. The dance had every element that I'd ever wanted in a routine—it had that fierceness and fire and power, while also being beautiful and showcasing my growth. I was more excited about that dance than I'd been about any of the other dances.

I was getting more and more excited. We were dancing to an incredible remix of the song, and during our performance, there would be live horns and drums, adding to the power of the music. It was my Latin explosion dream. It was who I really was—my culture, my passion, my heart, and who I was as an entertainer. This was the real Ally, exiting with a bang.

Still, we both wanted it to be perfect—Sasha had never won before, and I was the underdog—we kept practicing. There were so many different tricks in the dance that I had huge bruises on my legs from trying to nail them. But we kept working. I not only wanted to prove to America that I could triumph, but I also wanted to prove it to myself. As the rehearsal days wound down, I started taking my time, walking the hallways at night before I left, soaking it all in, just like I'd promised myself I would. And Sasha and I began to prepare for the end of our partnership.

"I've never had a partner like you before, and I'll never have anybody like you again," Sasha said to me. "Love you, Alz. Thank you for everything you've done for me, and thank you for being the best partner. We're friends for life."

"Thank you so much, Sasha," I said. "I love you, too. And I could not have done this without you. Thank you for changing my life. Thank you for giving me confidence that I never had before. I am so eternally grateful for you, and I love you."

Of course tears welled up in both our eyes.

Those last few days were definitely emotional for me. Just take my final fitting, when I got into the costume for my "Conga" dance. The wardrobe department had become like family to me. They had witnessed my growth and watched me shine. I had contributed to the design for this beautiful petite, formfitting bodysuit. I'd saved this particular design for years, always wanting to wear something like this, but never having the confidence to do so. Now I did, and I felt like I was in the best shape of my life. When I tried it on, I started crying.

"I never thought I would love myself this much, and love my body, and allow myself to wear something like this and actually feel beautiful in it and confident," I told the designers. "This is such an amazing moment for me."

I couldn't believe how far I'd come, how much more confident I was. Whether we won the mirror ball or not, this had been one of the best experiences of my life. I was nervous, but I had prepared as much as I could, and it was my final dance. *Just have fun,* I thought.

As we stood on the side of the stage, just before we went on, we beamed at each other. "It's time to shine, one last time!"

We did "Proud Mary" first. I got to sing during the opening, with a choir backing me, which was the perfect kickoff for my second-to-last dance. The first time we'd done this dance, it had been the beginning of my scores starting to turn around, so it had significance for me.

And then "Conga." Here was my chance to say: *I'm here, world. Look at how far I've come. I am a performer. I am a dancer. I have this fire within me that nobody's ever seen before, and nobody will ever be able to take away from me.*

This was it. My final dance. Sasha and I hugged each other and both said, "I love you."

"I'm so proud of you," he said. "Go out there and shine, Ally. Shine like never before."

I got up on that stage. I climbed into the set, which was this huge mirror ball trophy. I was inside the ball, waiting inside for my cue. I looked down at the silver ring my mom had given me that spelled out "Believe." I prayed. I thought of my grandpa. "This is for you," I said to him.

As soon as the set opened and I stepped down onto the stage, I felt this power and velocity like I had never felt before. I had the most fun doing this dance, and I couldn't have given an ounce more than I possibly did. I left it all out on the floor, for the audience and for America. And then that was it. That was my final dance.

When we were standing together afterward, Sasha and I started crying. And then we got our scores: all tens. And I received the most incredible comments.

It was the most perfect ending I could have imagined. We had wanted "Conga" to be a celebration of my evolution, of the show, and of life itself. That's exactly how it had felt. It was one of the most incredible moments of my entire life.

And then it was time to hear the results. We were shaking, both Sasha and me. We held hands and said a prayer. Then we had a group huddle with the final four contestants.

"Hey, guys, no matter what happens, amazing job," we contestants said to each other. "We love you guys. Yeah!"

And then we lined up on the stage, and the producers played messages sent to us by our families. I cried. Everybody cried, actually. And then it was time to announce the winner. First up was fourth place. It was Lauren. And then, drumroll, third place was—me! Of course, I would have loved to have taken that trophy home—actually, more so for Sasha than for me—but I truly could not have been prouder of myself. Neither could Sasha. I was so proud of him, too. Plus, I ended up earning the highest score of the entire season, something I was surely proud of. Of course I was happy for Kel, who got second place, and for Hannah, who did take home the mirror ball trophy. By this point, it was a big celebration. We were all just so happy to have had our *Dancing with the Stars* experience. It was such an unbelievable, joyous night. And there to cheer me on were my parents, my close friends, and my cousin Nick, who had given me a large framed photograph of Dada as a gift going into the finals.

It was over, but it wasn't over. We had such a short amount of time to do our final postshow press line, pack, to celebrate with our family and friends, and then to say our farewells. I said goodbye to my beautiful trailer, which had been my home on Monday nights. I said goodbye to my parents and other loved ones. I took it all in, one last time. And then we final four loaded into a van, which drove us to the airport, where we took a private jet to New York City to appear on *Good Morning America* the next day.

There was an amazing spread of drinks and food—sushi, filet mignon sandwiches, a cheese platter, fresh fruit, and desserts. It was amazing. Everyone was having the best time, laughing and riding high after our final performance. We were celebrating like crazy, talking about the next chapters in our lives and how much we were going to miss each other. I chose not to drink, because I had another exciting first ahead of me in just a few short hours—I was going to debut my new single, "No Good," on *GMA!* I knew I was already going to be exhausted, so I did everything I could to stay alert and take care of my voice.

We were all staying up, talking, and then we finally all tried to close our eyes for a little while before we landed. I think I slept for only thirty or forty-five minutes. I was so tired. When we landed, a camera crew greeted us outside of our jet, and we went straight to *GMA* for hair and makeup, and then it was time to be on. I think we were all running on adrenaline. I know I was. By this point, we really were like family, and so doing our interview was so fun. Then I sang "No Good," and at the end, I had all of the cast members come out and dance with me. It was so special.

And then one by one I said my goodbyes to each and every person. They had all been the most amazing spirits, a true family. Everybody told me how much they loved me and adored me and were thankful for my presence and energy. And I told each and every one of them how special they were to me. I was very sad to leave them, after all we'd been through together, and I surely would miss them. But we were all happy to go spend Thanksgiving with our families, and we all vowed to stay in touch. They will be my friends for life.

Finally, it was just Lauren and me, backstage at the very studio where our whole friendship had begun just a few months earlier. We'd become so close during the show that we didn't want to say goodbye. But eventually, it was time. I made a face. And I just kind of looked at her and she looked at me, and without any words, we both started crying.

"I'm going to miss you so much," she said.

"I am going to miss you more," I said. "We're going to be friends forever, and I love you so much. Thank you for coming into my life."

As we were hugging and posing for one last photo, Lauren leaned in close to my ear.

"I wouldn't have made it without you," she whispered.

I'd forged this special bond with a friend and artist I admired so much, while we'd both been undergoing this incredible adventure that so few people in the world would ever experience. I was filled with so much love and gratitude in that moment.

My time on the show was so special. It moved me, it changed me in so many ways, and it gave me memories I'll cherish forever, along with my *Dancing with the Stars* family.

I will eternally be grateful that the producers decided to ask me one more time to be on the show. I'll never forget it. Now it was time to dream of what would come next.

TWENTY-TWO

Time to Shine

People had seen my heart—just as my mom had promised me; just like I'd wanted them to, but had been afraid to hope they would. *Dancing with the Stars* was completely transformative for me. I finally believed that I really could dance, something I'd been conflicted about for many years. I finally discovered true inner confidence that no one can take away from me. I lost ten pounds and was in the best shape of my life. And I received a beautiful sense of love and community from the show's fans, which I'll always value and hold dear to my heart. *Dancing with the Stars* gave me so much more than just dancing.

First of all, Emilio and Gloria Estefan had watched my tribute to them with my dance to "Conga," and they'd given me their full support, and Gloria even gave me a shout-out on the finale. Even before that, Emilio had contacted my management about the possibility of our working together. He'd been asked to write and produce this year's song for the annual New Year's Day Rose Bowl Parade, and he had chosen me to sing it.

This meant the absolute honor of flying to Miami for a day at his legendary Crescent Moon studios to record his song "Reach for the

Stars." As soon as I walked in, I felt the magic of the room. And I couldn't believe it when Emilio had a personal message for me from Gloria, who had told him how proud she was of me, and how happy she was that I was there, adding: "Tell her to use my mic. I would love that." Now, *that* was a special honor. Of course, I was a little nervous to be singing in front of such a legend, especially someone who was one of my inspirations, but Emilio made me feel so comfortable. His engineer was so lovely and kind as well. It didn't take me long to let loose, and we had so much fun. I was instantly struck by what a wonderful, warm-hearted man Emilio was, and how incredibly next level talented he was. After we finished recording the song, Emilio gave me the biggest compliment.

"Wow, Ally, I knew you were a fantastic singer, but you honestly impressed me today even more. You went beyond my expectations, and you really are such a talented singer with such an incredible voice. I would love to work with you on more music and to work on your album with you," he said.

I couldn't have been happier. Then he played me more music. But we'd both had time for only a quick session, in and out in one day, and so we'd vowed to find time to work together again sometime very soon.

After spending Thanksgiving at home with my family, in December I was back on the road. One of the highlights was flying to Atlanta to perform at the Miss Universe pageant, which was a phenomenal opportunity. It is watched by one billion people around the world. I went home for the holidays and gathered with my family. It was hard, having our first Christmas without Dada, and being reminded that it had been a year without him. But on that same day that we had lost him, December 27, I got to make the most amazing trip. Selena's sister, Suzette, asked me to drive down to Corpus Christi because she wanted to meet with me. Obviously, that was a big deal. It was super last-minute, and only the day before I was due to fly back to LA. But of course I said yes right away. And my dad was able to get the day off from work to drive me. I also brought along my little cousin Cassandra, whom I call Cassie, and was twelve at the time.

Again we met Suzette at the museum, and she took us around. Then we all had a big lunch with several of her employees, including Daniel, whom I'd become good friends with since the first time I was there. When Suzette was driving us back to the museum, she let us know why she'd asked me to come see her.

"Okay, so I need everybody in here to keep a secret," she said playfully.

We all nodded enthusiastically.

"Ally, so we are having a huge Selena tribute concert in San Antonio at the San Antonio Alamodome, and I would love if you would be a part of it," she said.

Wow, my life could not have come more full circle. Not only had I watched Selena tribute concerts that Suzette had organized before, but the Alamodome was somewhere Selena had performed and where they'd filmed the movie. I could feel the significance.

"Suzette, yes, of course," I said, with the biggest smile. "Nothing would make me happier than to be part of that."

When I was a little girl, I had prayed: "Please, one day, let me meet Selena's family and let them let me to pay tribute to their sister."

Now it had come to pass, and it was unbelievable. When we got back to the museum we toured around some more, talking the whole time, and then went into the gift shop. In the past, Suzette had been so generous about gifting me with Selena merchandise. But on this day, I was planning to buy something special for my little niece, Cassie, whom I adored so much. She is like my little sister. I took Cassie around the room.

"Mama, you pick out whatever you want," I told Cassie.

She picked out a purple Selena hoodie that I was wearing and a blanket.

I was at the register, ready to pay.

"It's okay, Mama, this is on the house," the woman at the cash register said. "This is on Suzette."

I was taken aback by her act of kindness, and I offered to pay several times, but the employee said, "No, she wants to, please."

She was treating us, and that was final. She hugged us both and was so gracious when Cassie asked if we could take a picture with her. Again, she proved herself to be a kind, humble, fun, down-to-earth gal, just like Selena was. What a day it was. And I was able to give that experience to my cousin, whom I just love with all of my heart. It was very, very special.

The next day, I was on a plane to LA to get ready for my New Year's performance. The first year of my solo career had been beyond my imagination. It was a very successful year for me. I did so much, was proud of all of my work, and loved every minute. Having been an underdog it meant a lot to me that I did so much my first year, and I was just getting started. Gearing up for 2020, I couldn't wait for what was ahead. I wanted to push my dreams even further.

Then it was time to ring in the New Year. Ironically, when midnight chimed I was asleep, because I had a three A.M. rehearsal for my performance during the Rose Bowl Parade the next morning. It was still dark when we got to Pasadena. I arrived to the cameras, the lights, the choreographers, the dancers, and the talented group of students I had the honor of performing with, the Chino Hills High Dance Team and Drum Line, all ready to rehearse.

Although I was tired, it was really exciting rehearsing for the parade during the middle of the night on New Year's Day. It was cold, but I got through it and had so much fun during our final rehearsals. Then I went straight into hair and makeup to get ready to kick off the parade.

That day I had the great honor of opening the entire parade. I took my place and then performed "Reach for the Stars." The lyrics included the lines: "It's a new year, time to celebrate! These are the dreams, follow the light, reach for the stars, I can touch the sky, it's never too far." I felt these lyrics deep in my heart and sang them with such feeling. It was the perfect song to inspire the world. This was my first time performing on New Year's Day. It was such a fun, joyous celebration, and a wonderful way to ring in a new year, and also a new decade.

And then, a few weeks later, I joined the *Dancing with the Stars* tour, in which some of the contestants took turns joining the pro dancers to bring our best dances to cities across the country. It was amazing to reunite with my *Dancing with the Stars* family, and of course Sasha. As soon as we got to our first rehearsal, we immediately picked up where we left off. I was going to be doing my dances to "Conga," "Proud Mary," and my song "Higher." I couldn't believe it, but I actually remembered most of the steps. I guess it never left my body.

It was great to be back on the road, and I even got to have some hosting moments in the show as well, which was amazing. It was exciting to dance on a theater stage, and this time I didn't have to be judged at all. We just danced for fun, in front of a wonderful audience. It felt like a Broadway show and a dance show all in one. I loved how this was the most fun, unique show I'd been a part of so far. It was amazing, being in the dancers' world now, after I'd almost always having been the headliner. It was nice to have less stress for once, to just show up and have fun during my dances and then watch their incredible show, which highlighted their amazing dedication and talent. It was like getting to be on vacation with my friends and do something I had come to love, which was dance with Sasha. I was so moved by the in-person response I heard again and again from fans at our meet-and-greet. *Dancing with the Stars* fans have so much heart, and they were really wonderful. I was approached by everyone from teens to moms and grandmas, and I heard the most amazing messages of appreciation.

"You are a lovely young woman and dancer with a bright future ahead."

"You were our family's favorite, and you inspired my daughter."

"You inspired me!"

I savored these last few dances with Sasha in the four cities where we performed on tour together, because when they were over, it would be all about my music career again.

Another highlight for me during this time was making a long-time dream come true—having my own makeup line! I partnered with Milani Cosmetics for their 2020 Ludicrous Lights Collection, co-creating my very own lip glosses. I'd always played with my Mom's lipstick as a little girl, puckering up my lips and twirling around. What a full-circle moment. When I saw my posters and collection for the very first time in person at Walgreens, I could not have smiled brighter. There are three electrifying, glittery shades: Pink-aroo, Lollapa-blue-za and Peach-ella. They are also available at Walmart, and even my favorite hometown grocery store, H-E-B! My parents sent me a video of them at H-E-B with the collection, and they were beaming with pride.

In late January I traveled back to Miami, which I completely fell in love with—it felt like a second home. I had been invited to record for a full week with none other than Emilio Estefan at Crescent Moon. I was having to pinch myself every day.

From the first moment I returned to Emilio's studio, I was enveloped in the warmth of his wonderful personality; it radiates out into everything he's created.

"Welcome to Miami, baby," he said. "You're family. You're part of the family now."

For the first few moments, I was just in awe. How could I possibly express how much this meant to me? I listened to Gloria's songs almost every day. I knew her life story and all of the music she'd created by heart, and I was well aware of how much she'd inspired Selena. In this one moment, in this one room, so many of my passions and dreams were intertwined together, and it was so beautiful for me, as an artist and as a person. Emilio also helped shaped the careers of everyone from Shakira to Ricky Martin.

Everything in Emilio's world was the absolute best. One of my favorite parts about being in the studio with him was having cafecito, a version of Cuban coffee that's like a sweet, hot espresso shot. I don't usually drink coffee, but I ended up having two of them a day. Everyone was surprised that it didn't give me crazy jitters. But I loved how warm and sweet it was—a little treat that helped me to focus. We joked that it would help me to sing better.

Emilio is so loving and warm, and all he wants is to give back to the people around him and to humanity. Everyone he works with—his assistant, the engineers, everyone who's employed at the studio—are all genuinely good-hearted people. And oh my God, the music he played for me was incredible. I even got a sneak peek of Gloria's new album, and it was unbelievable. We spent hours listening to amazing songs, cowriting lyrics, getting rough mixes down. He is such a legendary producer, and he was kind enough to take me under his wing. When I was singing, he gave me some wonderful advice that I've really taken to heart. "Always be yourself," he said. "If something doesn't feel right, don't do it. Don't sing it. Don't say yes. Always follow your heart. At the end of the day, you're going to be singing this music for the rest of your life. And always put yourself, and your personality, into each song."

He wasn't one of those people who told you to express yourself but then didn't want to hear what you had to say. Even with all of his experience and success—he and his wife had literally changed the world and had been leaders in the entertainment industry for more than four decades, earning so many awards, including the Presidential Medal of Freedom, and opening their own hotels and Cuban-themed restaurants—he was so humble.

"With me, please feel that same way, and feel free and comfortable to voice whatever you want to say," he said. "If a key is too high, too low, or the levels aren't right, let me know."

One day, after we'd been working together for a few days, he sat me down, away from the recording area. It was just him and me, and he was so genuine and nice that it almost felt like I was talking to my uncle or my dad. "I believe in you, and I'm here to help in any way," he said. "I see who you are as an artist and as a person, and I just want to help you, with all the experience that I've had."

This moment had a lot of meaning for me. It was the culmination of the amazing feeling of having so many power players on my side, now including the Estefans.

He empowered me to always remember that I'm in charge of my voice and my career, and we recorded some incredible music together. The musicality was on another level. I can't wait for the world to hear them.

Because we were guests in his city, every day after recording, Emilio would take my manager Will and me out for dinner, along with the engineers from the studio and everyone he worked with. That's just the kind of generous, kindhearted person he is. On the last day we recorded, after we wrapped, it was time to revel in all we had just done together.

"Okay, baby, come on, let's go," Emilio said. "Let's go celebrate and have dinner at Estefan Kitchen. I want to take you."

I'd always wanted to go to their restaurant in the past but never could. I was excited to have the chance.

"Yay, let's go!" I said.

As we wrapped our final day of recording, I was so excited, but also a little sad because I felt like I was having to leave paradise. I was planning to live it up on my final night with Emilio and everyone else. I joked with him: "I brought my Louboutin heels, and I pulled out my Chanel purse, because I'm so excited to go to your restaurant with you. That is such an honor."

We were laughing as we got in the car to leave.

All I could keep saying was thank you. I must have said it a thousand times that night.

"You don't know how much this means to me," I said.

As we talked, Gloria of course came up in our conversation several times. He had already told me that it would just be us at the restaurant, but someday I knew I'd meet her.

"It's a dream of mine to meet Gloria. She's one of my biggest inspirations of all time."

"Well, that dream will come true one day," he said. "You know, dreams do come true."

You know by now that I love to eat, and of course I had brought my appetite. I knew the food would be amazing, so I was ready. As we pulled up in the parking lot and walked up to the restaurant I could already hear the music from several feet away. We paused outside the restaurant to all pose for a quick picture, and I took it all in—it was beautiful and so lively.

"We're here at Estefan Kitchen," Emilio said, with his arms spread wide in welcome, looking up toward the restaurant. "We're so happy, and we love to have a good time, and we love to . . . dance!"

Just at that moment, I turned to my right, and to my complete shock, there was the one, the only, Gloria Estefan, dancing the salsa, making her way over to me. I was the most surprised I'd ever been in my life. You know how sometimes Ellen or Oprah would treat guests by bringing on their favorite celebrity or artist? Well, that's how I felt. I had no idea Gloria was going to be there. I was totally stunned.

Completely and utterly floored, I put my hands over my mouth in pure disbelief.

"Hello! How are you?" she said.

I almost couldn't talk—I was so full of emotion. "Hi! It's so wonderful to meet you," I said, with tears in my eyes. "I just love you so much."

She couldn't have been nicer, and I instantly felt like I'd known her my whole life. I was in Heaven. I really had not expected to meet her. If I had, I definitely would have dressed up for her, in more than just my nice heels and purse, and I would also have brought her a gift. I was so casual from being in the studio, wearing a neon-yellow tank top with high-waisted blue jean shorts, and my hair was beach wave messy, and I wasn't really wearing makeup—only my eyelashes and a little lipstick. She was absolutely beautiful. Emilio had known she was coming this whole time, but he hadn't told me, because he'd wanted to surprise me. I wouldn't have changed a thing about the night, because it was so perfect.

The restaurant was incredible. As soon as we entered, we were welcomed in by this loud wave of lively Cuban music, with piano and congas and singers. Gloria was dancing to the band as we entered, and it was loud, exuberant, and full of life.

We sat down and had dinner together and celebrated. I honestly couldn't have dreamed up a more perfect night. Emilio was so loving, and Gloria was so loving and fun and vivacious and kind. I told her how much I loved her, which I could tell she deeply appreciated.

"Ally, that means so much to me, and so much to us," she said. "That's all we aim to do: inspire and help people. The fact that we helped you is a privilege."

After thanking her again, I made good use of my time. When we first sat down together, I was a little nervous. I was with one of my all-time heroes, and I couldn't help but feel shy. Will was just as surprised as I was, and he was so happy for me, because he knew how much this moment meant to me. "Ask her anything," Will encouraged me. "Don't be shy. They love you."

I was still feeling nervous, so I turned to Emilio, whom I felt quite comfortable with after our time together in the studio.

"What should I say?" I asked.

"Oh, Mama, you ask her whatever you want," he said. "She just loves you. You're family to us."

And then I went for it and asked her so many questions. She gave me priceless advice.

"Be yourself, girl," she said. "Don't let any label or anybody tell you what to do. We knew 'Conga' was a hit, and our label didn't believe it was a hit. We had to fight to get to where we are. So always remember to be yourself. Don't conform to what anybody wants you to be. Social media negativity, don't listen to that. Be your own person. You're incredible."

It was exactly the reminder I needed as I dug into the hard work of launching my solo career. And I couldn't have imagined a better person to hear it from or to look up to.

After we had eaten the best Cuban food of my life and talked and laughed, I was sad to find the night winding down. As we walked out, Gloria hugged me.

"I want to say, it's an honor to have you as part of our family," she said. "Really, it's a privilege. And thank you so much."

"It's my honor," I said. "You do not understand what this means to me. And thank you for everything you've done for me."

Life has been revealing new insights and gifts every day. I'm incredibly grateful for the opportunities that keep opening up. More than that, though, I'm thankful because I'm free to be myself. To be my type of artist. To sing my heart out. I've been through a lot. I've seen so much already, but I feel like my life's really just beginning. Even though I have more adult responsibility than ever, I feel like a kid again. That's how I excited I am!

This year has also dawned with plenty of new music, including my feature on the song "All Night" by the EDM DJ Afrojack. I had been a big fan of his. As soon as I first heard the track, I loved the vibe and its energy. I was excited to have that out in the world. It was so incredible to have it go to No. 1 on Dance Radio, all thanks to my marvelous fans. It was my very first No. 1!!

One of the biggest, most exciting dreams of mine came true when I returned to Miami in late February to plan and rehearse for my very first headlining solo tour, the Time to Shine Tour, which was due to kick off in early March. Touring has become *the* way to build an organic fanbase. I had been doing so for years with Fifth Harmony, and by the end of our time together, we were playing for arenas full of tens of thousands of fans. Now, in order to earn my own fan base, for my solo music, I was going to basically start over. This meant going back to playing smaller clubs, holding five hundred to a thousand people. For me, this was what it was all about. While I'd loved all of the TV I'd done, and how it had introduced me to new people in their homes, this was what I was really passionate about. Singing to my fans, in person, to show them my true heart as a solo artist and to show them that I truly am an entertainer. This was the moment I'd been waiting for my whole life.

But there was also a lot of risk involved. We had eight days to come up with a sixty-minute show. It was a huge crunch. At times it felt impossible. Fortunately, I was working with the most incredible, talented team. I was so excited to be reuniting with my amazing choreographer, Aníbal Marrero, his assistants, Susie and Paxton, and my dancers, called the Ally Boyz. It was like returning to my family. Susie owned a huge, wildly successful dance studio called Show Stopper Miami, and she was kind enough to let us rehearse there—whatever we needed. It felt like our safe haven. Every day, rehearsal was buzzing with creativity. At times we had four rooms going, with my dancers learning one song in one room, another song in the next room. Everyone was pouring every drop of energy they had into the show. We worked tirelessly, getting little to no sleep, enjoying our time together while we ate our meals at an amazing Cuban restaurant down the street. It was a labor of love that was rewarding beyond words. I will forever be thankful to my team for making it all come together.

I was proud to have so much solo music and features to choose from when I was putting together my set list. At the time, I had just released, "Fabulous," and I launched an online campaign for a fan to learn the "Fabulous" choreography and join me onstage. I loved "Fabulous" because it was a message about being yourself and loving yourself. Like my first solo song, "Perfect," I resonated with the song because of its positive message. I want my fans to know that I see how beautiful, and yes, fabulous, you are, even on your darkest days.

It's a good reminder for myself, too. I loved it because it narrated my journey. Even though the odds were against me—I struggled to find a place in the entertainment industry when my parents first brought me to LA as this little twelve-year-old Mexican American girl with a dream to sing for the world. I'd gone through the roller coaster of being turned down by multiple record labels before finding my perfect home at Latium/Atlantic. And I always kept my faith that God had a greater plan for me and that I had a greater purpose to help all of you. It was the moment for me to sing it, loud and proud, for the whole world to hear: "In my past / I put my heart in someone else's hands / Let everybody tell me who I am. / But now I understand / That if I'm gonna love someone / I'm just gonna love myself. / I already know I'm fabulous. / I don't need no one else."

I was feeling hopeful that it really was my time to show the world exactly who I was and what I could do. Finally, we said goodbye to our oasis that was Show Stopper, and headed to the airport together. I flew first-class to Chicago, seated next to Aníbal. We talked the whole flight about how happy we were to see this day and to be experiencing this together. We shared our dreams for the tour and were filled with gratitude that our hard work had led us here. And then as I touched down in Chicago to do the final prep before my monthlong tour, we had no choice but to make everything work. The night before one of our final rehearsals, I could barely sleep. In the morning, my team couldn't wait to unveil the intro that had been created for my show, and I was excited to see it. Overall, I was full of so many emotions and still having trouble believing this was all real—I was on the verge of my first-ever solo headlining tour.

When I got to the rehearsal space, everyone on my team was so excited to see my reaction as they cued up the intro. I had a videographer with me to catch my rehearsals and first show who was filming everything. When it began to play and I saw how carefully they had chosen images from throughout my journey—from me at nine years old, singing in San Antonio at the Market Square, to me jumpstarting my solo career—I was so touched, I began to cry. I was so moved by how well they had captured my story and everything it had taken to get to this moment, and how important it was that I had made it—not only for myself, but also for my parents, my extended family, my friends, and my incredibly loyal fans. I couldn't think of anything better in the whole world than sharing my heart—and my voice—in this way.

And then, things got hard. It was the last day of rehearsal, and on the first run-through, everything that could go wrong went wrong. My in-ears had been lost. I needed them to hear the music and cues, when I was singing onstage. And then, every single aspect of the show somehow failed. The video wall was not synched with the music. Our DJ had the wrong tracks for the mix. We realized our dancers had forgotten their wardrobe. It was devastating, and I completely lost it. I was so rattled. *What if we didn't pull it together in time? What if I let everyone down, most of all myself?* Our first show of the tour, in Chicago, was the next day. But we had no choice but to keep working, keep trying, keep praying. Finally, after such a stressful day of everything going wrong, we nailed it. We did a total of four run-throughs, which was exhausting. We all pushed our physical limits. But it was magnificent. By the final dress rehearsal, I was glowing. At the end, we all huddled together and cheered, because we could not believe everything we'd overcome, everything we'd accomplished, and we were more excited than anything in the world to show it to everybody.

That night when it was time to leave the rehearsal space, we stepped outside into the cold Chicago night and saw a tiny miracle. Perfect little flakes of snow were falling from the sky. One of my dancers got really excited because it was actually his first time ever seeing snow. That was such a special moment. It really felt like everything was happening just as it was supposed to.

"If this is not perfect, if this is not a sign, if this is not a gift from God, I don't know what is," I said, feeling the chilly flakes tickle my face. I held out my tongue to catch a few, just as I had as a little girl.

The next day, it was officially time to kick off my solo tour, and everything was pure magic. We pulled up to my first venue, the legendary House of Blues. Parked out back was my very own tour bus. Backstage were posters of my face for me to sign for my meet-and-greet.

"I feel like a little kid on Christmas morning," I said. And since you know how much I love Christmas, you know *exactly* how happy and fulfilled I was.

Everything was perfect. The fans at my meet-and-greet before the show were the sweetest—many brought me gifts, some cried, some threw their arms around me, one had even gotten her nails done like mine. I loved getting to know each and every one of them, including some fans who were attending their first concert. I was so filled up with love and joy. I had fans coming up to me and saying, "I'm so nervous, but so excited!" Some fans told me how much this moment meant to them because they knew how underrated, and underappreciated, I had been. They loved seeing me triumph now. It was a glorious beautiful moment for my fans and I to come together.

Backstage, as I was getting my hair and makeup done, I had one last FaceTime call with my parents back in San Antonio. "Go out there and have fun," my dad said. "This is your time to shine. We are blessed that God made this day come true."

They said a quick prayer over me.

My entire team had a group prayer backstage, to bless our show. Everyone, from my dancers, and Aníbal and Susie, to my DJ, and my entire crew, gathered hands and said a prayer, and then we went onstage. As I walked from the wings into my first position, I took it all in: my first show of my first solo headlining tour. I wanted to savor every moment of it. The crowd was massive. I was blown away by how many people were there. The energy of the crowd and the entire room was powerful—there was a sea of excited fans, from kids and teenagers to parents and grandmas. When I told the crowd that this was the first night of my first-ever solo headlining tour, they screamed with pride. It was like everyone in that room was right there with me—helping me to take my career to the next level, the one I'd been working toward for more than half of my life. My dancers were so hardworking and talented. They brought the most love, passion, and energy. We left everything on the floor. Everything came together, everything went perfectly, from the choreography, to the wardrobe changes, to the video wall. God anointed that show, and everyone in the room could feel it.

And we shined. We really did.

It was opening night of my first headlining solo tour, and I'd been so afraid that everything would go wrong. But all of our hard work had paid off. We nailed everything. Not a thing went wrong. And the crowd was right there with us. It was a moment I'll never forget, one of the highlights of my entire life. At the end, when I stood at the center of the stage, all of us holding hands for our final bow, it was a moment of pure joy, triumph, and victory. It felt like that scene at the end of a movie where the hero finally wins—that was me. I had done it, and no one could take this away from me. I had finally found my own harmony. And it was only the beginning.

Epilogue

What I'm learning during these unexpected, scary, heartbreaking times is that there are many different ways to shine, and we all have our part to play. After our triumphant opening night show in Chicago, we realized that we'd been so wrapped up in our bubble of getting ready for the show that we hadn't really been following the news. As we climbed onto our tour bus and prepared to travel to our next date in Toronto, we connected with the anxiety and uncertainty that was building everywhere in the world. No one seemed to know how bad the coronavirus pandemic would get, or what should be done to try to prevent its spread.

It became a day-by-day, minute-by-minute question of whether we would be doing our next show, whether it was safe for us to be out on the road. We had an amazing night in Toronto, but we could feel that the mood was shifting. People were scared and many stayed home. We understood why. But we pushed on to Boston. During those late nights on the tour bus, we bonded as a family. We would stay up late, eating cereal, watching movies, dancing, talking, and taking everything in. It was incredible for us to feel this amazing camaraderie, to feel that we all had stories, and we could relate to them so well.

We didn't know until six P.M. the day of our Boston show if it would be happening or not. We had decided that morning that this was going to be our last show. The news that we would have to cancel the rest of the dates and go home immediately to shelter in place was devasting. I was in the back of the bus, heartbroken and crying. I prayed to God: "I don't understand why this is happening, especially when I am finally just starting to see my dreams come to life, but I know I have to trust your Will." Everyone had poured their heart and soul into our show, and just like that, we weren't going to be able to finish the tour. We were just two days from going to New York City, which was going to be my first-ever sold-out solo show. I released a statement right before my meet-and-greet. We were all sad, from our crew to the fans. There was a somber energy in the room, but at the same time, we wanted to leave on a high note, and I'm grateful to all the fans who showed up that night.

We also wanted to get everyone home safely. My entire crew and I had one last big night out in Boston, where we celebrated what we had accomplished—nothing could take that away from us. And then the next day everyone flew home. Will and I returned to Los Angeles. I felt so grateful to know that my whole team was safe at home with their families and loved ones.

I soon realized that I was more connected to my community than ever. It has been so moving to feel like I'm able to shine a light for people during these dark times. I have sometimes had a rocky relationship with social media, but I've been happy to be reminded of how much power it has to bring people together. I've been moved by people who've been so open during this difficult time about their struggles to not let anxiety get the best of them. It has made me feel closer to my heroes and to my fans alike. I've been able to be myself, which is incredibly liberating. All we can do is try our best, each and every day.

I've been able to keep busy during this time and use my platform and passion to help in the ways that I can. I'm thankful to bring love and light and connection, not just through my voice, but through my heart. And I thank you all for giving me the opportunity to do so.

There have been times when I've asked God: *What happens next?*

That's where my faith kicks in, and I remember that God knows better than I do. He has a plan. And it will happen exactly as it's supposed to. I have high expectations for the future. I was supposed to perform at other festivals that were postponed, including Coachella, Ultra, and the Selena concert. I've had to keep faith that one day I will.

I feel so grateful that, at least, I had those four amazing nights of my tour, and I'll always hold those memories in my heart. And I know, without a doubt, that I'll be back on that stage again one day. Until then, these are my last words for you: *Thank you. May God bless you. I will always love you. We will always have this unbreakable bond. Thank you for allowing me to be me and to finally find my own harmony. I hope you can find yours, too.*

Acknowledgments

My Lord & Savior, Jesus Christ. My King. My everything. I thank You for making this book possible, and for writing my story even before I was born. For every dream that has come to pass. For every miracle You have performed. You've saved and changed my life. I owe everything to You. My beautiful Savior. I dedicate this to You.

Mom and Dad—I am at a loss for words. My heart, my champions, my soul. I love y'all with all of my heart. Y'all mean everything to me and more. God is so good for what He has done in our lives, and for blessing mine with you in it. We did it!!

Bobo—my dear brother. What would I do without you? I love you more than words. God could not have blessed me greater. You will always be special, and always mean so much to me. I love you to infinity, my brudder!!

Will Bracey—you have changed my life. Thank you for following your heart, and for always letting God lead. Thank you for believing in me, and for seeing me for me. Thank you for being brave and for protecting me like no one else can. I'll never be able to repay you for changing my life. Your gifts, leadership, work ethic, intuition, and heart are beyond inspiring.

Gigi—thank you for loving my brother and for making him happy. God bless y'all and the babies (doggy babies!).

The city of San Antonio—where I proudly got my heritage—thank you for being the greatest city in the world. I love you with all of my heart.

HarperCollins/Dey Street/Matt Harper—thank you for believing in me and my vision for my book. Thank you for your patience and guidance. I am incredibly thankful to have had the honor of your support.

Dupree Miller/Nena Oshman—I cannot articulate enough how thankful I am for you and your passion and belief in my story since day one. You were there to cheer me on, shower me with support, and fill me with positivity. From the moment I first talked to you, I knew we were in this together. My fellow Texan, it is beautiful to finally see my book come to life! Thank you.

Charles Chavez—the day I met you was one I'll never forget. Thank you for taking me under your wing. Thank you for taking a chance on me. Thank you for believing in me, the way I prayed someone would. Your efforts, passion, and guidance has changed my life. I can't say thank you enough, Chuck.

Latium Records—I love Latium! So grateful for my label fam. We have done so much together. I am so proud and happy to have created the records of my dreams, and to have such phenomenal support.

Nick Ferrer—thank you, Nick, for always being there to help at any and all times. I know if I need something, I can count on you. You are deeply appreciated!

Deby Chavez—thank you for your kindness, and for taking me in like one of your own. Your belief in me has meant so much.

Monique Chavez—thank you for giving me the priceless gift of my beautiful book cover. It is my dream cover, and I am so proud when I see it. You really put your heart into it, and I won't forget it. You have always been so kind, encouraging, supportive and loving since day one. Thank you, Mo!

Atlantic Records—My Atlantic fam! My dream label. I want to share a special thank-you to each and every person at Atlantic who has had my back and supported me in my solo career. It means the absolute world, and I am beyond thankful.

Grandma—you are my heart and the angel of our family. There is no one that compares to you. I will never be able to say how much I love you. My sweet, precious grandma. Thank you for always loving and supporting me.

Grandpa Paul—I miss you so much, Grandpa. I miss our jokes, your infectious laugh, and your hugs. I know you are making so many angels smile in Heaven, and I know you are watching over me and Grandma. We miss and love you with all of our hearts.

Dada—I know you are so proud of me, watching from Heaven, and are my mighty angel. I am so happy I can share your story. That is one of my greatest honors. I will never forget our time together. Thank you for showing me Jesus's love and miracle. I love you, Dada.

Rosa Rios in Heaven—I love you with all of my heart and miss you so much. Thank you for loving me like one of your own. I know you are with me and are so proud of me. You are always in my heart.

Darci Rios—you are so special to me. I am so grateful that God and your mom brought us together. You have been such a blessing in my life. I love you, Darci.

I want to send a very special thank-you to my parents' wonderful friends:

Mr. and Mrs. O'Brien

Mrs. Francine Gonzales and Mr. Ron Gonzales

Terry and Mike Perez, who inspired my parents and helped to guide them spiritually

Mike and Sam Miller/the Miller Family

Julie Corbett

I love you all so dearly! I will forever be thankful to you for your beautiful love and friendship to my parents!

Pastor Max Lucado—Pastor Max, thank you for sharing the love of Christ. It is my dearest honor to witness your wonderful heart and to know you. You have been such an inspiration to my family and me. You have blessed us so dearly. God bless you and your beautiful family.

My Oak Hills Church friends and community—thank you from the bottom of my heart for your mentorship and for always sharing the Lord's love with me. You have left an imprint on my heart. May the Lord bless each of you:

Deneen & Tim Geoke

Brett & Jenna Bishop

Chris & Katie Butler

Jeff Nelson

Daria Valdez

Stephen Fryrear

My Milani Cosmetics Family—what a dream to work together. You have given me such joy and love. Thank you for believing in me and for making my makeup dreams come true! I love my Milani fam.

Suzette Quintanilla and the Quintanilla Family—thank you for your unbelievable kindness, support, and love. There are not enough words to say how I feel.

Jake Updegraff—my Jakey! You are such a treasure. I am grateful for you beyond words. I love you so much.

Masey McClain—I am so blessed to know you, sweet friend. You have that Jesus sparkle. Thank you for sharing that with me.

My dancers/Ally Boyz—Jose, Chris, JP, David, Miguel—you guys are my family. I am forever thankful for our beautiful love, and the bond and passion we share. Y'all are true gifts to me. I love you.

Aníbal Marrero—my dear Aníbal. Thank you for believing in me and for putting everything into my visions and artistry, and for making my dream tour come true. You are an answered prayer and also a part of my family. God bless you. I love you dearly.

Alejandra Espinoza—thank you for your never-ending support and kindness. You are a beautiful soul.

Susie Garcia—thank you for believing in me since the first day we met. You saw something special in me and gave me such life and confidence. I love you so much.

Preston Wada—I love you, boo! Thank you for being the center of happiness and love for me. You are my ride-or-die.

Gaby Ruiz—thank you for always putting your 1000% into every show, especially on my first solo tour. I cannot share my gratitude.

Syphe—thank you for always bringing the energy and good vibes on my first solo tour, and on each show we did.

JoMari Goyso—thank you for believing in me since I first traveled to Los Angeles in pursuit of my dreams when I was twelve. I'll never forget that.

Sasha Farber—you know how much I love you! Thank you, once again, for changing my life.

Emma Slater—I cherish our memories on the show and our friendship now. Thank you for always being so sweet to me. I love you!

My entire *DWTS* Family—I love you with all of my heart and am forever blessed by my experience. There will never be another quite like it. We will always be family.

The ASPCA—thank you for allowing me to honor Bobbi's life as your ambassador. Thank you for the incredible work you do, and for changing my life by blessing me with LadyBelle and Minnie.

The March of Dimes—thank you for your generosity and kindness to my family when I was born, and to so many families like mine. I am so proud to be an ambassador.

My lovely neighbors Mike Rau and Tom Cestaro—I will always have infinite love for you. You are the best neighbors in the world, and I am honored to call you my friends. I don't deserve you.

Mark Burnett and Roma Downey—thank you for the wisdom and everlasting goodness you share. You both are real light to this world. You bless and inspire me enormously. Thank you for your help to make this book possible.

Dana Barron—I will never, ever forget the chance you gave me as a little girl. It was a once in a lifetime opportunity that changed my life. Thank you.

1500 or Nothin'/Larrance Dopson/Alex Dopson/James Fauntle-roy/Duke and Duchess Dopson—my 1500 or Nothin' fam! You guys are my world. Words cannot express my love and thankfulness. You took me in as a little girl with big dreams. You gave me a community of love and friendship, and for that, I'll always be grateful.

Rest in peace, our beautiful Duchess.

My school friends—Kayla Martinez, Aaron Gonzales, Kristen Va-ladez, and more—Thank you for being in my life and for supporting me since I can remember. I know I can always count on your amazing friendship, and you know my truest self. You have blessed me so much in my life. I love you guys.

Sarah Tomlinson—there are not enough words to express my grat-itude. Thank you for understanding how important this book is to me, and for allowing my heart to shine in the most beautiful way. God bless you for your truly remarkable spirit.

Cindy Coloma—thank you for your kindness and grace, and for helping to open the doors to my heart.

Clarissa and Gilda Hartley—thank you for being such a special part of my life. God bless you. Rest in peace, beautiful Gilda. I won't ever forget your amazing soul.

All the Radio DJs who are spinning my music—thank you for the incredible support.

Pastor Ryan Ries—I couldn't be more grateful for your prayers, guidance, and generosity. May the Lord continue to bless you.

Diane Warren—thank you for the remarkable opportunity to

work together. You are one of a kind and a huge inspiration to me. It is an honor to know you and have your support.

Karma, Ninja, Keyon, and all the dancers who danced with me in San Antonio in my younger years—I will never be able to say thank you. Y'all will always have a special place in my heart.

Tori Kelly—thank you for your sweet friendship throughout the years. I am so happy God connected us. Love you!

Crystal Lewis—thank you for inspiring me to sing since I was a little girl. Your music was one of the first songs I'd ever sang. Thank you for your support in my solo career. You will always be an inspiration!

Jaci Velasquez—your music has completely changed my life. Thank you for inspiring my faith. Thank you for being that voice. My admiration and gratitude will always be immeasurable. God bless you.

Flict—Pare! Thank you for being one of the first to believe in me when I first was transitioning into a solo artist. You have blessed me so much.

All of the amazing producers/songwriters I have had the honor of working with—thank you from the bottom of my heart for whole-heartedly believing in my art. I am blown away that I've been so fortunate to work with so many talented people. My heart couldn't be fuller.

To my Aunts, Uncles and Cousins—I would need another book in and of itself to write their names lol. I love you very much.

Crossroads Church in San Antonio, as well as their Pastor and Family—thank you for blessing my family and me with a home church when I was a little girl. Thank you for giving me my first ever chance to sing at church, too!

My first vocal teachers, thank you for your wisdom and guidance. I look back at our times together with such fondness. Thank you:

Alisa Clarity
Sonya
Analisa

Amy in Los Angeles

Network for Young Artists/Terry Lowry "Coach"—I will be grateful to you for the rest of my life. Thank you for the gift you gave me as a child.

My beautiful teachers:

Mrs. Merrill—Mrs. Merrill, thank you for changing my life. You will always be a special piece of my heart.

Mrs. Laureano in Heaven—I will always miss you and love you. You are forever in my heart. Thank you for making me believe I could do anything.

Thank you for giving me a chance in so many amazing ways when I was young:

Tom Heck P.A.C.E. program in LA

Jay Dominguez

Alberto Kreimerman from Hermès Music

Ron Hayes and Pinky

Annette Romo Schaefer

Micah John from the Jewish Community Center

Aunt Denise and Uncle Jesse—thank you for your love.

Thank you to my Uncle Conrad for giving me my first recording experience with the children's album. I love you!

Aunt Alma—thank you for always being so kind and caring to me.

Uncle Ernest—thank you for always traveling and supporting everything I do since I began. I love you so much!

To all my fans, old and new—thank you for making the dreams in my heart come true. I love you more than I'll ever be able to say.

About the Author

Ally Brooke grew up in San Antonio, Texas. Following her time in Fifth Harmony, the multiplatinum singer-songwriter kicked off her highly anticipated solo career in 2019 with back-to-back Top 40 charting singles and an impressive resume of genre-bending collaborations including "All Night" with Afrojack, which marked her first #1 as a solo artist on US Dance Radio. A life-long entertainer, Ally competed on ABC's *Dancing With the Stars* before embarking on her debut headline Time to Shine tour in early 2020 with scheduled stops including a sold-out show at New York's Gramercy Theatre. With total career streams already in the billions, Ally is only just getting started. She lives in Los Angeles, California.